Development and
Disenchantment
in Rural Tunisia

The author (*left*) with women from both town (*right*) and countryside (*center*). Dress remains an important indicator of identity, and the women of Medjerda debated the appropriate dress for the anthropologist. Country women felt the author should dress country style when working on the farm. Town women claimed that a European should wear the latest French fashions. All agreed the author should not don a *safsari*, or veil. *Source:* Courtesy of Marc Zussman.

STATE, CULTURE, AND SOCIETY
IN ARAB NORTH AFRICA
Series Editors
John P. Entelis, Fordham University
Michael Suleiman, Kansas State University

The states and societies of Arab North Africa have long been neglected in the scholarly literature dealing with the Arab world, the Middle East, and Islam, except in the context of dramatic international events. Yet this region has a rich historical and cultural tradition that offers important insights into the evolution of society, the complexity of cultural life, forms of social interaction, strategies of economic development, and patterns of state formation throughout the developing world. In addition, as the region has assumed more importance in geopolitical terms, both the United States and the Soviet Union have become more directly involved in its economics and politics. Few books of a scholarly or policy nature, however, analyze and interpret recent trends and changes in the constellation of relations between regional and global powers. This new series—the first in English to focus exclusively on Arab North Africa—will address important conceptual and policy issues from an interdisciplinary perspective, giving special emphasis to questions of political culture and political economy.

Books in This Series

Development and Disenchantment in Rural Tunisia: The Bourguiba Years, Mira Zussman

State and Society in Algeria, edited by John P. Entelis and Phillip C. Naylor

Polity and Society in Contemporary North Africa, edited by I. William Zartman and William Mark Habeeb

Development and Disenchantment in Rural Tunisia

The Bourguiba Years

Mira Zussman

Westview Press

BOULDER • SAN FRANCISCO • OXFORD

State, Culture, and Society in Arab North Africa

All photographs by the author unless otherwise attributed. Cover photo shows fellahin preparing the soil on a half-hectare farm, the smallest viable private parcel in the region.

Figures 1.1, 1.2, and 1.5 were previously published in Laurence Michalak and Jeswald W. Salacuse, eds., *Social Legislation in the Contemporary Middle East* (Berkeley: University of California International Studies, 1986), pp. 180–183. Reprinted by permission.

Published in 1992 in the United States of America by Westview Press, Inc., 5500 Central Avenue, Boulder, Colorado 80301-2847, and in the United Kingdom by Westview Press, 36 Lonsdale Road, Summertown, Oxford OX2 7EW

Library of Congress Cataloging-in-Publication Data
Zussman, Mira Fromer.
    Development and disenchantment in rural Tunisia :
the Bourguiba years / by Mira Zussman.
        p. cm.—(State, culture, and society in Arab North Africa)
    Includes index.
    ISBN 0-8133-8238-6
    1. Rural development—Government policy—Tunisia—
Case studies.   2. Rural development—Medjerda River
Valley (Algeria and Tunisia)—Case studies.   3.
Medjerda River Valley (Algeria and Tunisia)—Rural
conditions—Case studies.   I. Title.   II. Series
HN784.Z9C69 1992
307.1′412′09611—dc20   92-5749
                                                                          CIP

Printed and bound in the United States of America

The paper used in this publication meets the requirements
of the American National Standard for Permanence of Paper
for Printed Library Materials Z39.48-1984.

10   9   8   7   6   5   4   3   2   1

To Fatima,
who taught me
and made me laugh at my own mistakes

The great challenge to an historical anthropology is not merely to know how events are ordered by culture, but how, in that process, the culture is reordered. How does the reproduction of a structure become its transformation?

—Marshall Sahlins
Historical Metaphors and Mythical Realities

Song of Medjerda

مجــرده يامجـــرده يقولـوا
عليّك، شـــــر الغـــربة
وانت، ليـــلة البلـــدان
كل جمعـــة ســـوقك يحفِل
رجال مع نســـوان
فيك، ثروات غنية
ضيعات ومعامل شـــشـــية
لهمالهم وخضرة و جنيـرِية
يقدر تتضـــح تتنـــزه
على حاشـــية الـــواد العشـــية

mjerda, ya mjerda yagulu	Medjerda, oh Medjerda they say of you
ᶜalik sharr ul-ghurba	you bring hunger and loneliness
	to the stranger
w-inti lillat el-buldan	but you're the queen of the countryside.
kul jimᶜa sugik yahfil	Every Friday your market
rjal maᶜa niswan	gathers men and women together.
fik tharawat ghniy	Treasure lies within you —
dayᶜat w-mᶜamil shshiya	estates and *chechia* makers.
Sabtik min kul thniya	Your harvest is renowned —
tmatim, w-khudra, w-generiya	tomatoes, vegetables and artichokes.
yigdir titdassih, titnazzah	Promenade and be at ease
ᶜala hashiya el-wed el-ᶜashiyah	on the banks of the river in the afternoon.

—traditional folk song

Contents

Tables and Illustrations

Photographs

The author (left) with women from town (right) and countryside (center) *(frontispiece)*

Photograph section (following page 116)

Firing up the oven: Women begin the long process of baking bread

The finished product: Fifteen loaves of bread are baked daily

Lessons on the farm: Rural families enjoyed teaching the author the tasks of farm life

Bedouin encampment: A local political leader tries to convince a nomad to send his son to school

Spinning with a drop-spindle: Some country women continue to practice crafts such as spinning, weaving, embroidery, and pottery

Sheep-shearing work party: A male member of each household participates in the annual sheep-shearing

Outskirts of Medjerda: The path leads from town to the countryside and down to the banks of the Medjerda River

Smallest viable private parcel in the region: Soil preparation on a half-hectare farm

A fellah of Medjerda: The winter crop of artichokes

Aid from the Belgian Agricultural Extension Project: Hybrid *primeur* tomato seedlings at first delighted a "model farm" fellah

Couscous-making in the courtyard: A woman's female kin and friends help her prepare couscous

Cooking *ᶜarbi* in a *souri* kitchen: A Medjerdi woman's unique solution to indoor rainy-day cooking

Opting out of agriculture: The son of a farm worker returns home laden with luxuries after five years as a worker abroad

Women sitting *ᶜarbi* and men sitting *souri*: Men have individual settings at the table, women and children eat out of a collective bowl

Friday in Medjerda: The streets swell with fellahin

Visit of the prime minister: Medjerdis line the streets one Friday

Preface

My first introduction to the lower Medjerda Valley was in 1976 by Werner Kiene, then director of economic development programs in North Africa for the Ford Foundation, and by professors Ali Ben Zaid Salmi and Moncef Ben Said, codirectors of the Department of Rural Social Sciences at the National Agronomy Institute of Tunisia (INAT). The region of Medjerda turned out to be an ideal fieldsite, and I am grateful to the team at INAT for introducing me to the region. My fieldwork in the late 1970s was supported by two sources: A Fulbright Hays Research Fellowship and an International Doctoral Research Fellowship provided jointly by the Social Science Research Council (SSRC) and the American Council for Learned Societies. Subsequent travel grants from the Center for Middle Eastern Studies at the University of California, Berkeley, and California State University Faculty Research Grants also were instrumental to this study. Without the financial support of these organizations, this research could not have been conducted.

In Tunisia, I am indebted to the researchers of the *Centre d'Etudes et de Recherches Economiques et Sociales* (CERES) for stimulating discussions when I came into the capital, Tunis, and to the archivists at the *Archives Nationales*. In addition, I am grateful to the administrators of land-management agencies—in particular, those of the *Bureau de Contrôle des Unités de Production du Nord* (BCUPN), the *Commissariat Regionale de Dévéloppement Agricole* (CRDA), the *Office de la Mise en Valeur de la Vallée de la Medjerda* (OMVVM), the *Office des Terres Domaniales* (OTD), and the *Projet Tuniso-Belge de Vulgarisation*—for their assistance, participation, and interest in this study.

My greatest debt is to the people of the lower Medjerda Valley, whose generosity, hospitality, and warmth made the region dear to me. The fellahin of Medjerda understood better than I did what I was after. The impact of land reform policies on rural life came alive under their tutelage. At first, many thought it strange that I had come to learn instead of teach, that I saw myself as a student and not an expert. They were used to so many experts telling them how to live and work that the fellahin were at first skeptical and then amused by my willingness to learn. But the fellahin of Medjerda took it upon themselves to be the finest teachers. They opened their homes and their lives to me and made sure that I took careful notes, visited them frequently, ate properly, and asked the right questions. They introduced me to their extended families and neighbors and reminded me frequently to take lots of photographs, a few of which are included herein. The women taught me how to milk, churn, weed, clean sheepskins, pluck chickens, stuff *merguez* sausages, boil up a resin depilatory, and put on henna as well as to prepare a year's supply of couscous and harissa. They told me what was important—family and children—and felt my belly waiting for me to conceive. When I did, they predicted a boy and taught me how to care for him. More than anything else, the fellahin of Medjerda taught me about values and priorities. The individuals who helped me most know how deeply I feel my debt to them. The fellahin of Medjerda insisted that I find the old French colonial families who once ruled over the region so as to understand the colonial enterprise from more than one perspective. The study then expanded to other parts of Tunisia, where colonial families still lived, as well as to France. Eventually, the study came to include more and more archival research, in Europe and in other parts of North Africa, on the Protectorate period. Only some of this later work appears in this volume. Most exciting for the fellahin were my meetings in France with family members of the legendary mayor of colonial Medjerda. The colonial period came alive for me as a result of these encounters.

Earlier versions of the chapters that follow have benefited from the criticisms and comments supplied by Ameur Ben Arab, Frederick Barth, Kenneth Brown, Elizabeth Colson, Elaine Combs-Schilling, Adnan Daoud, Alain deJanvry, Morris Fred, Fred Huxley, Lamont Lindstrom, Laurence Michalak, and Lucette Valensi. I am especially grateful for the instructive correspondence with Jean Poncet during my research in Tunisia and France. Burton Benedict, Elbaki Hermassi, and, most of all, Nelson Graburn scrutinized the progression of this research and offered their continued support throughout the years. They have all done their best to steer me in the right direction. This book is only one of the paths I have taken in my study of Medjerda. My own students have encouraged me by their enthusiasm, insight, and support of Middle East Studies at San Jose State University. My family has been uncommonly patient in awaiting the completion of this study (only to see me begin the next). The encouragement of my husband, Marc, his accompaniment to North Africa on numerous occasions, and his continued participation in the research process have been instrumental to my fieldwork. In addition, he has provided me with a continual source of support, comfort, and childcare at those times when I never seem to leave the computer in the attic. Our children, Michael and Rayna, must be thanked for their cheerful explorations in North Africa as well as for their endurance of the writing process. Michael, conceived in Medjerda, is adept at finding his way through the medinas of North Africa, and Rayna keeps asking why I did not name her Fatima. My in-laws, too, have offered their unfailing support and encouragement, and my own parents have given me a lifelong commitment to the study of Middle Eastern culture.

Names of local people and places have been changed to protect their anonymity. Medjerda is the name of the entire fertile valley that traverses northern Tunisia. This study was carried out in the lower, or eastern, portion of the valley. The name is derived from the river, Oued Medjerda, which meanders throughout the length of the valley. Fellahin, farm managers, agency representatives and archivists provided me with copies of maps and documents that I did not even know existed. Most of the maps were constructed by combining regional geographical surveys with land agency farm plans and merging these onto a single topographical master. Both Figures 1.2 and 1.3 were compiled by combining over a dozen separate farm surveys supplied by three different state agencies. The regional farm plans tended to be on different scales which I had to standardize before proceeding. For this reason, the maps should be taken as schematic, rather than cartographically precise, and I take responsibility for any errors in this regard.

Standard Arabic transliteration is used and italicized throughout the text, with the following exceptions. Arabic words which are found in English, such as *couscous, souk, hadj,* and *hammam,* are not italicized. English language dictionaries have alternate spellings for these terms. I have used spellings which best approximate local pronunciation of Arabic dialect. Thus, a term like *souk,* or open-air weekly market, may at times be spelled *soug* or *souq* to reflect variations in local usage. Some spellings have come to English through the intermediary of French and it is the French orthography which has become standardized. A good example of this is the word *couscous,* which would have been written *Kuskus* had it entered English directly from the Arabic. The inconsistencies of transliteration reflect both local usage and the degree to which a term has been adopted by the French during the colonial period and its subsequent entry into English. The songs, sayings and proverbs found in these pages are taken from the courtyards and fields of Medjerda. There appeared to be a variety of versions of each, and those familiar with the region may have encountered alternate forms. The sayings and proverbs which head each chapter are transliterated in rural Tunisian dialect. The Arabic calligraphy, generously provided by my colleague, Hussein Al Hussein, Imam of the Masjid of Santa Clara, provides a more standardized rendition of the transliterated Arabic.

French terms are italicized, with the following exceptions. Words like *cooperateur* and *agro-combinat* are treated as English terms because they are the more common forms found in rural development studies on North Africa. The use of foreign terms and the variations in their spelling should be looked at as artifacts of different degrees of cultural contact and are as much a part of the data as the narrative.

I thank Ruhama Veltfort for her editorial assistance, Louis Collonge for computer assistance, and Rachel Mundy-Johnson for her patience and aid in the preparation of the manuscript. I am grateful to John Entelis, editor of State, Culture, and Society in Arab North Africa, and Barbara Ellington of Westview Press for their encouragement and support.

Mira Zussman

Development and
Disenchantment
in Rural Tunisia

مجردة اسهار الغربة / مجردة خبز الشربة

Introduction

mjerda isharr ul-ghurba | mjerda khubz u-shurba
Medjerda, land of injustice and exile | Medjerda, land of bread and soup

Long years after the departure of the French from northern Tunisia, the memory, imagery and influence of the colonized past has persisted. This imagery, phrased locally in an uneasy dualism of *ᶜarbi* (Arab) and *souri* (French) classifications, has pervaded the daily life of the fellahin of the Medjerda Valley despite decades of colonial absence.

The fellahin of Medjerda express their colonial reminiscences and contemporary experiences through what Sahlins has called "historical metaphors and mythical realities" (1981). Thus, local Medjerdi interpretations of present experience are couched in seemingly anachronistic categories from the colonial past: contemporary national interventions are associated with the French and referred to as *souri*, while local initiative and customary practices are considered *ᶜarbi*, or Arab. National policy directives and foreign development programs vividly, bitterly, and *nostalgically* bring to mind the years as laborers under French colonial landowners.

Throughout Tunisia, certain epithets characterize given towns, villages, and tribes. These epithets are standardized and almost always negative. Medjerda has two epithets by which it is known; one is positive and the other is negative, but both serve to heighten the *ᶜarbi/souri* theme. The first is the one by which Medjerda is best known to others throughout the country: *mdjerda isharr ul-ghurba*, or "Medjerda—injustice and exile." The second is one which the Medjerdis themselves promote: *mdjerda khubz u-shurba*, or "Medjerda— bread and soup." Both epithets recall the colonial occupation of the region. In the first, *isharr*, here translated as injustice, also means disaster—injury, evil, sin, evildoer, and culprit. *Ghurba* has a triple connotation: first, it refers to exile and banishment—life away from home and separation from one's native country. First, *ghurba* refers to the Moorish expulsion—exile—after the reconquest of Spain and their subsequent re-

1

turn to North Africa. Indeed, the people of Medjerda claim they originated elsewhere and came to the region seeking refuge and opportunity. Secondly, *ghurba* refers to those whose origins stem from the Gharbi tribe and region of Morocco, or from the Maghrib in general. Thirdly, it refers to Westerners, not only in the Maghribi sense, but also in the Western sense, *i.e.* European. Thus, the ambiguity of the term *ghurba* itself embodies the historical contradictions of the region's population: Are they Maghribi, i.e. North African or are they Westerners, i.e. European? To whom does the land of Medjerda belong?

The epithet readily conveys Medjerda's painful history and duality, and encapsulates Medjerda's origins, acknowledging the tribes and townsfolk who were forced to leave their homelands because of drought or political upheaval and who emigrated to this spot on the Medjerda River and came to call Medjerda home. In addition, it recalls the incursion of French, Italian, and other *colons*—who not only uprooted themselves, but also uprooted the *ᶜarbi* inhabitants and society which stood in their path.

The second epithet—"Medjerda: bread and soup"—offers a positive characterization of the same dual identity. The bread referred to is not the indigenous *khubz tabouna*, but rather French *baguettes* and Italian breads which are still baked with pride and care in the regionally renowned *boulangeries* of Medjerda-*souri*, just as they were in the colonial days. The soup referred to is the homemade Tunisian *shorba*. The epithet speaks of the delicious *souri* bread and heavenly *ᶜarbi* soup of Medjerda—both of which local people claim are famous throughout the country. French bread tastes best when dipped into Tunisian *shorba*: they complement each other and enhance each other's best qualities. They represent the best of both worlds. Between "injury and exile" and "bread and soup," lies all the ambivalence Medjerdis feel about their *ᶜarbi/souri* heritage.

The Town and the Region

As the proverb indicates, the town of Medjerda was founded by the Moors when they were forced to flee Spain at the end of the fifteenth century; it was built on the ruins of the much larger ancient Roman city. Stones from the ancient amphitheater were used to construct the town, as well as to reconstruct the Roman dam in the region, and Roman artifacts found under the plow decorate both the mud huts and the courtyards of the fellahin of Medjerda. The countryside appears more Roman or French than Andalusian, but the *medina* of Medjerda retains its Moorish architecture, particularly in its arcades, tile work, and bath-houses. Mosques and *koubbas* dedicated to saints rise above the maze of narrow lanes; whitewashed walls are punctuated by blue-painted fortress-like doors—many of which are lined with handsome Andalusian tilework. The founding families of Medjerda have kept alive their heritage and yet, since the last wave of Moors arrived in 1632, the Andulsi have dwindled and now constitute a minority in both the region and the town.

The town became known as "the land of *chechia* makers," for the Andalusians of Medjerda specialized in manufacturing the red felt hats worn by men throughout North Africa. The town prospered from its agriculture as well as from its textile industry. The fertile lower Medjerda Valley, which surrounds the town, was covered with vast olive orchards and wheat fields, while vegetable gardens were cultivated along the river. Every family had its land, its gardens, and its flocks grazing in the hills above the valley. Rural hamlets—*douar*—arose in the countryside and blended nearly invisibly into the earth.

The Medjerda River meanders through the valley, crosscutting the 51,000 hectares that make up the Delegation of Medjerda. The Djebel El Kebir rises over 600 meters along the western reaches of the region. The average rainfall is a plentiful 475 millimeters per year, but it fluctuates widely from year to year. In 1947, for example, there was a sparse 230 millimeters while in 1953 the 820 millimeters of rain caused heavy flooding. Winter cold can approach -3° Centigrade and the fierce summers are unrelenting at around 45° Centigrade (URD de Medjerda 1963). The soil is rich but salinated in parts of the region. The French claimed that at the turn of the century, much of the Medjerda's land was uncultivated and had been used primarily for grazing.

The French began settling the region almost as soon as the Protectorate was declared in 1881. They built a town of their own alongside the *medina* and filled it with *épiceries, boulangeries,* and *charcuteries.* The French town was dominated by the *église française.* The panorama of the countryside quickly became dotted with the red tile of French villas, villages and farmhouses. Water works were begun on a large scale during this period. Roads were paved and farm machinery was imported. The region evolved into a replica of the French countryside.

In 1905, the town of Medjerda had approximately twenty-five hundred residents and the region as a whole had not quite 15,400 people (Canal 1914). Rapid expansion of colonial farming attracted Italian migrant workers and impoverished nomads from southern and central Tunisia. The latter fled drought-ravaged lands and left their dying flocks behind them and arrived at the verdant colonial farms of the Medjerda Valley to become agricultural laborers. What had once been known as an Andalusian town became home to a conglomerate of peoples.

The growth of agriculture in Medjerda was further accelerated by the inauguration of a number of organizations and programs unique in Tunisia.

First, in 1895, was the founding of the *Ferme-Ecole de L'Alliance Israélite Universelle* which included four thousand hectares in the environs of Djemiliya. The school was dedicated to teaching farm methods to young Tunisian Jews so that they too could participate in the expanding field of agriculture. Although few if any of the graduates of the Ferme-Ecole became farmers—many turned instead to marketing or management—the school's 4,000 hectares were rapidly transformed.

Secondly, in 1901 the *Colonie Agricole Indigène de Djebel El Kebir* was established on the *habous*, or religious foundation, property of Henchir Mellasine. At this site, sixteen hundred hectares were ceded by the *Djemaᶜia*—the Administration of Religious Foundations—for the foundation of an agricultural school for Tunisian boys. Described later as "more military than pastoral" (Violard 1906:238), the school accomplished great agricultural feats by using young schoolboys to clear the rocky, brush-covered plain. While the *Alliance* school had emphasized theory over practice, the *Colonie Indigène* apparently did the reverse (Violard 1906:236-239).

Thirdly, an experiment at Bordj Toungar used Tunisian prisoners as the labor force for colonial estates. And fourth was the creation of the *Societé Foncière et Agricole* at Sidi Ugᶜud, an organization of colonial farmers who lobbied to obtain markets abroad, import of agricultural machinery, and oppose the immigration of Italian workers into Tunisia.

This last lays bare the rationale of the colonial regime for developing programs like those enumerated above, which had the purpose of recruiting and developing an indigenous work force and promoting modern agriculture among the indigenous population. French colonial farmers demanded more agricultural laborers at the same time that they insisted on fewer Sicilian workers. They feared that the Italians might begin as workers but would rise to compete with them in the land market. The French *colons* of Medjerda, however, were opposed both to the immigration of Italian workers and the training of the indigenous Arab labor. Whenever possible, they opted for a third alternative—mechanized farming. The *Societé Foncière* later evolved into the powerful *Societé d'Agriculture de Tunisie*, or French Agriculturalists' Union, which in the post-colonial period became UNAT and the *Dar El Fellahin*.

The borders of the Delegation of Medjerda have changed numerous times, but the town of Medjerda has remained the administrative center of the region. The town is the seat of the Municipality, or town government, as well as the *ᶜomda*, or district government, and the Delegation, or regional government *(see Figure I.1)*. Medjerda, once part of the Governorate of Tunis, by the 1970s had been incorporated into the newly formed Governorate of Zaghouan. The governorate in turn is responsible to the national government just as each lower administrative level is responsible to the next highest. Here we are concerned with farms throughout the Delegation of

Medjerda and the terms "delegation" and "region" are used interchangeably.

The town of Medjerda is only forty kilometers west of Tunis, the capital, but it has remained more provincial than Tunisia's southernmost oases. Medjerda has neither dunes nor beaches to attract the European tourists who roam over much of the country. There are no hotels and no restaurants and not even the Friday market draws outsiders. No Peace Corps personnel have ever been installed in the region, and Americans are a fleeting memory from the bombardments they exchanged with the Germans throughout the Medjerdi countryside during World War II ("Europeans fought it out among themselves in *our* fields," said one Medjerdi, summing up the war). The memory of these bombardments is jogged only on those occasions when a mine on the Djebel Es Sghir explodes spontaneously in the summer heat. People from Tunis do not come to Medjerda unless they are sent there—as administrators, teachers, policeman, or agrarian advisers—but the fellahin of Medjerda go to the capital to market their produce and make purchases.

In contrast to the nearby capital, Medjerda appears sleepy, insulated, and self-involved. Local men have enjoyed the protectiveness the town affords their families and, in fact, have endeavored to cultivate this atmosphere. Women are veiled when they walk through the streets of Medjerda; they handle little or no money, and they rarely—if ever—are seen in the shops, but radio and television bring the outside world into the family courtyard.

Peasants, Farmers, and Fellahin

This book is essentially the story of the fellahin of Medjerda—their experiences and understanding of their experiences with European colonizers and developers. After a century of colonization in North Africa, the word *fellah*—singular of *fellahin*—seems to have been assimilated into the French language to the point that it is used in common parlance and found in written accounts without an accompanying definition. Cassell's defines it simply as *Fellah* (Egyptian peasant); (pl. *fellaheen*). (1965:340). French language newspapers in North Africa use the term *fellah*—with the plural *fellahs*—interchangeably with *agriculteurs,* or agriculturalists. In the Tunisian French language press it is rarely if ever used synonymously with *paysans,* or peasants.

"Agriculturalist" is a bulky term and is as uncommon in English as it is vague. "Cultivator" implies exotic practices such as slash and burn cultivation in, say, the Ituri Forest of Zaire. The root of the Arabic term *fellah* means *to plow, till and cultivate.* The best translation therefore is simply *"farmer,"* yet Webster's defines *fellah* as "A peasant in Egypt, Syria, and other Arabic-speaking countries" (1961:304). By definition, then, this work clearly belongs within the genre of peasant studies. Despite this, however, I have some reservations about using the term *peasant*. I am concerned about inaccuracies which may be engendered in the reader's mind. My reservations extend to the term "farmer" as well. Hill (1989:8-29) resorts to using *"country people"* to avoid the *peasant* classificatory trap.

Jean Poncet, author of innumerable books and articles on Tunisian land and agriculture, and Lucette Valensi, author of *Fellahs Tunisiens* (1977), do not define the term at all. Cuisenier defines *fellah* in his glossary of *L'Ansarine* (1961) as *cultivateur* but does not elaborate on this in his text. Bardin went further than his colleagues by classifying fellahin into four types, based on the amount of land worked; he attempts, with self-admitted lack of success, to determine how many hectares per household member qualifies one for each category (Bardin 1965:35-51). Bardin further distinguishes fellahin from *khammes*—sharecroppers who receive one-fifth of the harvest—as well as from agricultural workers and those who rent land. The problem, of course, is that the *khammes* would classify themselves simply as fellahin working under a *khammes* contract.

Rich or poor, fellahin define themselves as a group—in distinction to, for instance, merchants or teachers or craftsmen. This characteristic prevails even though one fellah is landless, one cultivates a small parcel, and one is the owner of huge estates. Despite the veneer of equality, fellahin may be classified into valid socio-economic categories. One must recognize, however, that the veneer is functional in that it allows fellahin a sense of solidarity—voiced through the forum of the *Dar El Fellahin*, or Farmers' Union—at the same time that it allows the full play of patron-client relations with little shame or humiliation. As one fellah to another, *Si* X can petition *Si* Y for aid when in distress, fully confident that he will one day be able to return the favor.

Here we are concerned with colonial imagery and its persistence in the post-colonial period. The English term *peasant* appears to approximate what the French have meant by *fellah*—particularly when employing phrases such as *la mentalité des fellahin*, whose connotation is clearly that of *peasant mentality*. Country people, indeed, may not necessarily be peasants, but in both the colonial and post-colonial periods of Tunisia they have been considered as such.

Development and Disenchantment

By the mid-1970s, colonialism was a historical fact that had not been directly experienced by the younger generation. Independence, after all, had been declared in 1956. In spite of this, colonial metaphors continued to influence the daily lives of the fellahin and their economic strategies. These metaphors helped to determine their responses to state directives and promote an oppositionalism toward foreign aid projects. Rural development workers deemed opposition to their programs as simply another example of "peasant mentality." I had gone to Medjerda to explore the relationship of local rural people to the nation state and to reconcile the paradox between post-colonial nationalist pride and rejection of national policy. I was interested primarily in the personal experiences of rural people, the fellahin, and their interpretations of the political and economic changes which they had endured. I had assumed that the colonial enterprise would have influenced rural attitudes toward state control of agriculture to some small extent.

The classic works on French colonialism in North Africa lead one to expect strong post-colonial nationalism, pride, gratitude and a sense of relief at independence. But that was not the case in rural Tunisia. Post-colonial national policies were continual disappointments to the rural sector, and compliance with the new state's directives eroded rapidly, particularly in Medjerda.

The French Protectorate over Tunisia had ended much more amicably than had the French dominion over Algeria or even Morocco. Nevertheless, by the 1970s, the new Tunisian national authorities themselves were being equated with the colonizer, and foreign development workers were compared *unfavorably* with the French landowners of the colonial past. Colonialism might have been long dead but its memory continued to haunt the rural population.

The post-colonial period under Habib Bourguiba, first president of the Republic of Tunisia, was one of struggle for authenticity. Bourguiba sought to reconcile European and indigenous cultures to create an independent state based upon the best of both worlds. As Bourguiba himself attempted to strike a balance between the two, so did the rest of the populace. This struggle was nowhere more apparent than in the Medjerda Valley during the formative period of the new republic.

Bourguiba was faced not only with the transition from a colonial protectorate to an independent state but also with the challenge of initiating a sense of national identity which went beyond shared anti-colonial sentiments. The task, as he saw it, was to instill in his people a longing for national development which would supersede contrary personal economic goals.

Tunisians were asked to sacrifice themselves—as they had for the colonizer—but now they were to build an indigenous future whose citizens were predominantly Arab Muslims rather than French Christians. In the mid-1960s and 70s, Tunisia was one of a multitude of formerly colonized countries undertaking this enterprise of nation-building. The bitterness and indignation against the colonizer that predominated in such countries as

Algeria or Zaire were less pronounced in Tunisia because colonial penetration had been less extensive and the struggle for independence less costly.

Unlike many of the leaders of newly independent states, Bourguiba sought reconciliation and partnership with Europe. He perceived his mission as merging both cultural traditions, *ʿarbi* and *souri* —Arab and French— rejecting colonialism while accepting useful aspects of European culture and practice. Europe was neither to be forgotten nor forbidden. Yet, the persistence of colonial imagery in the countryside reflected ambivalence on the part of the heavily-colonized rural sector to the policy of reconciliation with the French which Bourguiba promoted.

The first attempts at creating a national identity, moreover, went well beyond symbols and imagery. Under Bourguiba, Minister of Finance and Planning Ahmed Ben Saleh instituted a policy of centralized control over political and economic action. As will be seen, however, economic centralization was met with major resistance. Between the years 1969 and 1979, Tunisian economic policy was reversed and the national government began to institute policies to decentralize rather than centralize farming, industry and distribution.

The new government's policies shifted repeatedly in these post-independence years. Every time state policy reversed itself, the abandoned policy was deemed simply an *experiment* which had failed, or only a transitional *phase* in nation-building. There had been numerous such experiments; some entailed centralized national control over rural affairs, while others were decentralized programs. Decentralization sometimes meant local autonomy but more often amounted to dividing large state agencies into smaller, more specialized ones. There was also an assortment of "intermediate" programs, although it appeared that they too were under national rather than local management.

The result was that by 1979, the countryside had become a patchwork of farms representing many stages of national development. Farms existed side by side which demonstrated a number of entirely different national policies now openly considered failures by either the public or the Ministry of Agriculture, or both. One extended family living in the same household was more than likely to be working concurrently under three, four or five entirely different land tenure systems.

Given this history and experience, the fertile lower Medjerda Valley provides us with a microcosm of the struggle between advocates of large-scale centralized systems, small-scale decentralized ones and every possible shade in between.

In the valley, it appeared that rural people had experienced and were dissatisfied with every development plan initiated from the capital. Even enthusiastic ideological support for a particular state policy was accompanied by rejection of its application on the ground. Socialists rejected cooperatives.

Entrepreneurs were dissatisfied with decentralization. Nationalists detested state farms. The region was filled with rural philosophers for whom "nation-building" was the focus of both despondency and mirth. As a result of their experience and observations, the people of Medjerda designed their economic lives to circumvent the fluctuations of the national political process.

Strategies for self-preservation, sometimes bordering on outright sabotage, had been refined under the French, and were judiciously employed. For many of the fellahin of Medjerda, the idea of the colonizer—the *colon*—continued to be the metaphor for the state long after independence. Thus, there was no explicit criticism of the national government, only of the colonial "survivals" which remained.

Remembrances of the Protectorate era evoked nervous anticipation of repeated history. Rural people in Medjerda feared another nightmarish cycle of what they considered unfair land expropriations and inexplicable agrarian reforms. Throughout the Bourguiba years, memories and reconstructed images of pre-independence Tunisia remained impediments to unconditional acceptance by the fellahin of *any* regional development plans that the state initiated. The countryside, it turned out, was filled with an infinite variety of pragmatists and skeptics.

The *ʿarbi/souri* dichotomy was used locally to articulate heartfelt and sometimes volatile feelings toward the state and its teams of European experts. There was no single monolithic native point of view about development or nation building, but rather a symphony of voices expressing perspectives that at times were harmonious and at times discordant. The unifying theme, if one could be said to exist, appeared to be a profound and pervasive disenchantment with national development, and dismay at the prospect of future encounters with the rural experiments of the state. The fellahin wanted development to work; they wanted to earn more and live better. They simply did not believe that the methods mandated by the state would facilitate their long-term goals.

Older fellahin were concerned that with the continual restructuring of land tenure and agrarian policy that there would be little they could offer their children as inheritance. Younger rural people, in response, expressed a powerful longing to emigrate to Europe—accompanied by an equal measure of Tunisian ambivalence regarding Europe and the European—but emigration eluded most. For the fellahin who remained behind on the farm, reactions to European development workers were influenced by earlier colonial experiences.

Foreign development workers, it turned out, were exacerbating their own ineffectiveness by continual, perhaps unconscious, condescension toward the rural population. Something resembling contempt crept over their brows as they diagnosed pervasive "rural oppositionalism" to their work in the region as evidence of a familiar yet unpleasant and unchange-able *peasant mentality*. Developers sensitive enough not to refer to the fellahin as stubborn, ignorant peasants spoke of them as happy fellows leading simple carefree lives who could not yet see the advantages of increased production. The anachronism of these views of *the native* was lost on them. Thus, both the fellahin and development workers exhibited attitudes about each other based upon evaluations of their own earlier experiences.

Whether local rural people were considered stubborn, ignorant or care-free, state and foreign development workers in the region agreed that non-compliance with program directives was primarily a symptom and that *peasant mentality* was the disease. The only debate was about whether or not the condition was curable.

Despite the above, developers perceived themselves as unappreciated altruists, rather than self-interested neo-colonizers, as some in the region liked to call them. The contrast between the self-image of foreign developers and the way they were viewed by the rural people in the region was particularly interesting in light of the fact that the fellahin never discovered that many of the region's European developers indeed had been colonial farmers or entrepreneurs before becoming employed by the foreign aid branches of their government.

Fellahin depicted themselves as agricultural and political realists, a striking contrast to the ignorant peasants they were portrayed as in news-papers published in the cities. As realists, they were interested in the long-term benefits of government programs. From their point of view, a government incapable of maintaining its own long-term stability was unlikely to fulfill any of its long-range promises to the countryside. Politicians and state-appointed program directors were accused of being motivated more by their own short-term financial or political gain than by lasting rural or national interest.

Various interpretations were given to the motives of development work-ers from the city or abroad. On the one hand, some fellahin were well aware that Medjerda meant nothing more to the developers than a rung on the ladder of promotions; and that developers, eager to go home to their own communities, had no long-term commitment to the region. On the other hand, there were fellahin who feared that foreign developers *might* take up permanent residence—and then the cry of "colonialism" was all the more urgent. The foreign aid givers were condemned on both accounts.

Not all representatives in the national government were oblivious to these irreconcilable mutual perceptions. However, the Ministry of Agricul-ture and its dendritic branches of sub-agencies pressured developers and fellahin alike to simply get on with the business of growing enough to feed the burgeoning population.

Fellahin joked that most of the "production" by the Ministry of Agriculture was in the proliferation of agencies rather than strains of high-yield wheat. But despite conflicts over what constituted appropriate agrarian policy, Tunisian self-sufficiency in agriculture was a universally lauded goal both in the countryside and the capital.

The common ground between the goals of the state and those of rural people eroded each time state policies were reversed. By 1979, that is, after more than two decades of office, President Bourguiba was applauded primarily for his good health and longevity. But he was by then in his eighties and there was no doubt that a change in government was forthcoming if not imminent. The fellahin of Medjerda prepared themselves for the inevitable.

Given the sum of these political uncertainties, there was little incentive in the countryside to comply with agrarian development programs very likely to be overturned before completion. This political rationale for what agricultural economists call risk aversion among peasantry entirely eluded the developers of the region.

I wanted to understand the qualitative experience of living first under colonialism, then under state centralization, and then under a number of different land tenure arrangements. How did these vacillations affect the relationship between rural people and the state?

The familiar struggle between rural autonomy and national authority is central to the dilemma of nation-building in Tunisia. Government policies attempt to dictate local practices and define economic roles, and they are met with resistance at every turn. President Bourguiba recognized and articulated this enduring problem on the third anniversary of agrarian reform in the lower Medjerda Valley.

> In this republic of 4 million people, how can we leave family units, which are states in miniature ruled by autonomous chieftains, to fend for themselves? The state, which sees beyond the individual, must intervene for the sake of national solidarity. (Bourguiba, June 11, 1961)

Bourguiba's statement, reminiscent of the classical concern with the relationship between family and state, inspired this investigation. How does a nation achieve balance between the requirements of the state and the needs of local people?

In Tunisia, competition between family and state for territory, resources, and allegiance became pronounced during periods of increased government attention to modernization of the rural sector, as was the case in the late 1960s and 1970s. This formative period provides an excellent opportunity to explore the early stages in the shift from centralized to decentralized policies and the impact of these changes on the relationship between rural families and the state. The authority of the central government in Tunisia has always been strong when compared to other North African countries. Its authority over land was exerted during the nineteenth century Beylical period, well before the establishment of the French Protectorate (see e.g. Valensi 1977).

I found that a century of fluctuations of national policy had exacerbated farmer oppositionalism and heightened the skepticism of fellahin concerning development programs. Foreign developers in the region had analyzed "risk aversion" in the lower Medjerda Valley, and had concluded,

> In addition to the farm size issue, older farmers are more risk-averse than younger farmers. Isolated farmers are more risk-averse than those farmers on the valley floor near the distribution centers, and farmers totally dependent on their farms for livelihood are more risk-averse than those with off- farm income. (Nygaard 1979:85)

Developers attempted to combat the risk-aversion they perceived by providing more aid to those fellahin whom they considered amenable to change. This policy did not go unnoticed by other fellahin who found themselves snubbed by development workers because they appeared too conservative. Moreover, this meant that developers furthered outside (i.e., non-local) entrepreneurs to invest in the region and made land available to these outsiders instead of to local fellahin. Such practices helped to further erode confidence in the development process. In fact, the fellahin do not consider themselves to be risk averse. Their choices in economic innovation simply do not always coincide with the national interest.

In the Field

The courtyard doors are closed to the outsider; entrance comes only when one becomes a neighbor, a friend, a member of the household—in a word: Medjerdi. The lane my husband and I lived on turned out to be vintage Medjerda; one of the oldest Andalusian lanes in the *medina*, or old *ᶜarbi* part of town, and inhabited by some of the most respected founding families. The hospitality and acceptance of our neighbors—and my husband's status as a medical doctor—gave us "standing" in the community. Medjerdis were surprised and impressed that we had chosen the Arab rather than the French quarter as our residence; we were apparently the first Europeans ever to do so. This choice recommended us to our neighbors more than any other credentials; Medjerda-*ᶜarbi* quickly became home.

The fellahin evaluated contemporary Europeans and their ways in the light of colonial parallels; thus a young, unknown European might be seen as a literal genealogical descendant of the *colons* of the past. In this way, I

FIGURE I.1   The Delegation of Medjerda: Political and Topographical Features: Valid 1975

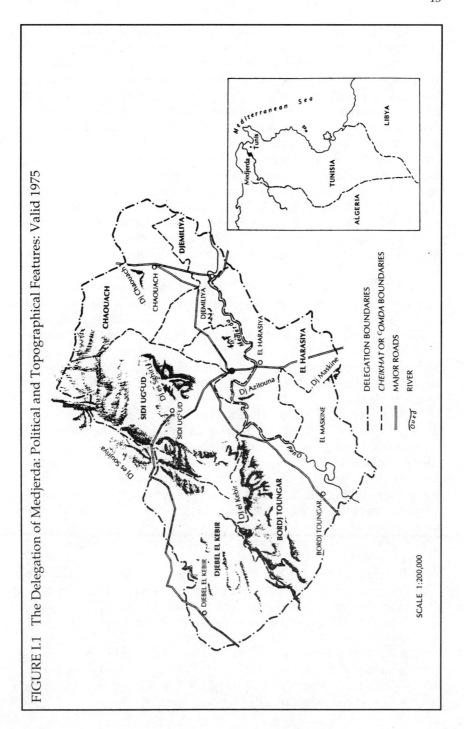

DELEGATION BOUNDARIES

CHEIKHAT OR ʿOMDA BOUNDARIES

MAJOR ROADS

RIVER

SCALE 1:200,000

was at first taken for the daughter of a French landowner returning to check up on *my* land. No category yet existed for American anthropologist, and the assumptions were that I would behave as the French had: I would drink whiskey, eat pork, dress skimpily, smoke in public, etc. Confusion arose when I failed in all these respects. The new assumption, which was both more comfortable and somewhat more accurate, was that I had come to learn how to become ᶜ*arbia*. A good number of the community dedicated themselves to assisting me in that task.

The presence of a European who came to learn instead of to teach was both an opportunity and a novelty not to be missed. No American, I was told, had been in Medjerda since the battles of World War II. One suspicious old fellah wondered why my husband was called Marc—a French name which had belonged to the most powerful colonial mayor of Medjerda—instead of "Johnny," like the soldiers he remembered from his youth. In this way, I began to learn about the categories used to distinguish competing ways of life.

I was told to seek out the storytellers of the French colonial days. I was handed old family documents and photographs to peruse in order to better understand the responses of the fellahin to change. I was told to look for the old French families who had dominated the region; to find them in France itself and to hear their side of the story. I found myself in the national archives of Tunisia and France—an anthropologist surrounded by historians asking why I wasn't "in the field." Ultimately, I did find "the colonizer" and hear his story.

Each of our neighbors owned agricultural land in addition to having an urban occupation. Fieldwork progressed swiftly from moving in to meeting neighbors to visiting farms. A drive through the countryside—always in the company of others—meant stopping to meet and talk to many other farm families along the way. Often enough, we never reached our intended destination. Within the first six months of research I had visited the six cooperatives of the region, the agro-combinat farms, and scores of private and agrarian reform farms. During the second six months I concentrated on intensive visiting of selected farms. It is difficult to say exactly how many families were visited regularly (that is to say, weekly) during this period—probably between ten and twenty—for I soon discovered that I was encountering the same families over and over as they visited each other. About sixty extended family households participated in the overall study, and in time, I inevitably discovered that almost everyone I had visited was in some way related to the others. If my own farm visits diminished on occasion, fellahin and their families came to my door in Medjerda mid-week to remind me of my obligations and to re-establish contact. Friday market day in town invariably found our house filled with farm women, much to the dismay of some of our more status-conscious neighbors.

During the first days of fieldwork in the countryside, I discovered to my horror that although Medjerdis understood my university learned Tunisian Arabic, I did not understand theirs. Before long, however, I was made aware that I had learned urban, rather than rural dialect. Medjerdiya women enjoyed helping me master the local manner of speaking and to appreciate the innuendos of *rural vs urban* Tunisian Arabic, and I learned to listen for and savor the differences in the accents of informants. Speech, like dress and mannerisms, proved to be an indicator of tribal or urban origins (or aspirations) as well as adherence to family customs. In Tunis, meetings with administrators and scholars were almost always conducted in French. This was partly because French was still very much an administrative and academic language in Tunis, partly because my Arabic was never as fluent as the French of my *Tunisois* informants; furthermore, meetings often included foreign project workers who spoke no Arabic at all. Having mastered rural Tunisian dialect, my countrified modern standard Arabic has since brought people to tears or laughter or a warm encouraging hug in such disparate places as the Rif Mountains and Baghdad.

Archival research on the colonial period began in Tunis at the National Archives in the Casbah, and proceeded to France. My understanding of colonial Medjerda is based in part upon interviews with former colonial families of the region and family archives, documents, photographs and momentos of both former *colons* and Medjerdis—all of which helped to bring the past to life.

The archives, statistics, maps and documents testify to the official land transformations of the region. But what I learned from the fellahin themselves was how regional metamorphosis *felt*. I became interested in the colonial era because it was still so vivid in the minds of the fellahin, and with the aid of the written record I was able to verify much of what I was told.

This chapter has presented some of the historical and geographic background of the region, and introduced some considerations and problems of agrarian development in Medjerda and in Tunisia as a whole. The chapters which follow proceed stratigraphically and reflect the various layers of Medjerdi experience, in terms of both chronology and meaning. Each chapter presents a different facet of the development process.

The first chapter discusses post-colonial land reform policies, with particular emphasis on the transformation of land-holdings in the period between 1969 and 1979. It is shown that there was, in fact, more land managed by the state—albeit indirectly—under the decentralization policies of the 1970s than existed during the cooperative era. A specific example, that of Sidi Ugᶜud, is given to illustrate the complex history of the region over the past century.

The second chapter delves into the contradictions of Medjerdi society brought about by colonial occupation, in terms of the local metaphor of *ᶜarbi/souri* classification. The third chapter explores the roots of Arab identity, and includes an analysis of tribal, urban, and class distinctions made in the region. This chapter contrasts the values and priorities of these different groupings, as well as documenting the relations between them. It is intended to demonstrate the long-standing diversity of the region and to belie the notion of a universal *mentalité des fellahin*.

National and foreign agrarian programs, primarily consisting of decentralized agricultural extension, are discussed in the fourth chapter. Here, it becomes apparent that there is a formidable duplication of effort on the part of numerous agencies to provide extension services. Not surprisingly, large-scale landowners play a substantial role in regional development and provide a link between local farmers and representatives of state agencies. As in chapter one, an example is used to illustrate the difficulty of agricultural extension even in a project applauded by local farmers.

The fifth chapter chronicles the individual experiences of eight fellahin. Here, class, tribe, colonial experience and personal disposition all contribute to the formation of different economic strategies and philosophies of life. The sixth builds upon this theme and further explores the choices and strategies of the fellahin. It includes a second look at the impact of colonialism upon the world view of Medjerdis, demonstrating how local perceptions of western and indigenous models affect the development process. Ambivalence regarding both Arab and European practices is shown to be a major impediment to progress for some farmers; for others, reinterpretation of traditional values has been successfully combined with selective acceptance of foreign ideas.

The final chapter discusses the general findings of the study, and concludes that the struggle between wary conservatism and innovative risk-taking takes place within all fellahin and that *both* attitudes are formed in response to long personal experience with the ambiguities, contradictions and frustrations of past and present agrarian reform.

اذا تقارك الأرياح يقع الدراك على المركب

1

Land and Cynicism

'itha it'arik lariyah, yag'a drak'ala markib
when the winds argue among themselves, the boat is out of luck

The French dominion over North Africa stimulated the pen and outrage of forceful chroniclers of colonialism like Fanon, Berque, and Bourdieu. Their writings led us to imagine an era of cultural as well as political independence in the post-colonial North African nation states. Hermassi (1972) reminded us that Morocco, Algeria and Tunisia not only experienced very different forms of colonial domination but also began with dissimilar political traditions. However, the impact of *la France* would not end when the colonizer departed. As Bourdieu put it, "each...may henceforth assume full responsibility for his own actions and for the widespread borrowings he has made from Western civilization; he can even deny a portion of his cultural heritage without denying himself in the process" (1962:157). Decades after the departure of the French, the memory, imagery and influence of the colonized past lingers in North Africa. In northern Tunisia, colonial imagery colors both the daily life and economic decisions of rural people. The fellahin of the Medjerda Valley have cultivated their memories along with their fields. Both continue to flourish.

During the past hundred years, Tunisia has experienced pendulum swings in national policy between centralization (state control) and decentralization (local autonomy—variously and ambiguously defined). Colonial centralization predominated during the French Protectorate period (1881-1956), with a proliferation of grass-roots colonial farming associations after World War II. During the post-colonial period, national policy continued to fluctuate, alternately espousing the virtues of national unity or local initiative. These vacillations have resulted in a long-standing cynicism and resistance by fellahin toward state directives. The ambivalence and hostility of the fellahin extend well beyond those policies and national directives dealing with purely agrarian reforms, and are particularly felt toward those aimed at transforming what is persistently referred to as "peasant mentality" (*L'Action* 1976-79).

Post-colonial oscillation of national reforms has left the countryside dotted with residual farm types from each development era. The lack of continuity between policies has helped fellahin maintain the pervasive belief that political uncertainty is the only certainty and that, despite the change in personnel and rhetoric, the post-colonial approach to the rural sector bears striking resemblance to that of its predecessor.

A Medjerdi farmer described the proliferation of the state land management bureaucracy in this way: "The OMVVM is the mother, the OTD is the father, and all the others [other agencies] are their sons." The smaller agencies and the state-managed farms have been shunted back and forth between these parent organizations, with serious consequences in all quarters.

A single case offers a microcosm of the past century of tumultuous land reforms in Medjerda. What emerges is a picture of familiar experiences repeated over and over again; first with the French *colons*, next with Tunisian administrators, and then with foreign developers. The scenarios enacted on specific state farms, cooperatives, agrarian reform and private parcels have varied sufficiently to give rise to ironies which affect the lives of the fellahin and the day-to-day functioning of the farms. They have been predictable inasmuch as they have engendered unending frustration on the part of the so-called "beneficiaries" of agrarian policy.

The case of Sidi Ug^{c}ud, an agricultural town in the region, points out the dangers of successful accommodation to unwanted land reforms. The legend of Sidi Ug^{c}ud's genesis legitimizes the region as ^{c}*arbi* territory in the minds of fellahin for the same reason that it negated their claims in the eyes of the French—it was legend. The *colons* succeeded in expanding their domain precisely because the legal status of land tenure at Sidi Ug^{c}ud was ambiguous—"legend" was no substitute for written title to the land. Later, the French agricultural community thrived due to the ruthless efficiency of its leadership. Later still, in the period of post-colonial reorganization, Sidi Ug^{c}ud's history of colonial profitability made it a low-risk site to use as an example. Fellahin who expected a return of their maraboutic property were sorely disappointed. They assumed—indeed, some claim they were promised—that full cooperation would be rewarded with the return of the domain to local authority. Their agricultural success, however, insured the reverse. Medjerda's history of land reform is replete with similar examples of locally perceived injustices (see Zussman, 1986).

The Example of Sidi Ug^cud

Medjerdi legend has it that long ago, a marabout, or saint, came out of Tripoli walking behind his mother. It was a long trip on foot and his mother told him *ug^cud*—"sit down, rest; you are tired." The holy man sat down to rest, but he fell sick and died within a few hours. The marabout, thereafter, was called "Sidi Ug^cud," since no one knew his name. He was buried on the spot where he died, and a shrine was erected at his tomb. He left no heir to claim ownership of the hilly chaparral at the foot of the Djebel El Kebir; nevertheless the land was considered his maraboutic domain. In time, farmers and herdsmen began to use the land and made offerings to the saint in the form of pilgrimage, sacrifice and donations to maintain the shrine at his tomb. The area became known as Sidi Ug^cud, but no village was established there. Sidi Ug^cud, in the the western province of the Delegation of Medjerda, remained a pasturage of beautiful rolling hills at the foot of the Djebel El Kebir, enjoyed freely by Medjerdi fellahin, their cattle and their flocks.

The French Colony

When the French Protectorate was established in 1881, the equivocal land tenure of Sidi Ug^cud caused difficulties for those who farmed or grazed their sheep in the area. While they had no legal claim to the land, neither was Sidi Ug^cud *habous* land—that is, an official religious foundation exempt from sale or fragmentation. Within two years of the establishment of the rotectorate, Sidi Ug^cud was settled by the French and became one of the earliest French agricultural communities in Tunisia.

By 1885, the French Ministry of the Interior had received hundreds of requests for land at Sidi Ug^cud from landless French workers and farmers. By 1888, Sidi Ug^cud was a thriving, well-established French village surrounded by 3,000 hectares of carefully cultivated vines, cereals, and fodder. Colonial inspectors considered the Domaine de Sidi Ug^cud to be a "remarkable example of French agriculture utilizing the most modern agricultural methods known." The inspectors found French relations with the indigenous population of Medjerda to be satisfactory, and declared that "the streets of the Arab quarter are clean, and its inhabitants give us testimony of their gratitude for improvements which are to their advantage" (FMFA Archives, 1888). The French farmers responded to this positive evaluation by requesting the expansion of colonial farming in the region from 3,000 to 30,000 hectares.

The French colony at Sidi Ug^{c}ud was presided over by the Commandante Gerodius, who "ruled his world with military precision and paternal benevolence" (FMFA Archives, 1888 p. 146). Four hundred people lived in the village in houses grouped around the Commandante's large villa. Gerodius, along with three other landowners of the area, formed an agricultural association, the *Societé Foncière et Agricole de Sidi Ug^{c}ud*, which later grew to become the powerful French Agriculturalists' Union of Tunisia—the *Societé d'Agriculture de Tunisie*. The Commandante was unanimously elected its president. He brought in one hundred thirty Sicilians to be agricultural workers at Sidi Ug^{c}ud, built houses for them, and established a school for their children—inasmuch as the French children, the offspring of landowners and their foremen, were sent to the French school in Medjerda-*souri*.

The introduction of Sicilians into the area brought Gerodius into conflict with other landowners of the association, who claimed that there were too many "foreigners" (i.e., Italians) in Tunisia. The irony of this appraisal appears never to have been acknowledged. The Commandante countered that his "compatriots at the same level [French agricultural laborers] would be less sober and less respectful" than the Sicilians (FMFA Archives, 1888 162).

The Commandante clearly indicated that what he wanted was both efficiency and servility, but the latter quality would not be appropriate among the French. In time, the dispute over French vs. Italian workers grew and was heatedly debated in the colonial newspapers. Despite prior claims of good relations, intergroup conflict became the norm and complaints multiplied concerning "the increasing number of crimes against the French by both Italians and Muslims" (FMFA Archives, 1888). The first gendarmerie and rural police force of Medjerda were created in response.

The possibility of hiring *indigènes* on colonial farms was not considered until the outbreak of World War I. Tunisians both were sent to France as laborers and hired by colonial wives—who had taken over farm management from their war-mobilized husbands—to replace conscripted European farm workers. The term *"indigènes"* was employed by the French to refer to the local Arab-Berber Muslim population. They were called—and continue to be called by members of old *colon* families—"the indigenous ones," as if their identities were rooted only in their physical presence in the region much like the chaparral and wild boar of the Djebel El Kebir overlooking the fertile valley.

During the war, the French farmwomen of Sidi Ug^{c}ud nevertheless established bonds with local Arab families whom they took into their employment; these ties were to endure well past the colonial demise. After the war, many of these wives were awarded the *Mérite Agricole* for their desperate efforts to manage the neglected and abandoned colonial farms, as well as for being "an example to the indigenous population" (FMFA Archives, 1888 1917-29). The award also was given to Tunisian farmers who had accepted French cultivation techniques, and on the whole it was seen as an incentive to raise production throughout the region, including on "indigenous" farms.

Despite the efforts of colonial farm women and indigenous innovators, the post-war period was one of economic crisis in agriculture. Many colonial farms had been abandoned for five years, during which time crops perished, animals died, and equipment disappeared. The association begun by Gerodius spoke for all colonial farmers when it demanded French aid to offset the heavy losses. When France put pressure on colonial farmers for more agricultural imports, the *colons* complained once more of their inability to attract workers and their consequent incapacity to expand agriculture. Upon their return, however, the French landowners were still averse to increasing their reliance on Arab labor. Instead, their solution was to rely more heavily on mechanized farming and avoid the implications of further recognizing an indigenous bond with the land.

Here, however, the French community of Sidi Ug^cud met with a new obstacle. The French government insisted that the *colons* buy only French-made farm equipment, but would not expedite shipments—which sat in the Marseille harbor for months. As a consequence, the *colons* feared that France was abandoning them, and they were forced to reconsider the expanded use of indigenous agricultural labor. Thus, the local inhabitants, mostly Djlass and Mejri, were inducted into French agricultural production.

Because of the Commandante's management, the farmlands of Sidi Ug^cud were better off than most. In 1920, while other colonial agricultural communities were struggling to rebuild their farms, the association opened a cooperative winery—the first of its kind in Tunisia—called the *Cave Viticole de Sidi Ug^cud*, and began producing its own wine, Côteaux de Medjerda. Arab workers were taught viticulture and the mechanics of farmer cooperation, and the region of Medjerda gained a reputation for turning failure into success well before the commencement of the second World War.

The region prospered in the period between the wars, but soon Medjerda was occupied alternately by German and American forces, experiencing major battles and bombardment. French farmers were mobilized once again; they served as civilian guides and translators in the Special Detachment of the British Forces, in the U.S. Strategic Services Section, and in the Tunisian Resistance (Auboire Letters, 1942-56). Tensions between French and Italian farmers in the region were eased by the fact that the Italians had become French nationals prior to the war.

Colonial families dispersed from the town of Sidi Ug^cud; those who remained in the region often escaped the bombardments by hiding with their Tunisian workers and servants in their mud huts along the forested slope of the nearby Djebel el Kebir. The fellahin of Medjerda never forgot the experience of French women and children living essentially ^c*arbi* lives for weeks or months at a time. The *colons* became part of Tunisian households and learned to live in the mud and straw *gourbis* of "their" *indigènes*. The ability and willingness of the *colons* to adapt to ^c*arbi* life during the war later contributed to the profound ambivalence felt by Tunisians during the struggle for independence; children who remembered fondly playing together on the slopes of Djebel el Kebir for years after the war were nevertheless at odds over the colonial enterprise.

Struggles for Independence

After the war, requests for colonial land multiplied and parcels were awarded on a point system which assigned a numerical value to agricultural experience, degrees, dependents, military resistance, captivity, wounds, campaigns, and decorations. Those with the greatest number of points—a maximum of sixty—held the highest priority in land awards. This method of land distribution was later used as a model to reward heroes of the struggle for independence against the French in 1956. Until that time, however, colonial farming at Sidi Ug^cud expanded and prospered. When independence appeared to be imminent, some *colons* sold their farms, gathered their belongings, and left for France. Others formed partnerships with Tunisians, transferring title to the farm while maintaining its management. Such partnerships enabled the *colons* to select and train their Tunisian successors and guarantee continuity on their farms. Still others maintained their farms as if independence had not been achieved, and refused to believe that the French government would not intervene if they were threatened with expropriation. This group of *colons* was the least prepared for the onset of expropriation in 1962.

The first step in the post-independence "Tunisification" process was the nationalization of colonial farms. Sidi Ug^cud's ready-made agricultural association and cooperative winery provided a framework on which to build the first indigenous agricultural cooperatives, which themselves were prototypes for the projected expansion of the cooperative movement. The fellahin of Sidi Ug^cud were already well-versed in the mechanics of cooperation, in that the French prototype had been one of a loose association of farmers pooling their capital (not their land) to invest jointly in the Côteaux de Medjerda winery. As might have been expected, the French *Cave Viticole* changed its name and affiliation to the UCCVT and became the first Tunisian state cooperative winery. Shortly thereafter, however, the Land Improvement Agency of the Medjerda Valley (the OMVVM) took over management of all the private French landholdings of Domaine Sidi Ug^cud and transformed it into the prototype, *Pré-Coopérative de Sidi Ug^cud.*

The pre-cooperative (PC) of Sidi Ug^cud comprised the farms of the

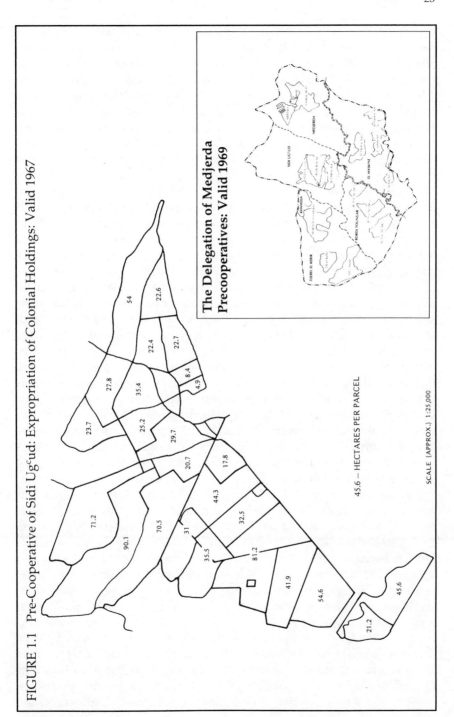

FIGURE 1.1 Pre-Cooperative of Sidi Ug\u1d9cud: Expropriation of Colonial Holdings: Valid 1967

The Delegation of Medjerda
Precooperatives: Valid 1969

45.6 — HECTARES PER PARCEL

SCALE (APPROX.) 1:25,000

twenty *colons* who had belonged to the association, and encompassed 935 hectares of unirrigated rolling hills. Half of this was devoted to vines, the other half to olive orchards. Tunisians who had been workers on the colonial farms—primarily the Djlass and Mejri—became cooperateurs on the same farms they had previously worked for the French. Their militant efforts during the struggle for independence had been tied to their own expectation of emancipation of the land, but in this they were disappointed.

In the exuberance of the period, the farm workers exalted in the conquest over their French masters and confidently anticipated that their success at PC Sidi Ug^{c}ud would ultimately be rewarded with perhaps fifty to seventy hectares of dry land for each of them and their families. The new government, however, had debts to other heroes of the independence movement, and soon the fellahin of Sidi Ug^{c}ud were joined by unknown families from throughout the delegation and beyond, who were rewarded with residence in the prosperous region as the OMVVM sought to reach its goal of settling one hundred cooperative families at Sidi Ug^{c}ud.

The Djlass and Mejri, who from the days of their neighboring ancestral territories to the south had long-established kinship bonds and marriage alliances, were devastated at the prospect of sharing "their" land with strangers. They had the skill and experience to work the land and manage the winery, and felt Sidi Ug^{c}ud had already reached its demographic limits. Instead of being able to look forward to a comfortable parcel of dry land, they now calculated that, divided among so many, each prospective individual parcel would be insufficient to support their growing families, even with their expertise in agricultural production at Sidi Ug^{c}ud. Perhaps they would need to keep the entire PC successful, not only to accomplish their long-term goal of parcellization, but simply in order to survive. Perhaps with the cooperative bonuses they could purchase parcels of land further up the mountain. The fellahin of Sidi Ug^{c}ud began to consider their options.

More colonial farms at Sidi Ug^{c}ud were regrouped to provide the core for a second pre-cooperative, Bordj Er Roumi, and together the two PCs were intended to form one permanent *Unité Coopérative de Production* (UCP). Bordj Er Roumi had not been under the Commandante's vigilant eye, nor had its farmers been members of the Cave Viticole, nor were its workers familiar with cooperative production. The fellahin of Sidi Ug^{c}ud began to anticipate setbacks both in agricultural production and in their hopes for individual family parcels. The cooperative became unwieldy and unmanageable; yet it continued to expand.

Over thirty UCPs were planned for the Delegation of Medjerda; by 1969, seventeen already had been formed. Two state land management agencies in the capital—the OMVVM with jurisdiction over irrigable land, and the OTD *(Office des Terres Domaniales)* which was to manage dry land—had worked together to define the boundaries of each cooperative farm and what they termed its potential carrying capacity, i.e., the number of cooperateurs and their families which could be supported on a given PC. Also calculated were the number of guaranteed work days, the number of seasonal workers to be employed, and the average income per cooperateur per year. The seasonal workers were to be selected from among the families settled on the PC and their wages were meant to supplement the family income. Intended land improvements and production increases over the subsequent ten years were projected, along with water requirements for OMVVM irrigation projects and revenue increases for each member of the cooperative.

The new independent government made it clear that these cooperative agricultural communities were planned; they were designed to speed up the development process and educate the rural population—not only in terms of production, but also in terms of household management and family planning. The pre-cooperatives looked good in print—but at the ground level, the view was different.

Sidi Ug^cud somehow prospered again, but Bordj Er Roumi and most of the other PCs in the region quickly went bankrupt. The monumental failure of PC Bordj Er Roumi—the inability of its fellahin to work cooperatively, to grow viable produce or to generate adequate income and profit—led inevitably to the dismantling of the cooperative and the parcelling out of twenty to thirty hectares of dry land to each family who had participated in the fiasco. The fellahin of PC Sidi Ug^cud were mortified. A former PC member recalls this period vividly:

Moncef's Tale

At the time of independence and after, I worked for the Neo-Destour. Everybody knows me, even as far as Testour. In 1964 or so, the Destour sent me out to tell the *colons* that they had to leave their land. I even went to the farm at Sidi Ug^cud where I was born (in the *gourbi* behind the French villa where my father had been a worker) and I was the one who told Monsieur Jean that he had to leave his farm.

Many families left the very next day. They took what they could, but they left a lot of things. Of course, they knew their days were numbered and had already made arrangements in France. Well, the next few months people were waiting around to see what would happen. The work had just about stopped and nobody knew what to do. For a few months it was pretty much laissez-faire. Whoever was there would take what he could or work whatever land he wanted. There was no bookkeeping. The sheep were allowed to roam all over the grape vines. There were lots of payoffs and graft. Everything had come to a halt.

Ben Salah came forward and had the idea of the pre-cooperatives and convinced Bourguiba that they were a good idea and he was the one who formed the pre-cooperatives. They put in charge of the PCs those people they thought would be responsible. They found unemployed civil servants and made them the *responsables*. I myself was given a job in charge of the warehouse on the PC where my land is now. This was in '68.

At the end of the year all the harvest was to go to Tunis from all the PCs and the profit was to be divided equally among all the members of all the PCs. Twenty million francs were spent putting it all together and at the end of the year we only got back 10 million—not even enough to pay our creditors. The rich PCs were supposed to give to the poor ones and all the profits were supposed to be shared equally. But the pre-cooperative at Sidi Ug^cud was the only rich PC. To reimburse all those pre-cooperatives that had lost money on their harvest, they took from the rich ones like Sidi Ug^cud and called it a loan. It was a real *chakchouka* [vegetable stew]. Too many loans everywhere. People were stopping each other on the street saying, 'Hey, where's my money?'

A lot of us wanted our old jobs back, but the *m^catmed* [the Delegué or regional governor] who died last year, said no—instead what we'll do is make it your private land, your personal land. Ben Salah said okay, go ahead and make it the private land of the poor, take the land of the pre-cooperatives. So Ben Salah came to Medjerda and said that everyone should share and everybody applauded Ben Salah. He told the rich landowners to lend their tools, their tractors, and their know-how to the poor ones. And he asked them if everyone agreed and everybody applauded and agreed. He was actually here, and people listened and applauded.

And the next day poor fellahin came to ask to borrow a tractor and to borrow tools or whatever from the rich landowners but no one would lend us any machinery. The day before, they had all applauded, but the next day nobody would give. The workers said 'Let's band together and go to the sheikh to apply the law.' And we took the tractors in a group by force with sticks in our hands. The situation was awful and it went on two weeks like that.

Bourguiba's son went to Bourguiba and said to him 'Do you want a revolution in the streets? The people won't swallow the pre-cooperatives.' And Bourguiba answered that Ben Salah had told him that the cooperatives were rich and had shown him wells that they had dug for new water supplies. But the people knew that the wells were just shallow holes that they had made the day before and put water into them and said that the cooperatives had dug the wells. And that Ben Salah had shown Bourguiba huge fields of watermelons that the PCs had grown and that showed that they were prosperous.

But we knew that the watermelons had been bought at the souk and placed in the fields to make them look prosperous. And when Bourguiba came to inspect, everybody was clapping with the same rhythm and chanting '*Bour-gui-ba—Dz-bi-sag-ik*,' ['Bourguiba, push with your foot.'] meaning that if Bourguiba pushed with his foot he would roll the watermelon away and see that it was not attached to the vine. But he didn't hear or didn't understand.

When Bourguiba found out from his son that he had been lied to, he called in Ben Salah and asked why he had lied. He put him in prison and also put the Minister of Agriculture in prison. We on the pre-cooperatives waited to see what would happen… The *m^catmed* asked, 'well, what about splitting up the

PCs and putting about thirty families on each one?' So they decided on the *lotissement* of Bordj Er Roumi into 30 parts. Lots were handed out and we didn't have to pay for them. But who knows?

We have papers signed by the Ministry of Agriculture. It tells us what we can do and what we can't do with the land. If it says vegetables, then you can't plant grain or fruit trees. And the rich pre-cooperatives—the ones that did well and loaned all their money to the poor ones—they stayed cooperative. But the money they lent out was totally lost. The cooperateurs at Sidi Ug^{c}ud never saw their profits to this day; perhaps the money never reached the other PCs in need. [At this point, the fellah illustrated by taking money out of his pants pocket and placed it in his shirt pocket, indicating the possibility of graft on the part of the director].

Sidi Ug^{c}ud Epilogue

The fellah quoted above was one of those active in the struggle for independence and one of the most sympathetic to the goals of the cooperative movement. As he said philosophically, "It's good for the poor man, but for the rich—they're better off when they run their own farms." Yet after his experiences during the cooperative period, he, like so many of his neighbors, became skeptical that any government program could be implemented successfully.

When the cooperative movement collapsed in 1969, PC Sidi Ug^{c}ud was the only OMVVM cooperative in the Delegation of Medjerda to remain intact. In 1972, Bordj Er Roumi was parcelled out to its former cooperateurs. Not thirty, but forty-seven landless families received agrarian reform plots, ranging from ten to thirty hectares. The successful PC of Sidi Ug^{c}ud became a permanent cooperative and was again retitled, this time with the less tentative appellation of UCP of Sidi Ug^{c}ud. Management was transferred from the OMVVM to the OTD, and then later again to the BCUPN—a small separate agency created in the late 1970's devoted exclusively to management of the remaining agricultural cooperatives.

UCP Sidi Ug^{c}ud continued to be productive enough to award bonuses to the successful cooperateurs. According to them, however, management lacked the cooperative spirit. Directors, who were appointed in Tunis, had veto power over all decisions voted upon by the cooperative members. Furthermore, each received a hefty bonus with each successful year.

Cooperateurs say that some directors received production bonuses even though they frequently did not remain at Sidi Ug^{c}ud long enough either to furnish the director's villa (once owned by Gerodius) or even to find their own way to the fields. In addition, cooperateurs claim that the UCP was more successful than official records showed, but their bonuses did not reflect these profits. UCP directors at Sidi Ug^{c}ud and at other agricultural production cooperatives respond that profits were reinvested in the farm— providing new housing, electricity and plumbing for their resident families as well as replacing old, poorly-yielding vines and other crops. The transient directors invested in the permanence and viability of UCP farms while the cooperateurs continued to look forward to the termination of cooperative farming—whether it was profitable or not.

Time and again, we see the cooperateurs make the cynical gesture of taking money out of a pants pocket and placing it in a shirt pocket; they say directors sit in the office and profit from fellah labor, either through bonuses or theft. A director, say the cooperateurs, may be replaced if he is found to be dishonest, but his replacement—sent from the capital to a rural cooperative that he does not want to manage and his family does not want to inhabit—will be no different.

Sidi Ug^cud's cooperateurs have felt that they have been victimized by outsiders long enough. Cooperateurs, they claim, have the least autonomy and fewest benefits of any agriculturalists in the region. They are not eligible for membership in the workers' union because they are not officially workers, and they are not eligible for membership in the agriculturalists' union because they are not officially farmers.

This lack of status is symbolized by the BCUPN's inability to decide whether to provide cooperateurs with the yearly gift of blue workers' overalls because such action would imply that they should receive other workers' benefits as well. Unlike either workers or farmers, the cooperateurs have no national union to represent them. They can come to collective decisions on each farm, but these must be approved by the state-appointed director—who will indeed veto requests even if they happen to be unanimous. The UCP director is on site to make sure that state policy is carried out, not to facilitate collective local decision-making. His allegiance to the state has made it clear to local fellahin that the term "cooperative" is a misnomer, and that the only difference between the UCP and the state farm agro-combinats is that cooperateurs have not been permitted to enjoy the status, benefits or representation of workers.

The incentive to work cooperatively—once valued with pride at Sidi Ug^cud—diminished as the cooperateurs watched the parcelled farms of their "failed" Bordj Er Roumi neighbors prosper. They continue to want the cooperative disbanded and parcelled out to them and insist that the land would be more productive if each was given his own parcel.

These cooperateurs have become the last remnant of a movement officially declared a failure. Their experience, and Sidi Ug^cud's history, has taught them that success is punished and failure rewarded. They remain landless; their neighbors, the landed. They say they are left with only one outlet through which to vent anger and frustration: sabotage. Their goal has been explicit and acknowledged by the central BCUPN office. That goal is to make Sidi Ug^cud fail so that once and for all, the land they were born on can be parcelled out to them and called their own.

Proliferation of State Land Agencies (1969–1979)

The agricultural development plans of the 1970s sought to reverse the problematic "centralization" policy of the 1960s, which was typified by the cooperative movement. The goal of decentralization has raised a number of unresolved problems. First, what is meant by "decentralization," and how far should it go? Does it call for the Ministry of Agriculture to reduce its management role on large state farms to a solely advisory capacity, or does it call for the full privatization of state lands—as sought by the cooperateurs. Second, if only some state farms are privatized, which ones are the best candidates? Third, how can the fellahin be assured that the privatization policy, too, will not be reversed, and once farm management is given to them, how can they be sure it will not be taken away soon afterward?

Decentralization has not brought about the dissolution of all state farms and cooperatives. What has occurred instead is a decrease in the number of farms directly managed by state agencies, in favor of the formation of agrarian reform parcels which are indirectly administered by the state. This can be demonstrated vividly by comparing a map of Medjerda in 1969, at the height of the cooperative movement (Figure 1.2) with a map of state land in the delegation ten years later (Figure 1.3). The result of these transformations was the decentralization of the state administrative bureaucracy, not the redistribution of land (Table 1.1). Thus, whereas at the dawn of independence, there were only two agencies devoted to land management in the country—the OMVVM for land within the irrigated perimeters and the OTD for the dry land regions—by 1980, there were at least six different land management agencies (refer to Figure 1.2). Both the agencies and the farms have become more specialized and the tenure system has become more complex than ever before. In addition, the specific boundaries of farms, both private and state, are literally on the drawing board at all times. This constant flux of farm boundaries and administration is seen by some as the search for a perfect system; by others, simply as constant flux.

The land tenure system of the 1980s in Medjerda reflected the incomplete dissolution of the centralization policies of the 1960s and the uneven application of the decentralization policies of the 1970s. The farms vary in their degree of autonomy from state to private farms and from direct to indirect administration under the Ministry of Agriculture. Contrasts are easily discernable and often discussed by the fellahin, who have relatives, sometimes within the same household, living or working on every type of farm to be found in the Delegation of Medjerda. These include the state-run agro-combinats, production and distribution cooperatives, specialized state-managed farms, and agrarian reform parcels, all of which are under the administration of almost a dozen separate agencies under the Ministry of

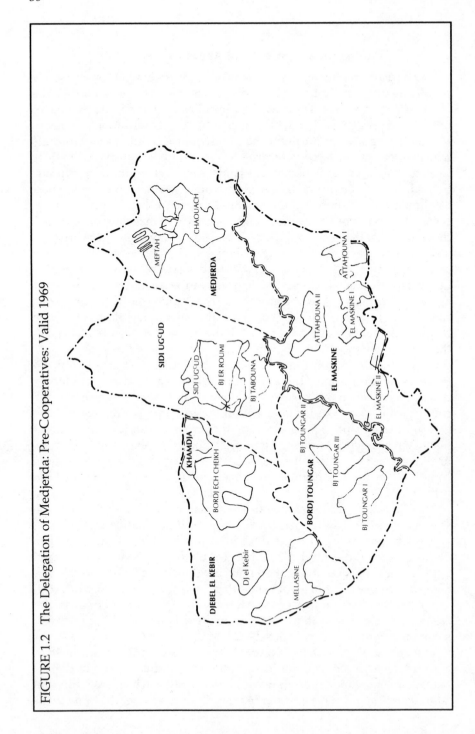

FIGURE 1.2   The Delegation of Medjerda: Pre-Cooperatives: Valid 1969

FIGURE 1.3   The Delegation of Medjerda: State Land Use: Valid 12/79

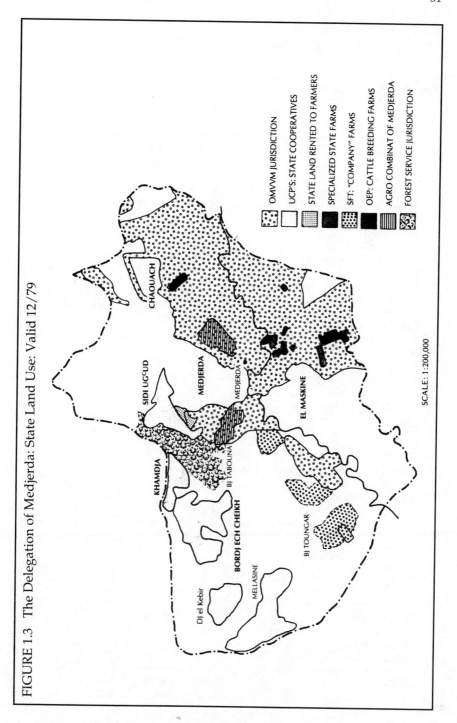

OMVVM JURISDICTION

UCP'S: STATE COOPERATIVES

STATE LAND RENTED TO FARMERS

SPECIALIZED STATE FARMS

SFT: "COMPANY" FARMS

OEP: CATTLE BREEDING FARMS

AGRO COMBINAT OF MEDJERDA

FOREST SERVICE JURISDICTION

SCALE: 1:200,000

CHAOUACH

SIDI UGᶜUD

MEDJERDA

MEDJERDA

KHAMDJA

BJ TABOUNA

EL MASKINE

BORDJ ECH CHEIKH

MELLASINE

BJ TOUNGAR

Dj el Kebir

TABLE 1.1   Transformation of State Land:
            Delegation of Medjerda 1969–1979

Transformation of OMVVM Holdings

Pre-Cooperative	Location	No. of Hectares	Transformed into:
Meftah I	Chaouach	681	OMVVM Agrarian Reform Parcels
Chaouach II	"	1361	" & 182 ha. – OEP
Attahouna I	El Harasiya	604	" & 55 ha. – Haras
Attahouna II	"	624	" & 237 ha. – OEP
El Maskine I	"	816	OMVVM Parcels
El Maskine II	"	522	" & 91 ha. – CCSPS
Bordj Toungar I	Bordj Toungar	879	" & 708 ha. – SFT I
Bordj Toungar II	"	544	" & 280 ha. – SFT II
Bordj Toungar III	"	840	" & 751 ha. – SFT III & some sold at Bordj Tngr
Bordj Tabouna	"	789	" & 757 ha. – AG Bordj Tbna
Bordj Er Roumi	Sidi Ug^cud	1062	" & sold
Sidi Ug^cud	Sidi Ug^cud	935	UCP Sidi Ug^cud

Transformation of OTD Holdings

UCP's	Location	No. of Hectares	Transformed into:
Khamdja	Djebel El Kebir	544	Complex Agricole de Djebel El Kebir
Bordj Ech Cheikh	"	901	
Djebel El Kebir	"	777	
Mellasine	"	1717	

Transformation of Private Holdings

Private	Location	No. of Hectares	Transformed into:
Ex-Ferme Khazem	Sidi Ug^cud	580	UCP Bordj Ech Cheikh
Oliveraies	Medjerda	450	AG Medjerda
Henchir Hamada	Chaouach	121	OEP Chaouach
Ferme Montarnaud	Bordj Toungar	138	AG Bordj El Achoura
TOTAL		**14,885**	**hectares**

Agriculture. In the post-Bourguiba era, which is beyond the scope of this volume, the privatization policies of the 1990s have been met with wary and tentative enthusiasm. Privatization is the policy the fellahin have been awaiting for decades—but will it continue to mean that Medjerda's best land will be sold to entrepreneurs from outside the local community?

State Farms and Cooperatives

The largest and oldest state agency that manages land, *the Office des Terres Domaniales* (OTD), has jurisdiction over land that lies outside the irrigated perimeters. It has epitomized the centralization policies of the early post-independence development plans, and until recently has managed four different categories of farms: small parcels, pilot farms, agro-combinats and production cooperatives.

The OTD has had under its authority approximately two hundred hectares of small land parcels within the irrigated perimeters near Sidi Ug^{c}ud. These parcels are independent of the larger state farms. The land is rented out to small-scale fellahin on a renewable, annual basis. In addition, the agency manages a number of large-scale "demonstration parcels," or pilot farms throughout the country. Using these farms as examples, they have hoped to promote new techniques in agriculture to private fellahin. In the region of Medjerda, the OTD operates no pilot farms; its greatest impact here has been through its management of agro-combinats and UCPs.

State Farms: Agro-Combinats

The agro-combinats of Tunisia were developed to promote agro-industrial production, such as Medjerda's specialization in cattle-breeding and milk-processing. These state farms encompass 210,000 hectares of rich agricultural land, most of which are in the northern part of the country, primarily in the Medjerda Valley. The Agro-Combinat of Medjerda consists of two farms and covers over 1200 hectares. Everything produced on OTD farms is sold directly to other state agencies for processing or distribution.

Directors of agro-combinats are assigned by the central office in Tunis. Workers on the farm are considered salaried employees of the state. They are members of the national workers union—the UGTT—and receive national health care, retirement, and other worker benefits. Some live directly on the agro-combinat with their families; others live off the farm but receive equivalent benefits.

On each state farm certain tribal patronyms predominate. Each ^{c}arsh includes anywhere from two to ten households living in close proximity to one another; their residency pre-dates the formation of the agro-combinat, and frequently pre-dates French occupation. Families who are long-term farm residents view the agro-combinat very differently than do workers who live in town and commute to the farm. Workers who live some distance from the state land they work appear to have forfeited their claim to future residence both for themselves and for their descendants. Families in residence, on the other hand, work hard to preserve the idea of their territorial stake and never let state administrators forget their priority.

Directors of state farms straddle the line between official discouragement of this concept of family territory and unofficial non-interference as each *ʿarsh* brings more relatives and flocks to reside in their compound on the agro-combinat. Rural developers have been increasingly concerned with population growth on state farms and cooperatives; however, state farm directors themselves are each supplied with a large, new or recently renovated villa on the farm. In addition to his villa on the farm, the Sahli director of Medjerda's agro-combinat maintains a house in the suburbs of Tunis, as well as another in his native town of Sousse. Furthermore, he will most likely be posted elsewhere when the eventual confrontation between the fellahin and the state takes place.

Agro-combinat directors are expected to carry out the state's farm policy regarding production decisions and labor issues, and to refer disputes they cannot settle directly to the OTD central office. Workers may make suggestions regarding farm policy or methods, but it has been made quite clear to them that they have no decision-making authority where production matters are concerned. Unlike the cooperateurs, however, agro-combinat workers have never been under the illusion that they have decision-making authority.

The Agro-Combinat of Medjerda did not exist in 1969, but was created later by the OTD from private land northeast of Medjerda which formerly had been planted with unprofitable olive orchards. It therefore stands as a warning to private farmers that expropriation is not an empty threat: it has happened to fellahin who have not at least attempted to maximize production, not just to *colons* who can return to their homeland in France. A second farm was added to the agro-combinat—land from PC Bordj Tabouna. All of this land had been first expropriated by the OMVVM and later transferred to the jurisdiction of the OTD, where it remained. In this case, transference from one agency to another indicated the OMVVM's initial intention to convert the property to irrigated farming. The move to OTD administration indicated to local farmers that perhaps, as they themselves had always maintained, the land had been more cost effective as dry land after all. The land, however, was neither returned nor was it reoffered for privatization.

Production Cooperatives: Unités Coopératives de Production

By the end of the 1970s, there were 220 UCPs in Tunisia, covering over 230,000 hectares. These UCPs were the last remainders of the cooperative movement which had planned an even more extensive program of cooperativization had the movement succeeded (see Figure 1.4). While the UCPs were similar to the agro-combinats in that directors were chosen by the central administration in Tunis, here the director was to function merely as an "advisor and representative" of the government to the farm administration. UCP Sidi Ugᶜud maintained the fiction of this type of advisory administration that had been envisioned in the 1960s. In 1979, however, the less successful UCPs of the Djebel El Kebir were regrouped once more and formed into a highly centralized single agricultural complex under a single director, whose office was in Medjerda and whose function encompassed far more than the simply "advisory". It was the job of this director—once one of the directors of PC Sidi Ugᶜud—to make these unprofitable mountain cooperatives work.

Once again, Sidi Ugᶜud remained the only successful agricultural production cooperative in the region. Whereas in the case of PC Bordj Er Roumi the so-called penalty for failure was the redistribution of private land parcels, here in PC Sidi Ugᶜud the so-called reward for success was increased centralized control. This forced the fellahin to diversify their economic lives further and to seek innovative strategies for obtaining legal title to a private parcel of land.

Cooperateurs on each UCP elected their own president and executive council. The president, rather than the director, was supposed to manage the farm as well as to represent the cooperateurs' interests in dealings with the central administration. In addition, cooperative members had a general assembly in which to voice their opinions or objections to OTD or local UCP policy. In this forum, they also were expected to vote on how best to utilize their shared profits. Elections were to be overseen by state officials, who came from the capital and thus they were held only when scheduling arrangements convenient to the central Tunis office could be made. Meetings to elect officers or make production decisions were therefore not regularly held; they were scheduled erratically, or not at all. When the general assembly did meet, members of some UCPs voted to use their profits to construct new housing, thereby greatly improving the living-conditions of many cooperative families. These UCPs planned to install electricity and piped potable water after the housing projects were finished.

In principle, the general assembly was to allow the cooperateurs to have more of a voice in running the farm than had the salaried workers of the agro-combinats. To effect this, however, it was necessary that the assembly be allowed to meet. Further, as has been seen, OTD directors were able to veto decisions made by the UCP presidents or their executive council—including the decision to hold elections. This made it clear that cooperateurs had no real authority or autonomy. When some cooperateurs threatened tongue-in-cheek to vote to dismantle a UCP altogether, a scheduling problem emerged and elections were postponed indefinitely.

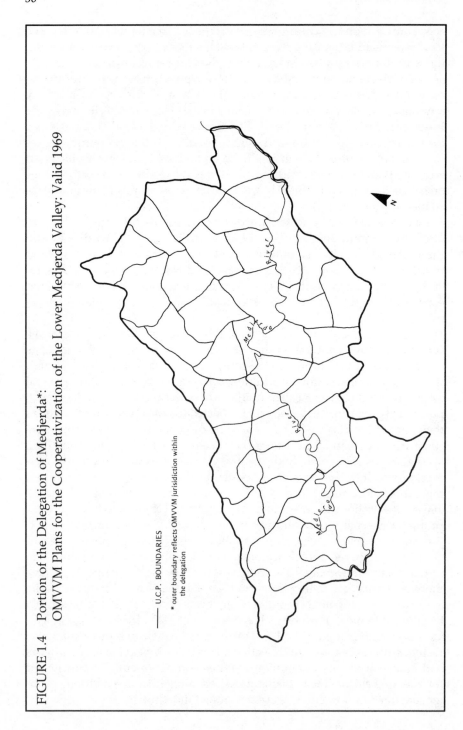

FIGURE 1.4 Portion of the Delegation of Medjerda*:
OMVVM Plans for the Cooperativization of the Lower Medjerda Valley: Valid 1969

——— U.C.P. BOUNDARIES

* outer boundary reflects OMVVM jurisidiction within
the delegation

Where agro-combinat workers are salaried, UCP cooperateurs receive shares of the UCP profits. This share is advanced to them in weekly installments and they can request additional advances drawn against their end-of-the-year bonus. UCPs engaged in cooperative projects generally have little or no profit left over for end-of-the-year bonuses. Thus, cooperateurs who have received advances against bonuses which never materialized end each year in greater debt to the UCP—a debt which can only be resolved if a subsequent year produces enough profit to warrant the year end bonus. When it arrives, this end of the year boon might, at best be enough to cancel out the cooperateur's indebtedness; he will never see the cash. Cooperateurs trapped in this cycle and desperate to get out of debt are all the more embittered when directors invariably choose to reinvest UCP profits in cooperative projects, rather than distribute year-end bonuses.

In keeping with the decentralization policy current in Tunisia of the late 1970s, the OTD decided to disengage from many of its holdings. OTD ambivalence, however, guaranteed that this would not mean actual redistribution of parcels to fellahin. Instead, the office was reorganized and the administration spent a good deal of time trying to decide which lands to maintain and which to liquidate. The OTD vacillated between whether to specialize in managing small parcels, like the OMVVM, or to continue concentrating on the large state farms. According to state agricultural administrators, the UCPs profited from decentralization in the late 1970s and began to enjoy a greater degree of autonomy. By December, 1978, they were "liquidated" to an entirely new branch of the Ministry of Agriculture, the newly formed *Bureau de Contrôle des U.C.P. du Nord* (BCUPN). Fellahin duly noted that this kind of autonomy simply added another layer of bureaucracy to their so-called independence.

The fight over the future of the state farms and cooperatives raged in the newspapers of the late 1970s. There were accusations of mismanagement, corruption, and lack of democratic procedure on the cooperatives. In theory, the UCPs were owned and managed by the cooperateurs. The problem was stated succinctly by the editors of the opposition newspaper, *Democratie*:

> Those in charge claim that the UCPs are at the same time property of the State and the people. In fact, UCP land remained the property of the State, and the cooperateurs are nothing more than in the domain of production and not at the level of ownership. (*Democratie*, 9 Dec 1978 – my translation)

This same observation that the state had given fellahin a mixed message with regard to their role on production cooperatives had been made by Zamiti and others almost ten years earlier (see RTSS No. 21 May 1970). *Democratie's* solution was to make the UCPs wholly autonomous—autonomous, that is, except for the state technical advisers who would "introduce a high level of technicity, create enthusiasm among the cooperateurs, and insure democratic proceedings, as well as insure that the profits go to those who work the land," (RTSS:1970). The irony lies not so much in the fact that these goals were incompatible, but in *Democratie's* advocating what already was the legal status of the UCPs vis à vis the state.

The agro-combinats fared no better. Those at *Democratie* and at the Ministry of Agriculture agreed that the state farms suffered from misman-agement, open conflict between workers and administration, and lower production than there might be, but they attributed these problems to different causes. *Democratie* claimed that all production decisions were in the hands of the bureaucracy (*"c'est la fonctionairisme"*), while the Ministry of Agriculture responded that there was a "destructive mentality" on the part of some workers on the agro-combinats to "abort production, to force the State to give up its lands, and to blame the whole thing on poor State management" (*Le Temps*, 9 Nov 1978).

All agreed that there were problems, as well as that the OTD held under its jurisdiction the best agricultural land in the country. The Ministry of Agriculture held firm to its position that the state lands were to be "an example for the private sector to follow" while *Democratie* concluded that it was regrettable that the best land in the country was proving more a burden than a boon to the national economy.

The debate and confrontation which existed in the press was not in evidence in Medjerda. Cooperateurs and farm workers were suddenly reluctant to discuss either the future or the past of the farms, particularly in public. In Medjerda debate has always been synonymous with dispute. It makes Medjerdis uncomfortable: *"'itha it ʿark l'ariyah, yagaʿ drak ʿala markib—*when the winds argue among themselves, the boat is out of luck." They have learned that when the people in charge are involved in contention, it is they themselves who will suffer.

Specialized State Farms and Cooperatives

The state farms in this category have indeed served as an example to the fellahin, both those who are private landowners and those who work public land. The specialized farms have been innovative experimental centers where fellahin can see for themselves the results of new grain, new breeds and new methods. they observe, in particular, how long they must wait to obtain one of the new agrarian wonders, and above all, what the cost is. The more conservative fellahin may follow a particular innovation five or ten years before exploring its adoption.

The *Office d'Elevage et Pâturage*, or Cattle-breeding and Pasture-land Agency (OEP), is concerned specifically with managing state farms which specialize in raising stock or sheep and growing new strains of animal fodder. The OEP, which was formed in 1965 as a branch of the OMVMM, was later transferred to the OTD, and became a separate agency under the Ministry of Agriculture in the early seventies. Employees of the OEP—including a foreign project director—were unclear about this progression and remained under the impression that they still worked for the OTD years after the implementation of this act of "decentralization."

The OEP operates three separate types of farms in the region of Medjerda. First, it manages the agro-combinat at Bordj El Achoura—only part of which is in the Delegation of Medjerda. This farm is devoted to raising cattle for both milk and meat, and raising pigs for tourist restaurants. Second, it manages the GRAFOUPAST Farm, which was started in 1979. This venture operates in conjunction with the Institute for Research in Experimental Agriculture (INRAT), and specializes in strains of *graines, fourrages* et *paturages*—from which its name is derived. Third, it manages the "Habibia Project" in animal husbandry in conjunction with a Canadian Project. Canadian participation in this project began in 1974 and terminated in 1979. OEP projects and farms cover 1258 hectares, which are dispersed throughout the delegation.

The *Societé des Fermes Tunisiennes* is a branch of the *Banque Nationale de Tunisie* (BNT), which is a state-owned bank. There are a total of six SFT farms in Tunisia, all within the jurisdiction of the OMVMM. They are categorized as semi-autonomous, as are the UCPs. Three of the six SFT farms are in the Delegation of Medjerda, and were once part of the pre-cooperatives of Bordj Toungar. The SFT rents portions of the larger farms to small-scale fellahin on one-year non-renewable contracts. According to one renter, SFT management has opposed long-term rentals because of a fear that those who move in may exercise squatters' rights in some future land reform program. SFT fears of losing control over its farms are well-grounded: classified studies conducted at the OMVVM have found that "the SFT is just as mismanaged as the OTD, and SFT farms are productive, but lacking in profits" (personal communication, OMVVM). The OMVVM is still accumulating evidence that could have resulted in major changes on farms now administered by the SFT. The OMVVM, however, has had to confront accusations of mismanagement of its own.

The *Cooperative Centrale des Semences et Plantes Selectionees* (CCSPS) Farms are centrally administered from Tunis. They comprise a network of plant nurseries throughout northern Tunisia. CCSPS directors, like other state administrators, are chosen through the Ministry of Agriculture and work in conjunction with INRAT, specializing in the breeding of fruit trees. The nurseries sell their young plants or trees to fellahin, state farms, and cooperatives. The goal is to upgrade the quality of fruit trees and to introduce varieties that are particularly suitable to the weather and soil conditions of the region. The CCSPS farm of Medjerda is located on 68 hectares at El Maskine. It has been visited with interest by local fellahin in El Maskine, but does not appear to have made a serious impression on fellahin further afield. While regional state farms and UCPs have obtained new strain seedlings from the CCSPS farms, many fellahin regard the specialized state farms as curiosities and not worth major consideration.

Expansion into the Private Sector

Fellahin living and working on state farms and cooperatives look longingly at their brethren on private and "agrarian reform" parcels. Acquisition of family plots of land has been serendipitous; in the Delegation of Medjerda land has rarely come on the market to local fellahin and privatization continues to be more of a longstanding dream than a reality for the fellahin of Medjerda. For the most part, families who have acquired land have simply happened to be occupying a plot scheduled for *lotissement*, or allotment. Land that has transferred ownership either from out of the state domain or through private sale, has not come on the open market. Local fellahin watch in frustration as farms they have dreamed of acquiring appear one day under the title of a complete stranger to the region. The sale of prime Medjerdi farmland to "outside" entrepreneurs has infuriated local fellahin to the same degree that it has delighted state administrators, for they have selected young innovators with capital to invest who have proven themselves successful in other regions of the country. Provincial Medjerdis, they say, would only plant more olive trees and watch the flocks of sheep wander through the groves. The new investors, on the other hand, will build factories and bring businesses of national stature to the region. These are the people for whom privatization was meant. For the fellahin of Medjerda, however, OMVVM agrarian reform parcels have been the only route to acquiring new private family farms.

Agrarian Reforms of the OMVVM

The *Office de la Mise en Valeur de la Vallée de la Medjerda* literally means the "Medjerda Valley Land Improvement Agency." Its precursor under the French Protectorate was the *Commissariat de la MVVM* (CMVVM), organized as late as 1953. The CMVVM acted as a liaison between the government and agriculturalists in an effort to carry out government development projects (see Chennoufi 1977). These projects included: (1) construction of a dam/reservoir on the Melegue River (completed April 1954), (2) Construction of a hydro-electric dam at Taulierville El Aroussia, in the Delegation of Medjerda (completed summer 1956), (3) construction of a large irrigation canal at Taulerville and an irrigation network, (4) soil and water protection projects (from erosion, floods, salination, noxious water etc.) and soil and water studies; and (5) agricultural extension services, including experiments in innovative agriculture. These innocuous sounding projects gave no indication of the role the future OMVVM would play in the lower Medjerda Valley.

After independence, the Tunisification program affected well over 50% of the land in the lower Medjerda Valley. The Law of 9 July 1958 inaugurated the OMVVM and gave the Office jurisdiction over all the land recovered by the state within the boundaries of the CMVVM projects. The OMVVM distributed land to rural Tunisians in accordance with the Agrarian Reform Laws, but not the actual title; the OMVVM retained its jurisdiction over all agrarian reform parcels in the region.

The OMVVM distributed two kinds of lots in the lower Medjerda Valley. The first, known as *Promotion Paysanne*, split up parcels of from four to twelve hectares, allowing the recipients to "rise to the level of small-scale landowners working the land with their own hands" (*Revue Medjerda* 1960). In some places the redistribution program called for grouping the fellahin into newly constructed villages and having them commute to their land parcels, but most of the agriculturalists were dispersed throughout the countryside, each living on his own farm. The second type of lot, called *Minimum Vital*, gave each fellah two or three hectares, a house and common pastureland, and these fellahin were expected to work as seasonal laborers for their neighbors (Chennoufi 1977). None of the lots were free; they were to paid for within twenty-five years—a deadline long since past.

The law differentiated agrarian reform parcels from private land (i.e. titled land or land bought from Europeans before expropriation went into effect), and until the land was paid for it "belonged" to the OMVVM. The Agrarian Reform Law of 11 June 1958 exclusively addressed land in the Lower Medjerda Valley, and spelled out the specific obligation of the fellahin to their land. The main points were:

1. Land cannot be fragmented or in any way divided smaller than four hectares, while the upper limit of land ownership is fifty hectares per agriculturalist. (Articles 5 and 15).

2. Agriculturalists in the irrigated perimeters are obligated to irrigate at least two-thirds of their land when appropriate, and pay the OMVVM for the service of irrigation at rates established by the law (Article 2).

3. Improving the land is an obligation of the fellahin within the irrigated perimeters. The law includes an annex listing the crops suitable for different soil types, and regulations are given regarding the spacing of fruit trees approved for the area (Article 19).

4. The OMVVM can proceed against those who do not exploit their rural property rationally. The law specifically includes proper distribution and use of irrigation water on the land (Article 15).

5. Landowners can be required to join and participate in production, marketing, and service, or agri-industrial cooperatives created by the OMVVM (Article 22).

6. Landowners not conforming to the law can be expropriated by the state and their land transferred to the holdings of the OMVVM. The OMVVM, however, can renounce its right to expropriate landowners who exceed the allowable number of hectares (i.e. above fifty hectares) if the land is intensively cultivated and employs inadequate work force (Articles 7, 8, 12, and 14).

In brief, the agrarian reforms made the OMVVM much more than a government commission dedicated to building dams and irrigation canals. The agency could determine what 'rational agriculture' was and expropriate landowners who did not comply; it could abrogate its right to expropriate if the Office found the land to be rationally cultivated. It could transform land tenure patterns as it saw fit. The OMVVM was a financially autonomous organization which not only sold irrigation water to the fellahin and state farms, but also collected land taxes, payments, and rents from them. Needless to say, the fellahin on agrarian reform parcels did not have the right to sell their land until it was paid for in full and until the full price of water usage over a twenty year period was also paid. Agriculturalists who did not pay for their irrigation water could be sued by the OMVVM.

In 1964, before many of the fellahin had been given their agrarian reform parcels, the OMVVM exercised its rights to cooperativize the lower Medjerda Valley, although their entire plan was not completely realized. (See Figure 1.5) In compliance with Ben Salah's socialist experiment, the OMVVM regrouped private and agrarian reform lots alike into either service cooperatives, which utilized family labor, or into large production pre-cooperatives.

The collapse of the cooperative movement five years later meant the redistribution of agrarian reform parcels and the return of only well-documented private parcels. Because of the rapid succession of tenure forms, agrarian reform farmers remained unclear about their land payment obligations: Were they still expected to pay for the land, and if so, how much and to whom? Were their previous payments recorded, and did they count toward current landholdings? What was the deadline for the last installment? Many fellahin never even considered making payments on their farms at all; some believed that they would never be asked to comply with the law; others believed that the land would be expropriated regardless of their payments. These fellahin, like the cooperateurs and agro-combinat workers, always await what one man called "the politics of the future."

Private Farms

Only fifty-four percent of the agricultural land in the Delegation of Medjerda consists of private landholdings. Approximately 10,300 hectares of this land are within the irrigated perimeters of the OMVVM, while 15,000 hectares are outside of its jurisdiction. Private parcels vary from a fraction of a hectare to loosely confederated ᶜarsh land in the hundreds of thousands of hectares. Farms vary not only in size, but also in the mode of acquisition. Thus, private farms may be classed as pre-colonial acquisitions, colonial acquisitions, and post-colonial acquisitions.

Pre-colonial acquisitions comprise farms primarily owned by those of the old Medjerdi elite who were able to maintain their own landholdings throughout the Protectorate because they held legal title and resisted purchase offers. The size of these holdings varies more widely than any in the region, both because of the collectivization of ᶜarsh land—holdings of tribal groupings and large extended families—and the fragmentation of inherited parcels.

The largest ᶜarsh holdings are primarily on hillsides or on the slopes of the Djebel El Kebir. The land is considered to be owned collectively by the entire ᶜarsh, although legal title may be listed in the names of a number of related individuals. When asked: "How much land do you have," a fellah may therefore reply "Six thousand hectares between here and Kairouan."

The landholdings in this group are the epitome of ᶜarbi farming both in tenure and in mode of production. They combine large-scale herding of sheep with dry-farming grains and olive oil production. Bedouin families frequently camp on this land; they tend the flocks of the landowners in exchange for permission to graze their own sheep. Few large-scale land-holdings exist within the irrigated perimeters, since these—generally, untitled *habous* land—were expropriated either by the French, or by the OMVVM after independence. In many instances, these private parcels are fragmented to such an extent that they are not worth the effort of cultivation. As a result, they are frequently abandoned by their owners or rented to fellahin who have adjoining farms. The OMVVM has drawn up plans to regroup and redistribute these segments so that each farmer will receive a single parcel of land equivalent in size to the sum of his various landhold-ings; such a regrouping was designed to encourage easier cultivation and irrigation of the lands under consideration. Under this plan, fellahin would be relocated to yet another new parcel; they would be expected convert to irrigated farming, as well as to work the land. The OMVVM has stated that the private land within its jurisdiction that is not developed is subject to expropriation. However, internal reorganization at the OMVVM has led to incomplete implementation of this regrouping plan.

Colonial acquisitions included farms that were purchased from the *colons* at the dawn of independence both by members of the old Medjerdi elite and by Sfaxi, Sahli, and other entrepreneurs who settled in Medjerda in the early 1960s. The farms are of moderate sizes—averaging fifty hect-ares—and are both irrigated and unirrigated. Most of these farms were

FIGURE 1.5 Land Tenure System: Delegation of Medjerda

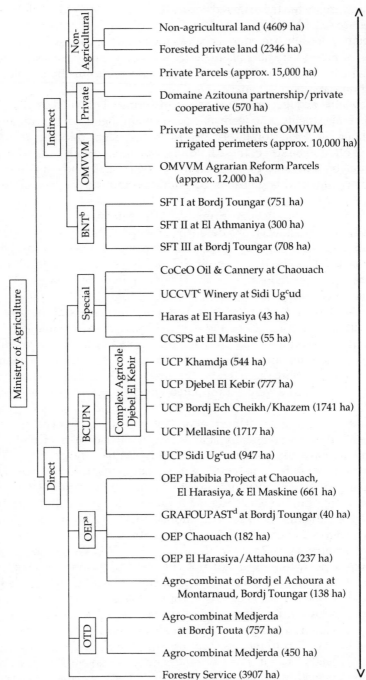

Non-agricultural land (4609 ha)

Forested private land (2346 ha)

Private Parcels (approx. 15,000 ha)

Domaine Azitouna partnership/private cooperative (570 ha)

Private parcels within the OMVVM irrigated perimeters (approx. 10,000 ha)

OMVVM Agrarian Reform Parcels (approx. 12,000 ha)

SFT I at Bordj Toungar (751 ha)

SFT II at El Athmaniya (300 ha)

SFT III at Bordj Toungar (708 ha)

CoCeO Oil & Cannery at Chaouach

UCCVT[c] Winery at Sidi Ug[c]ud

Haras at El Harasiya (43 ha)

CCSPS at El Maskine (55 ha)

UCP Khamdja (544 ha)

UCP Djebel El Kebir (777 ha)

UCP Bordj Ech Cheikh/Khazem (1741 ha)

UCP Mellasine (1717 ha)

UCP Sidi Ug[c]ud (947 ha)

OEP Habibia Project at Chaouach, El Harasiya, & El Maskine (661 ha)

GRAFOUPAST[d] at Bordj Toungar (40 ha)

OEP Chaouach (182 ha)

OEP El Harasiya/Attahouna (237 ha)

Agro-combinat of Bordj el Achoura at Montarnaud, Bordj Toungar (138 ha)

Agro-combinat Medjerda at Bordj Touta (757 ha)

Agro-combinat Medjerda (450 ha)

Forestry Service (3907 ha)

Ministry of Agriculture

Indirect

Direct

Non-Agricultural

Private

OMVVM

BNT[b]

Special

BCUP'N

Complex Agricole Djebel El Kebir

OEP[a]

OTD

PRIVATE FARMS

STATE FARMS

[a]Office d'Elevage et Pâturage   [b]Banque National de Tunisie   [c]Union Cooperative de Cultivation Viticole Tunisienne   [d]Graines, fourages, et pâturages

acquired through the formation of Euro-Tunisian partnerships during the transition period. They retain the continuity of *souri* farming practices, including viticulture and mechanized production. The largest, Domaine Sidi Mansour, encompasses 570 hectares, and thus far exceeds the OMVVM hectarage limitation on irrigated land. The farm is owned by a partnership of Sfaxi investors—well-connected in both the Ministry of Agriculture and other branches of government, and thus they are unlikely to be expropriated by the OMVVM. The Domaine employs great numbers of workers and produces high yields, and the farm's partner/manager plays a crucial role in regional politics, as well as in the rural development of the region.

Post-colonial acquisitions comprise those farms purchased since the cooperative period and average fifteen rather than fifty hectares. Given the land history of the region, one may appreciate the fact that land is rarely, if ever, bought or sold privately. The few parcels purchased in the late 1970s were farms disposed of by state agencies, not by private landowners. The purchasers were the wealthy young entrepreneurs previously mentioned. These men and their families live outside the delegation, have non-agricultural professions in the capital, and have hire local managers to run the farms. These farms are small agro-industrial businesses specializing in cattle-breeding, yogurt production, and raising *souri* chickens and eggs. Small-scale local fellahin, desperate to acquire additional land, generally petition the OMVVM, OTD or any other agency that holds neighboring land. These petitions are handled by the agriculturalists' union, which acts as an intermediary. This method has proven to be both time-consuming and ineffective. Reliance on personal connections is more effective, as will be seen, and many fellahin hope to acquire more land through future governmental regrouping of private parcels. They vie with one another for the attention of developers, hoping to profit from expropriation of abandoned or poorly-worked farms owned by their neighbors.

When Success Breeds Failure

The land history of Medjerda has deepened the cynicism and sense of fatalism of the fellahin. Many of the experiences they underwent during the colonial period appear to have been repeated in the post-colonial era. Government authorities, though Tunisian, have had neither kinship nor family ties to the region. Thus, like the French *colons*, they are "outsiders" who have come to expropriate, distribute, regroup, and redistribute land parcels. Land tenure in Medjerda has been in constant flux. Decentralization has meant the proliferation of agencies managing or giving directives on the farms. It has not meant the dissolution of all state farms. Disappointed workers, cooperateurs, and fellahin have become demoralized and unproductive. Their interpretation of the problem is that the land reform program has undergone too much change, while at the same time the conditions of their lives have not changed at all.

Families who live on the agro-combinat have worked on the same farm for generations, irrespective of who owned the land. They preceded the agro-combinat and they hope to outlive it—expanding their households, grazing their sheep, and planting crops for home consumption. They were never under the illusion that the land belonged to them; as a consequence, they are not terribly bitter about not owning it now. Their standard of living has improved as both wages and benefits have increased—but they anticipate and prepare for future reforms.

The cooperatives—which in "rational terms" were "national successes"—were continued by the government, but the cooperateurs, according to their own value system, have led the most unsatisfactory and unsuccessful lives. In contrast, the cooperatives which failed were disbanded and their cooperateurs "rewarded" with individual agrarian reform parcels.

Those who were awarded agrarian reform parcels also have anticipated further land reform and/or the day when they will be required to pay for their land—an event for which they are ill-prepared. In any case, they expect their "ownership" may be interrupted by what they call "the politics of the future." Their belief that the land will be subject to reallocation while their personal belongings will not has led them to reduce agricultural investment in favor of accumulating luxury items. These fellahin consider title to one's own land the only basis of a security which would allow them to make agricultural investments without fear.

Meanwhile, agrarian reform, which initially affected only state land acquired from colonial expropriation, has come to encompass private landholdings as well. The OMVVM's plan to regroup private parcels places the same restrictions on private farms as have existed on agrarian reform parcels. Thus, in what must appear to be the ultimate irony, private farms—despite their owners' legal title to the land—may face expropriation for non-compliance with OMVVM directives. Although this plan was never fully implemented, fellahin with title to their own parcel of land have begun to invest in non-agricultural enterprises in the interests of their own future security.

جا كاري، والآ مالك؟

2

Uneasy Dualisms

dja kari, wala malik
He came to rent, but stayed to rule

According to Medjerdis, there are two entirely different ways of doing things and explaining the world—two models from which to choose. Distinctions are made between *ᶜarbi* and *souri* ways. *ᶜArbi* reflects the Arab way, while *souri* evokes the way of the French, or European. The fellahin of Medjerda selectively combine elements from each world view to accommodate their own needs. The distinction between *ᶜarbi* and *souri* categories is not wholly analogous to binary oppositions such as nature/culture, male/female, traditional/modern and so on, although these elements are prominent in the *ᶜarbi/souri* classification system. *Souri* is as much an idealized, anachronistic version of bygone times as is *ᶜarbi*. It is an image based upon limited access to the colonial dominion; the term *"souri"* itself is an *ᶜarbi* category and a reflection of the Tunisian struggle for a national identity. The two versions of reality coincide on a daily basis despite the departure of the colonizer and are highlighted in the uneasy encounter between Medjerda's fellahin and state and foreign rural development advisers.

The word *ᶜarbi* literally means Arab; in Medjerda, however, *ᶜarbi* refers to objects and practices considered to be local, rural, proper, or primitive. Berber customs, for example, would be considered *ᶜarbi* as would Roman artifacts, for although neither one is "Arab," nevertheless both of these are indigenous to Tunisia and well preceded the arrival of the French. The term *souri* is derived from one of the Arabic words for "Syrian" and connotes things European. Jacques Berque provides an explanation for the Tunisian propensity for calling "Syrian" that which is European.

> On the whole, everybody was becoming Europeanized after a fashion, or rather 'Syrianized,' *itasauer*. For in Tunis the European is known as 'Syrian'. This minor lexicographical puzzle may be explained as follows: Tunisians following the pilgrims' way from 1900 onwards may have been struck, as they passed through Cairo, by the appearance of the Syrio-Lebanese who were then transporting the Beirut *nahda* (Renaissance) into Egypt; the influence of Europe was identified with that of the Levant; one became 'Syrian' because one stood in relation to the traditional milieu as those Cairo Syrians stood in relation to the fellah of old, or the old Cairo bourgeoisie. (Berque, 1967:200)

What Berque considers a "minor lexicographical puzzle" was of some significance in classical Islam. The necessary ingredients for understanding the *ᶜarbi*/*souri* distinction and its symbolic manifestations are found precisely in these rather obscure Syrian roots:

> Situated on the western face of the Arabic peninsula, the Hijaz, the cradle of Islam, is bounded on the north by Syria and on the south by Yemen. Now it is altogether remarkable that the Arabic word for Syria should be *Sam*, which is unquestionably related in etymology to *su'm*, "unhappiness," "misfortune," "ill augury," and *mas'amat* which the Koran uses to designate the left. We have already seen that the verb *sa'ama* has in fact two meanings, "to bring bad luck" and "to turn left"; it is now relevant to mention a third meaning, "to go to Syria." The ancient Arabs therefore tended to confound the left with the north. The fact that the word *simal* indicates the north and also designates the left side makes this supposition a certainty. Furthermore, in keeping with this association, the north brings famine with it. The author of the *Taj-al-arus* informs us that when it blows for seven consecutive days across Egypt, the inhabitants prepare their shrouds, for it is by nature analogous to death: dry and cold.
>
> *In contrast, the south is laden with blessings.* The south wind is the bearer of prosperity and fertility; it is also synonymous with good relations. The South is Yemen, the flourishing land, the *Arabia Felix* of the classics. Its etymology is taken from the root *ymn* which implies ideas of success and happiness, and from it are derived the terms *yumn*, "felicity" or *baraka*, and *yamine*, "right." Here again geographical location is intimately bound to man's position in space and is subject to the same mystic influences. (Chelhod, in Needham 1973:246-7, my emphasis).

The extension to Europe in the North, its association with misfortune and contrast with felicity, *baraka*—the right and the good—is a theme which is visible throughout Medjerda's modern history. This symbolism not only affected the relationship between the colonized and the colonizer during the protectorate era, but also extends to contemporary European agricultural developers.

Symbolic associations with Syria have been transformed in the Tunisian context and have coalesced with a familiar North African theme described by the Tunisian historian-philosopher, Ibn Khaldûn, in *The Muqaddimah*, in 1377: the opposition between two ideal types—Bedouin and sedentary life (i.e. southern desert vs. northern city).

> Sedentary people are much concerned with all kinds of pleasures. They are accustomed to luxury and success in worldly occupations and to indulgence in worldly desires. Therefore, their souls are coloured with all kinds of blameworthy and evil qualities. The more of them they possess, the more remote do the ways and means of goodness become to them. Eventually they lose all sense of restraint. Many of them are found to use improper language in their gatherings as well as in the presence of their superiors and womenfolk. They are not deterred by any sense of restraint, because the bad custom of behaving openly in an improper manner in both words and deeds has taken hold of them. Bedouins may be as concerned with worldly affairs as (sedentary people are). However, such concern would touch only the necessities of life and not luxuries or anything causing, or calling for, desires and pleasures. The customs they followed in their mutual dealings are, therefore, appropriate. As compared with those of sedentary people, their evil ways and blameworthy qualities are much less numerous. They are closer to the first natural state and more remote from the evil habits that have been impressed upon the souls (of sedentary people) through numerous and ugly, blameworthy customs. Thus, they can more easily be cured than sedentary people. This is obvious. It will later become clear that sedentary life constitutes the last stage of civilization and the point where it begins to decay. It also constitutes the last stage of evil and of remoteness to goodness. Clearly the Bedouins are closer to being good than sedentary people. . . . (Ibn Khaldun 1377/1970:94)

Ibn Khaldûn considers these two ways both as conflicting communities and as extremes within the continuum of a single society. He places the fellahin next to the Bedouins, and claims that "agriculture is a way of making a living for weak people" (Ibn Khaldûn 1377/1970:309); thereafter he dismisses the fellahin as powerless and inactive in the process of government. This view has persisted to the present time and reflects the image many fellahin have of themselves.

Unfamiliar with the Syrians of Cairo, unaware of the symbolism associated with Syria or Ibn Khaldûn's philosophy of history, the fellahin of Medjerda have a less elaborate explanation for the term *souri*. According to them, the word *souri* is derived from *fransouriya*, a variant of *fransaouiya*—meaning "French." Some fellahin have claimed tongue-in-cheek that it derives from *casri*, or "modern." The full flower of symbolic value has persisted through the ages; however, whatever the origin of the term—on the local level at least—it has nothing whatever to do with Syria. To urban Tunisians it refers specifically to anything from France, and to the farm people of Medjerda, it is a catch-all term which refers to anything considered non-indigenous—be it from France or from Tunis, scarcely forty kilometers away. *Souri* evokes for the fellahin not only unknown or foreign concepts, but also memories of an all-too-familiar colonial Medjerda—a time when the farms they call their own were European farms and the town of Medjerda was administered by French *colons*, or colonizers.

The contrast between *ʿarbi* and *souri* is strongest in areas that were heavily penetrated by the French. It encompasses peoples, ideas, language, costumes, foods, vegetables, farm techniques, farm animals, types of roads, and even, ways of sitting down (see Table 2.1). The merging of these quite different traditions is distinctively Tunisian and is most prevalent in the heavily colonized north. The distinction is used as well by some neighboring Algerians and Libyans, but appears to be altogether absent as far west as Morocco.

At one end of the *ʿarbi/souri* continuum is a "Frenchified" urban bourgeoisie, who either speak French or a Tunisian dialect heavily infused with French. The more urban and wealthy an individual is, the greater the *souri* attributes in language, customs, and values. At the other end of the continuum is the Bedouin, who speaks what is considered the closest language to classical Arabic and epitomizes the ideal, or pure *ʿarbi* way of life. The farm people, neither "Frenchified" urbanites nor nomadic Bedouins, find themselves clustered somewhere along this continuum.

Foreign and government agricultural-extension workers coming to the region from the capital advocate practices considered by all to be thoroughly *souri*. The stated goal of the developers is to "change the mentality of the fellahin"—ostensibly in a more *souri* direction.

To the fellahin, however, *ʿarbi* is the superior path of adherence to long-valued customs that are simply "better." It follows, therefore, that Islam is superior to Christianity, the *hammam* public baths get one cleaner than showers, a clay *kanoun* charcoal burner in the lap is warmer than a bottled gas heater half a room away, a flock of sheep is more secure than money in the bank, sheepskins are more comfortable than chairs. *ʿArbi* chickens are healthier while *ʿarbi* eggs have better color and taste, fresh food is healthier than packaged, and nothing tastes better than milk straight from the cow.

While the foregoing reflects ways in which *ʿarbi* is felt to be better, *souri* farming leads to bigger yields, higher income, and large-scale production.

TABLE 2.1 Mejerdi Classification of *^cArbi*/*Souri* Traits

Sphere	Trait	*^cArbi*	*Souri*
Personal	Origins	Arab, Berber	French, European
	Religion	Islam	Christianity
	Language	Arabic	French, European languages
	Education	Qur'anic *mekteb* or unschooled	Secular education, university studies
	View of Success	*Maktoub, baraka or kteff;* personal contact	*Pistons*, schooling, use of machines
	Coloring	Dark skin, eyes and hair	Light skin, eyes and hair
	Hair Texture	Curly, frizzy	Straight or wavy
	Handedness	Righthanded for food and "clean" activities	Indiscriminate use of left and right
	Women's Dress	*Meliya:* country women; *Safsari:* town women; *Hjab* for observant women	European clothings, pants & second-hand *frippe;* skimpy clothes, Bareheaded
	Men's Dress	White *jibba:* townsmen; *kashabiya:* rural men Red *chechia (fez)*	European suit, ascot, walking stick, fedora, wristwatch
	Footwear	*Shlekka* (rubber sandals) Slip-on shoes or barefoot	Closed-back shoes; boots; laces
	Music	Folkloric; religious Rhythmic percussion Symbolic rhythms Songs in Arabic *Mezwed* (goatskin bagpipes); *Darbuka* or homemade drum	Secular; commercial melodic, harmonic Idiosyncratic European songs Symphonic, brass, guitar; Rock music Cassette tapes
	Communication	Personalized; face-to-face	Mechanized; radio, TV

(continues)

52

TABLE 2.1 *(continued)*

Sphere	Trait	ᶜArbi	Souri
Household	Rural Abode	Goathair tent or mud and straw *gourbi* No water or electricity	Colonial farmhouse, villa Internal water and electricity
	District of Town	*Medina: houma ᶜarbi* walled, Arab section of town. Religious center	Colonial section of town *Houma souri* Administrative center
	Town Abode	*Dar ᶜarbi* with courtyard House attached to neighboring houses Paneless windows facing into the courtyard Water spigot only in courtyard and toilet	Red-tiled urban villa Unattached house Windows with panes facing public street Garden with flowers Running water in kitchen Always electric lighting
	Streets	*Trig ᶜarbi*; narrow, cool, unpaved, circuitous	*Trig souri*; wide, hot, paved, angular
	Heating	*Kanoun*; clay charcoal or mesquite burner	*Gaz*; bottled-gas heater Electrical heater
	Igniting Kanoun	Light olive-oil soaked cloth amidst the coals Already-burning coals	Pour gas on coals; Heat coals on hotplate Matches
	Lighting	Roman oil lamp; kerosene lantern	Electric lights Flashlight
	Table	*Midah*; low, round wooden table	*Tabla*; tall, formica & metal, rectangular table
	Seating	*Jild*; sheepskins on ground rag rugs, straw mats Reclining or squatting	*Kursi*; hard-backed chair metal & formica or wood Upright position
	Bedding	Sheepskins on rag rugs or padded straw mats Wool blankets	Metal bed frame with foam mattress Electric blankets
	Utensils	Bread or spoon	Forks and knives
	Cookware	Clay or hand made	Metal store-bought
	Meals	Homecooked, offered freely	Restaurant meal, paid for

(continues)

TABLE 2.1 *(continued)*

Sphere	Trait	ᶜArbi	Souri
Household	Cooking Baking	*Kanoun* grilled, boiled or heated; *Tabouna* country oven (outdoor adobe) Fresh ingredients, home processed foods & spices	Bottled-gas hotplate Electric/gas stove; Store/bakery bought Canned, packaged food
	Serving Food	One bowl shared by all	Separate plate for each person
	Buttermilk Churn	Goatskin or ceramic *shegwa*	Metal churn, or purchase butter and buttermilk
Hygiene & Health	Bathing	On farm: basin in courtyard In town: *hammam* public bath Weekly or less often Social occasion Prolonged and enduring	Shower or bath at home Daily Bathe in private Brief and superficial
	Haircare	*Tfall*; sudsing argil clay	Bottled shampoo
	Dental Care	*Shouek*; bark dental polisher. Monthly	Toothpaste and daily brushing
	Depilatory	*Sukr*; sugar & lemon juice resin (for women) Performed collectively All body hair removed except thin eyebrows & headhair	Razor/shaving cream or soap (for men) Individually Only facial hair for souri men *Souri* women do not depilate
	Cleanliness	Women say men should shave pubic area and armpits after marriage	Remain unclean
	Menstrual Care	Washable, reusable cloth home made	Disposable products Store bought
	Children's Rites	Boys: circumcision at latency age Girls: formerly facial and body tatoos	*El-meh* (Baptism) Male and Female. Age variable
	Birth Control	Olive oil soaked cotton vaginal supositories	Pills or I.U.D. Tubal ligation

(continues)

TABLE 2.1 *(continued)*

Sphere	Trait	ᶜArbi	Souri
Hygiene & Health	Healer	Folk or religious healer Folk healers have been banned but still practice	Physician/nurse or pharmacist
	Medicines	Herbs, *naffa* & sand on wound; blood-letting	Injections, ampules, pharmacy tablets
	Headache Remedy	Heated clove & olive oil compresses	Aspirin or vitamin tablets
	Blood -pressure Control	*Ṭashlit* blood-letting to lessen volume Rest to increase volume	Injections, ampules, tablets
	Temperature Regulation	Equalize body temperature with environment: e.g. Sip cold water to go out into the cold	Retain stable body temperature: e.g. Drink something hot to go into the cold
Farming	Farm Ideology	Way of life and profit Sell at weekly *souks* Differentially valued; e.g. nomads and formerly nomadic families claim to abhor farm life even when they are successful at it	Business for profit Daily markets/export
	Farming Education	Long-term personal and/or family hands-on experience	Overspecialized textboods & photos *En principe* classroom theories and abstractions
	Preferable Crops	Olives, durum wheat, tomatoes, artichokes, peppers, carrots, melons	Vineyards, soft wheat, fruit, imported seed, salad vegetables for urban restaurants
	Preferable Animals	Sheep and local breeds	Pigs and imported breeds Turkeys, called *djedj souri* or *souri* chickens
	Sheep	Fat-tailed sheep Small, local breed	Thin-tailed with horns Large, foreign breed–not highly regarded and not raised
		Healthy & succulent	Sickly, weak and stringy

(continues)

TABLE 2.1 *(continued)*

Sphere	Trait	*ᶜArbi*	*Souri*
Farming	Cattle	Small, hardy local breed High endurance ot heat Low maintenance	Large, imported from Holland and Switzerland Low heat tolerance and costly maintenance
	Chickens	Large, brown, free-ranging Home-raised, rarely at market. Lean & tasty	Small, white, cooped Fatty and tasteless but abundant at market
	Dogs	Small, speckled, faster, excellent at herding and guarding camp or farm	Slow, attractive, not suitable for herding or guarding; Pets
	Feed	Free-ranging grazing or pecking	Concentrate with chemical additives. Dole out on schedule
Foods Grown Eaten	Food (general)	Specific seasonal combina- tions. In-season, cooked Fresh vegetables, Home-baked or home- processed	Any other combinations or out-of-season *primeurs*, Raw vegetables, Imported packeted, processed or store-bought
	Drink	Strong tea or coffee heavily sugared	Weak tea or coffee Coffee with milk Wine and other alcoholic drinks
	Meat	Lamb, *merguez* sausages Small portion to share Religiously sanctioned	Pork, pork sausages Large individual portion Religiously proscribed
	Eggs	From *ᶜarbi* chickens Large, with orange yolk Flavorful but rarely at market. Unprofitable despite higher price at market	From *souri* chickens Small, with pale yellow yolk, Rubbery but cheap and always available at market
	Milk	From the cow, unprocessed Difficult to purchase	Homogenized, sterilized, packaged and purchased
	Dairy Products	Fresh and processed at home or locally Difficult to purchase	Factory processed and packaged. Purchased

(continues)

TABLE 2.1 *(continued)*

Sphere	*Trait*	*ᶜArbi*	*Souri*
Foods Grown/ Eaten	Bread	*Khubz tabouna;* home-baked large round durum wheat flour. *Khubz ghnā* fried in a clay baking dish on the *kanoun*	Baguettes; French or Italiian bread made with white soft flour
	Pastas & Grains	Couscous, *mhammes* and other home-made pastas Bulghur locally milled	Rice, spaghetti and macaroni; store bought
	Lettuce	Romaine (Roman Lettuce) For urban market only	Butter lettuce For urban market only
	Turnips	Round, with some red on them	Long, white variety
	Radishes	Long radishes	Small, round radishes
	Carrots	Large carrots	Young, small carrots
	Spinach	Green variety	Gray or white variety
	Tomatoes	Round tomatoes	Oval Italian tomatoes
	Other Produce	Local varieties	Imported varieties

For example, it would be impossible to have five thousand *ᶜarbi* chickens running loose, pecking around, and laying eggs wherever they pleased—despite their good taste and the higher price they could bring at the souk. *ᶜArbi* chickens and eggs are consumed at home on the farm, though they are rarely seen in the marketplace. Five thousand *souri* chickens, on the other hand, are easily cooped and fed—even on a tiny farm—and lay their eggs in convenient depositories. They are found in abundance at the souk and vendors agree that one *ᶜarbi* is worth three *souri* chickens on the market (see e.g. Michalak 1983:101).

Souri therefore signifies accumulation of material wealth—not only of chickens, but also of many other desirables. These may include medical care, appliances, machinery, electricity, new seed strains, *"pistons,"* and a *souriya* wife. While *souri* things are seductive and tempting, they are generally frustratingly out-of-reach. In addition, they are associated with *souri* ways—many of which the fellahin find repellant and polluting. Among these ways we may find eating pork, drinking alcoholic beverages, and

personal practices considered non-hygienic. It is impossible to overempha-
size the fact that ambivalence characterizes the *ᶜarbi*/*souri* relationship, just
as it characterized the Bedouin/sedentary relationship once described by
Ibn Khaldun. As indicated earlier, *ᶜarbi* living represents and constitutes a
life of primitivism and poverty. *Souri* living, however opulent, brings with
it manners and customs that are deemed offensive. "The European," like
"the Bedouin," is both paragon and pariah, and fellahin straddle the line
between both ways—for they find it impossible to follow either the *ᶜarbi* or
the *souri* path exclusively.

Each fellah's household and farm blends *ᶜarbi* and *souri* modes in a distinctive way. I have documented over sixty common attributes with both
ᶜarbi and *souri* manifestations in daily rural life. However distinctive the
blend in a given household, there are, nevertheless, patterns to be discerned.
The *ᶜarbi*/*souri* choices made by fellahin may change during different stages
of the life cycle and according to the currently advocated national values
and fashion. Yet no Medjerdis ever wholly reject one side or the other, for
it is the dualism itself which is part of their distinctive colonial and post
colonial Tunisian heritage.

Colonial Space and Architectural Order

Like many towns of the region, Medjerda was geographically divided
into *ᶜarbi* and *souri* halves during the colonial period (see Figure 2.1). The
ᶜarbi half of Medjerda—which was known as Medjerda-*ᶜarbi* or *el humah
ᶜarbi*—or the Arab quarter—was founded on the rubble of an ancient Roman
town by Moorish Andalusian settlers in the fifteenth century. The medina,
or old Arab quarter, consists of a maze of gravel lanes which branch off from
the central market square. The narrow streets have no sidewalks, and are
bordered with high white-washed walls. No windows face the street, only
the ornately decorated heavy blue-painted Andalusian doors. Some retain
the threshold tilework still found in Sevilla, Cordoba and Granada. Behind
these doors lie courtyards and rooms bursting with the activity of women
and children or tiny shops, where conversation lingers.

Medjerda-*souri*, or *el humah souri*, which was built by French colonial
settlers at the end of the nineteenth century, is still a distinct quarter of the
town and visually contrasts to Medjerda-*ᶜarbi* in every aspect. Here we find
wide streets and paved avenues that branch off from the large brown-stone
church and run perpendicular to each other. Shops and houses are interspersed, and the buildings often do not touch each other. Instead of inner
courtyards, the red-tiled villas once even had gardens which faced the
street. People say that French homes in Medjerda-*souri* were on display from
the street through their large and unshuttered windows. Medjerdis who
have moved into the *souri* part of town have shuttered the windows; paved

58

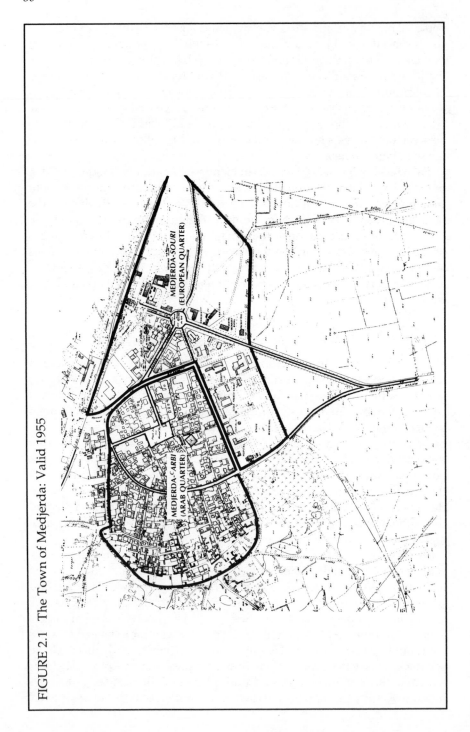

FIGURE 2.1　The Town of Medjerda: Valid 1955

and enclosed the old French gardens. Bourdieu describes the imagery of colonial space thus:

> They began by attempting to discipline space, as if through it they hoped to discipline men. Everything was characterized by uniformity and straight lines. Built on prescribed sites, in accordance with set standards, the houses were laid out in straight lines along wide streets, which could serve equally well to outline the plan of a Roman camp or a colonial village. In the center is the square, with the characteristic triad of the villages of France—the school, the town hall and the war memorial. It is as if the authorities thought that they could create village life by creating their outer symbols.(1961:169)

The irony, of course, is that the medina itself had its genesis in the merger of European and Moorish styles. The exiles of 15th century Spain synthesized the finest elements of European and Islamic architecture into a proud imagery of breathtaking elegance. The Moors brought with them their concept of an urban ideal, and painted their memory of Andalusian grillwork and tilework, masonry and woodcraft on the Tunisian canvas. Before the arrival of *la France*, regional identity had been more Mediterranean than Middle Eastern, more Andalusian than Arab.

The inescapable colonial penetration replaced this merged identity with a bipolar image of the Mediterranean world. Each quarter came to constitute a separate world for its residents. To most *colons*, the "Arab" quarter was an entirely invisible world. A map of Medjerda drawn by a former *colon* dramatically displayed this invisibility, for on it the older, *ᶜarbi* quarter has been entirely deleted. Streets fade off into the empty page as if Medjerda had housed only a European town. Not surprisingly, a colonial map of the Medjerdi countryside indicated only French colonial farms. Andalusian Medjerda was considered by the French as a quaint anachronism with pathetic pretensions to grandeur. From their perspective, there was nothing European about the medina; it was decidedly other, or Arab. Thus, it is possible to speculate that it was the French who created the idea of Medjerda-*ᶜarbi* with every blow of the hammer with which they constructed its counterpart, the *souri* quarter of town.

As invisible as *"les indigènes"* may have been to the French, the reverse was not the case. The local population reckoned with European ideas, technology and people every day, even long after the departure of *la France*.

As the colonial era receded into the past and the town expanded, the *ᶜarbi/souri* dualism was only somewhat diminished. An influx of people from the countryside brought about the growth of new quarters surrounding the entirety of Medjerda, contrasting as sharply with the self-contained identity of Medjerda-*ᶜarbi* as did the European-inspired Medjerda-*souri*. The *ᶜarbi* and *souri* quarters of town have retained distinct identities and are inhabited by people from differing backgrounds. In Medjerda-*ᶜarbi* we find the old, wealthy Andalusian families and other highly-regarded founding families of the town. The narrow streets and walled boundaries prevent expansion. Custom prohibits the construction of multiple stories, although on occasion they have been an option for Andalusian families unwilling to leave the quarter. With so little capacity for expansion, the growing extended family branches into Medjerda-*souri* and the newer quarters. Younger sons with their wives and children move into the old French quarter, where post-colonial urban investors have come to settle.

Upon the departure of the French, Medjerda-*souri* property was purchased by incoming Djerbi, Sfaxi, and Sahli speculators; these individuals became the post-colonial elite of the town. Medjerda-*ᶜarbi* houses most of the town's coffee houses, butcher shops, the old souk, Qur'anic and secular Arab schools, maraboutic shrines, mosques, and hammams. Medjerda-*souri* boasts the *douche moderne*, or public showers, the secondary school, the French bakeries, and the *Auberge du Bon Acqueil*— the only spot in town where men can drink beer and wine, though they are not allowed to take them out. The location here of the post office, the tax office, the police, and all government agencies further identifies the national government with the colonial overlords of the past. After Independence, however, the prominent and proverbial French War Memorial was replaced by a huge bust of Habib Bourguiba, leader of the resistance against the French and first president of the independent republic.

Medjerda-*ᶜarbi* is considered the religious center; Medjerda-*souri* is the administrative center. The *ᶜarbi/souri* halves of Medjerda came to reaffirm the spatial separation of sacred Islamic spaces from those considered European, secular and profane.

Post-colonial Medjerda, however, expanded well beyond the perimeters of both the Arab and French quarters of town. Nine distinct quarters have emerged—each with its own architectural style (from neo-Andalusian villas to squatters' *gourbis*) and attributed identity (from "real" Medjerdis to "not real" Medjerdis to "mountain people"). Most interesting among the nine is *Hayeh Soyah*. Named for one of the first Arab families to construct a house beyond the borders of Medjerda-*souri*, *Hayeh Soyah* has both middle class (i.e. non-fellah) and "real" Medjerdi aspirations. Authenticity and respectability are solidified through the blending of Medjerda's pre-existing *ᶜarbi* and *souri* architectural forms. Streets are midway between the narrow, convoluted passageways of Medjerda-*ᶜarbi* and the straight, wide avenues of Medjerda-*souri*. There are sidewalks, but no windows or verandas face the public street. In their place are solid whitewashed walls and iron gates lining the dusty, ever-so-slightly curved road. However, walls and gates are only half again as high as those of Medjerda-*ᶜarbi*. *Hayeh Soyah's* outward appearance is one of compromise, moderation and an easy accommodation of two opposing images.

Once within the walls, compromise becomes disjuncture. The home has a definitive central courtyard which is approached through an ᶜ*arbi* maze of indirection. Windows face the courtyard only. But the kitchens have been supplied with counters, cupboards and sinks complete with running water. These kitchens have been designed with a *souri* use pattern in mind. The counters support bottled-gas hot-plates, forcing women to either stand for hours while cooking or climb upon the counter in order to sit comfortably cross-legged over their broth; the cupboards are too small to store four-foot-high crockery; and indoor running water attracts mosquitos and other insects. ᶜ*Arbi*-style cooking is done at floor level, and this kitchen design is too cramped for even one woman to cook this way comfortably. Cooking with the help of more than one daughter requires careful choreography. In homes of *Hayeh Soyah* one may find that the indoor water pipes have been disconnected, and stately earthen jugs crowd the limited floor space. While cooking most frequently takes place in the courtyard, girls nevertheless excuse their lack of culinary skill by blaming the overburdened kitchen.

ᶜ*Arbi / souri* contrasts are apparent throughout the region. Djemiliya, the delegation's second largest town, is so divided into ᶜ*arbi* and *souri* halves that the two divisions actually function as distinct towns separated by a narrow bridge across the Medjerda River. Djemiliya-*souri*, like Medjerda-*souri*, lies to the north of the old ᶜ*arbi* town. To all intents and purposes, it is a fiction to think of Djemiliya as one town at all. Sidi Ugᶜud, to the northwest of Medjerda, was once entirely *souri*. At its peak stands the ruined church and cemetery that once dominated both the village and the valley. The fertile countryside is dotted with red-tiled roofs of French colonial farmhouses and barns—which are mostly rundown, uninhabited or already in ruins. Many Medjerdis take pleasure in the presence of *souri* ruins. Those with long memories have a visual reminder that French authority indeed has ended; their grandchildren play among the ruins looking for *souri* treasures in the rubble of villas, churches and cemeteries. Restoration is the exception rather than the rule and is frowned upon by many.

The French farmhouses that remain standing are two-storied and have columned porches. Roman ruins may be seen decorating the gardens that were used by the *colons* for sitting or picnics. During the colonial period, most of these farmhouses had access to electricity, which was supplied by private generators; they also contained indoor plumbing—including hot tap water supplied by a bottled-gas water heater. Gas, for heating and cooking, was available in bottles which were exchanged in town on a monthly basis. Many of the colonial farmhouses were built with formidable fireplaces—large enough to heat a Normandie villa in the dead of winter—despite the scarcity of wood throughout the country. Furniture tended to be custom-made or imported from France; including polished hardwood armoires, buffets, and dressing tables. Many such furnishings are in evi-

dence today covered with dust and cobwebs— unmoved, unused in decay-
ing expropriated French farmhouses. Some are found in dark antique shops
along the Rue Zarkoun in Tunis. In back of the colonial farmhouses there are
still the one-room mud and straw *gourbis* of the household help and farm
workers, who often inherited (formally or informally) the homes of their
souri patrons on the eve of expropriation. Farmhouses that were awarded
through private legal transactions were later reevaluated and reassigned to
fellahin on the basis of their participation in the independence or cooperative movement.

Most of the colonial farmhouses no longer have electricity, or indoor taps
or hot water; their walls have crumbled and their gardens are overgrown
with weeds. In some cases, attics have become pigeon roosts. In the region
or Delegation of Medjerda—which has a population of about 55,000—only
two colonial farmhouses and farms had been purchased and renovated by
the 1980's, by wealthy young entrepreneurs from outside the region. These
houses have been adorned elaborately and furnished with the most modern
European kitchen and bathroom appliances to be found in Tunisia. The
flower gardens (so common in Andalusian Spain but absent in Andalusian
North Africa) are maintained with "useless" (i.e. neither edible nor salable)
decorative flora in true *souri* extravagance. The fellahin of Medjerda, in their
abhorrence of the purely decorative, are the ultimate economic maximizers.

In one of these modernized *souri* villas, the patio has been transformed
into an *ᶜarbi* courtyard and the sheds in the back into *ᶜarbi* sitting and storage
rooms replete with sheepskins on rag rugs and a *kanoun* brewing the perpetual pot of tea. Huge earthen jugs, stacked and lined against the walls of
the storage rooms, are filled with the year's supply of homemade couscous,
mhammes and bulghur. The family actually lives within these rooms. In this
case, the fellah, although deeply committed to *souri* farming, lives a rich
ᶜarbi home-life behind a façade of unused modern *souri* comforts.

Most of the region's population lives in some form of *ᶜarbi* housing—
either in countryside *gourbis* and newer *douar* or Arabic houses, or in the *ᶜarbi*
section of town. In contrast to the *souri* farmhouses, the *douar* are one-storied
houses made out of whitewashed cinderblock. The roofs are flat and are
covered with straw or tin. The basic model has one room which is used for
living, sleeping, and eating, and another room which is used for cooking
and storage. There is always a courtyard and sometimes a partition for a
toilet. Families often add *gourbi* or cinderblock rooms to the house as sons
marry and the family grows. The furnishings in most country *douar* include
a metal frame double bed, an armoire, rag rugs, and sheepskins; sometimes
there is a formica-type table and a chair or two. Parents sleep in the double
bed, sometimes with an infant; children sleep on sheepskins and mats. The
midah or low round wooden table, is brought in and used to serve meals.
Dishes are cleared by picking up the entire *midah*—dishes, scraps, utensils,

etc., and hauling it out to the courtyard for cleaning. The *tabouna* oven used for baking the daily loaves of flat bread, or *khubz tabouna*, generally stands outside the courtyard proper. The region's towns as well as many of its villages have the additional conveniences of electricity, cold tap water, or plumbing that drains into a centralized network. Families in the town of Medjerda rarely have a *tabouna* and buy their bread from the local bakery instead of baking their own.

Nomadic families, harvesters, and charcoal makers, who travel from farm to farm, live in tents. The Bedouins live in woven goat-hair tents. One side of the tent is designated for adults; the other for children. The son who brings his wife into the household sets up his own smaller tent next to his father's. Just as there are five-*gourbi* farm families, so are there five-tent nomadic families herding together on the fields they rent from the fellahin and state farms. The olive harvesters use canvas tents while traveling; their families remain in *douar* and *gourbis* at their home in central Tunisia. The charcoal makers live in a makeshift tent made out of plastic bags. The tent is too small to divide into sections. When it is not raining, the children sleep out-of-doors.

Uneasy Dualisms

ᶜArbi/souri divisions correlate with many customs that reflect gender roles. In matters of dress, cooking, sitting, and eating, women follow *ᶜarbi* ways; their husbands characteristically follow *souri* ways—though in the more rural areas, men are more likely to lean toward the *ᶜarbi*. A dinner scene thus reveals women dressed *ᶜarbi* in a *meliya*—or more rarely, the *hjab* religious head-covering that is seen more and more frequently in towns. They sit with the children on sheepskins around a low, round wooden table, the *midah*. The women and children share one bowl of food which they dip into with bits of freshly baked country-style loaves of round *khubz tabouna*, which they tear with their hands. (The *tabouna*, like the courtyard, represents female space in that it is an earthen, fiery, volcano-shaped oven which metamorphizes what was once grain or seed and produces the staff of life; crude, perhaps, but wholesome and sustaining). The bits of bread are used as utensils for spooning sauce or stew. *Souri*-attired husbands and sons are dressed in western, second-hand *frippe*, sit on chairs at a high, rectangular table, and are served food on individual plates. They use metal utensils and eat carefully sliced bakery-bought freshly-baked baguettes. Where women always sit on sheepskins or straw mats, men more often sit on chairs; where women eat at a low, round wooden table, men eat at a high, formica table; where one is round, the other is rectangular, etc. Contrasts are sometimes intensified, as when women eat in the bedroom or kitchen after men have been served and have finished their meal in the courtyard, or perhaps in front of a television set. What follows elaborates upon these male/female differences and outlines *ʿarbi/souri* distinctions throughout the life cycle. These distinctions play an important role in determining farm and work strategies.

Women have had little contact with the *souri* world. Older women who remember the *colons* have a command of French which extends no further than *"misyu," "merci ʿalik,"* and *"Santa Maria."* Their essentially *ʿarbi* lives have revolved around the *kanoun* and cooking, the courtyard and the children—and if they live in town, the *hammam* and the marabouts. They do have *ʿarbi/souri* alternatives; however, these choices are generally expressed through the options individual husbands may or may not present to their wives. These options include *ʿarbi* or *souri* birth control, nursing or bottle-feeding, *ʿarbi* or *souri* clothing, cooking utensils, dental hygiene, health care, etc. (see for example, Hermanson, 1976 for dual-use patterns in Tunisian health care practices and Gallagher, 1983 on colonization and the collapse of indigenous Tunisian medical institutions).

The *souri* alternative in each case is costly; the *ʿarbi* alternative is either free, inexpensive, or payable through the barter of vegetables, poultry, or sheep. Decisions concerning vegetables and sheep lie within the male sphere, while those concerning chickens lie within the female domain if the chickens are *ʿarbi*. *Souri* chickens and eggs are decidedly within the male domain and the sole woman who raises and sells them is considered a regional aberration locally (and a national heroine by the state). Women should not sell chickens or anything else at the souk in Medjerda, nor are *ʿarbi* chickens likely to be exchanged directly for *souri* items. *ʿArbi* chickens, or other *ʿarbi* items, however, may be bartered by women through a process of indirection. Gifts can be made to someone to whom the whispered suggestion for a dress from the souk—a *souri* item—can bring the desired result. The *souri* alternative always entails cash payment; it is therefore almost exclusively a male alternative. Farmwomen, as well as many townswomen, do not have access to cash and do not frequent the market-place.

Men are generally more knowledgeable about the *souri* world and its alternatives, while women simply know that it exists. This seems to hold true even for men and women who were brought up in the same homes and on the same colonial farms. On the whole, women may learn about their so-called *souri* options through the radio or through rumor, inasmuch as most husbands do not inform their wives about the choices that are possible.

Women who live in town generally wear European second-hand *frippe* (purchased by their husbands) at home but do not venture beyond the courtyard without wearing a *safsari*, however they do not walk through town unless they must. The *safsari*—similar to the Algerian and northern Moroccan *haïk*—is, according to some women, a symbol of Andalusian rather than Arab identity, just as the *hjab* represents Islamic, rather than

Arab, identity. Nevertheless, Tunisian women with no Andalusian aspirations don the *safsari* when venturing into the public sector. Wealthy women never appear on the streets; they move about town or throughout the region by chauffeured automobile—with the back windows curtained. A car may thus be considered a type of veil for women, or perhaps being inside a car is equivalent to being within the confines of one's own home. European—i.e., *souriya*—wives are not bound by the customary veiling of women. *Souriya* wives are not necessarily born in Europe; one, indeed, is a third generation Tunisian—but of Maltese origin.

Among the poorer fellahin, *souri* choices other than in farming—such as owning an automobile—would be considered extravagant. Among wealthier fellahin, they constitute real possibilities from which to choose. Two contrasting cases follow which illustrate the gender dynamics of *carbi/souri* choices.

The Bejaouis: Ali and Naima live in a one-room *gourbi* with seven of their eight children. Ali works his six-hectare farm with the help of his children and younger brother. After eight children, Naima asked Ali if she could go to the clinic in Medjerda-*souri* to find out about birth control—which she heard about on the radio. Naima suffers from migraine headaches which so debilitate her she can do no work, but remains curled up in the dark *gourbi* holding her throbbing head. When pregnant, the headaches diminish, but she is dizzy and nauseated throughout the nine months. Her legs become swollen, painful, and ribboned with large varicose veins. Her home childbirth experiences, she says, were nightmares, and have not gotten easier through the years. In addition, she finds nursing painful, but says that Ali never brings home enough formula for the baby. She mixes the powder with milk from their tubercular cow. Ali replied that she could go to Medjerda. Dressed in her finest *meliya*, Naima boarded the family *karita*, or donkey-driven cart. Once in Medjerda, Ali smiled and said, "You may go to the *hammam*, you may visit with Habiba. But stay away from the clinic." And he rode off to sell his vegetables at the souk. Naima went to Habiba's and then to the clinic, and confirmed as she suspected, that she was pregnant again. Once again at her cousin's house in town, she sat her ten month old baby girl on the floor and curled up in Habiba's lap to cry. When Ali came to pick her up, he commented, "Look at her, she is just like a cat: always sleeping.'" Later, when he learned that Naima was pregnant again, he said, "Next time you can go to the clinic" (i.e. after the birth of the next child).

The Tunsis: Moncef and his wife Mounira live in the *souri* part of town along with Moncef's mother and his ten year old nephew. Moncef raises *souri* chickens and imported livestock and feeds them an experimental concentrate. He uses high-yield seed in the fields of his three farms. He lives in a former colonial villa which he had remodeled according to the latest Parisian decor. His wife studied for two years at the University of Tunis before their marriage. Moncef, in discussing his life and philosophy, told me in French:

> I wanted Mounira to finish school. I took her to the doctor and got her birth control pills. She did not take them and got pregnant. I took her back to the doctor in Tunis so that he could follow her pregnancy to term, and then I took her to the hospital for the birth. I bought her bottles and infant formula. I believe in the proper spacing of children, so after our son was born, I brought her back to the doctor for more birth control pills. Again, she did not take them, and got pregnant. But this time I took her to Tunis for an abortion. I only want two children. These things must be done right. I want my children to have the best possible life. If there are too many of them, this is not possible.

Mounira is sitting in her bathrobe in an *ᶜarbi* corner of the lavish European bedroom: she is brewing a pot of strong Tunisian tea on the coal-burning clay *kanoun* while sitting crosslegged on a white sheepskin on the floor, embroidering with her mother-in-law. Explains Mounira, "If I had wanted to stay at the university I would not have gotten married. Now that I am married I want to have children. Besides, everyone knows that birth control pills are not healthy for a woman's blood."

In the first case, the husband refuses the *souri* alternative; in the second case, it is the wife who refuses. In both cases, however, the husband decides family policy, while the wife attempts to work through subterfuge.

When a rural woman goes into labor, the family's usual *gabla ᶜarbiya*, or midwife, is called in to attend her at home. Some women, particularly young, terrified women having their first child, beg their husbands for a clinic delivery. They have not been taught the stages of labor and childbirth and are unprepared for the intensity and duration of their uterine contractions. Older female relatives carefully watch over the new mother-to-be but expect her to learn more about childbirth from experience than from precept. Husbands whose wives have not previously miscarried tend not so much to explicitly refuse their wives a clinic delivery as much as they delay so long that the child is born at home. Men who are firm believers in *dwa' souri*, or Western medicine, arrange for their wives to deliver at a clinic under the guidance of a physician. The cost of a clinic delivery far exceeds that of a home birth not only because a physician's rates are higher than that of midwife's, but also because the hospital stay is billed by the hour. Young husbands hope to minimize the the entire cost of the birth knowing that the infant will precipitate further expenditures for which they already are ill-prepared.

Once a child is born, there are further *ᶜarbi/souri* possibilities. Binding the baby, similar to swaddling, is said to be a *souri* custom adopted from the *colons*—although the French do not bind their infants and former *colons* claim they never did. The custom, however, is universally practiced by women in Medjerda. A long strip of cloth is wound tightly around the baby starting at the shoulders down toward the feet, where the cloth is tied. Only the infant's head and neck are free to move; the infant cannot smother, mothers say, since he sleeps face-up. Older babies are sometimes bound with their arms free. The number of months that a baby may be bound varies, and some babies are still bound a good part of the day at ten months of age. The form and manner of binding infants in Medjerda, while disclaimed by the French, does have antecedents in the Andalusian Jewish (i.e. Sephardic) families who once were an integral part of the fabric of Medjerdi life. These mothers used embroidered rather than unadorned binding cloth. When outgrown by the baby, the cloth would be donated to the synagogue to be used as a Torah binding. Local Medjerdi women, perhaps knowing that the custom originates with some "other" have come to simply dub the custom as emanating from the *souri* world. Or perhaps the identification of Sephardic Jews in Tunisia with *la France* did indeed make the custom *souri*.

Breast feeding is considered ^c*arbi*; bottle-feeding, *souri*. Most farm women nurse their infants and consider breast-feeding superior to bottle-feeding for the baby's welfare. However, complications—such as discomfort, infection, abscess or loss of milk may lead a woman to long for bottle-feeding. When this happens, a real financial burden is faced by many farm families since bottle-feeding requires a constant cash outflow in families who generally have no cash at all except after harvest season. The husband may buy formula and bottles in town in order to keep a young infant adequately supplied. Mothers prepare formula in the same manner as tea; they pour a handful of powder into the bottle, add water from the earthen water jug, and stir with the tea spoon. Bottles are rinsed out with jug water, as are the tea glasses. When formula runs low, women in these families must either dilute the formula or begin feeding their infants solid foods; by then, they have, of course, lost the option to nurse. Older babies have a more "^c*arbi*" bottle feeding: milk is flavored with *harissa* (hot chilli pepper paste, olive oil and spices) so that they can get used to the taste of real (i.e. solid) food.

Going to school, especially beyond the sixth grade, has been considered *souri*—particularly by rural people. Many courses are taught in French and some Medjerdis still believe that secular education will lead to a highly paid position that does not entail manual labor. The prevailing belief in Medjerda, however, is that a higher education leads to a "higher" level of unemployment—commonly called with derision, *chomeur deluxe*, or high-class unemployment. The *chomeur deluxe* would rather sit in the coffee house and wait for a non-existent white collar position rather than defile himself with the sweat and toil of agriculture. Staying home and preparing to be either a fellah or a wife and mother is considered *ᶜarbi*. A father either encourages a child to stay with his schoolwork, allowing him time away from farm duties to study at home, or he encourages him to master farming. Frequently one child in the family will be encouraged to study while the others help out on the farm.

When a child fails at school, it signals the end of his education; in such cases, the school principal discourages farm children—particularly the girls—from continuing. My impression is that girls do not appear to attend much school if they live on a distant farm, despite statistics on rural school attendance to the contrary. Mothers claim their husbands will not allow daughters to attend school; fathers claim the schools are too far for girls to walk unchaperoned. Were the schools nearer to home, some fathers say, they would gladly send the girls as well.

A few exceptional rural fathers without means have solved the "distance" problem by sending a daughter to live with relatives in town in order to provide her with an education. The pressure for these farm girls to achieve is high; the dream is for them to become a teacher or marry the son of a "wealthy" man. When a girl's education is interrupted, either because of failure or betrothal, some girls—like Mounira—eagerly accept the change. Others experience disappointment, shame, and depression. A few attempt or successfully commit suicide. Mastering *ᶜarbi* home skills is much less anxiety-provoking. If a girl were determined to produce an income, she would do well to become adept at acceptable *ᶜarbi* skills such as pottery, weaving, embroidery, or sewing. However, sewing on a machine—a *souri* skill—would require a generous father, brother, or husband in order to purchase the machine and supplies.

If the girls have a *souri* dream at all, it is more concerned with the attributes they would like to see in their future husbands, rather than with their own unlikely careers. However, here, too, their ambivalence is in evidence. To the beat of a *darbuka* or a kitchen pot, they can be heard to sing songs that contrast the qualities of *ᶜarbi* and *souri*-style lovers. An example follows:

Ya liri ya liri goulu l'Amar	O dear one, O dear one tell
Amar Yajini	He should come to me
Eliri ya liri ya ṣamara	O dear one, brown skinned girl
Eshbiki etghiri?	Why are you jealous?
Manhibush hak haka	I don't like him like that
Ushaaru kil-hakaka	His hair is like steel wool
Labisley jardu shlekka	He wears old rubber sandals
Wigini ᶜogbelil	He comes to me in the middle of the night
Wagouli ya liri	Calling O dearest

Manhibush iṣalli	I don't want him to do his prayers
Inhibu yiskr wa-yighani	I want him to get drunk and sing
Wa-yjini wa ygabilni	And come to me and approach me
Wa-ygouli ya liri	And call me O dearest
Manhibush tha'if	I don't want a frail old one
Inhibu zghayr wa thrif	I want him young and sweet
Eliri ya liri ya ṣamara	O dear one, dark one
Eshbik itghiri?	Why are you jealous?
Yitkayef fi-larti	He smokes Larti
Wa-ygouli aysh marti	And asks pretty-please be my wife
Yagouli ya liri, ya liri	And calls me O my dearest
Ya liri	O my dearest
Manḥibush smin	I don't want a fat one
Inhibu yilbess idjin	I want him to wear jeans
Wajini ᶜogbelil	And come to me in the middle of the night
Wa-ygouli ya liri ya liri ya liri	Calling O my dearest ...
Inhibu yimshi li-monobri	I want him to go to the Monoprix
ilbis sirwal 'Charley'	And put on bell-bottom pants
Shaᶜaru kil-hibbi	His hair like a hippie's
Wa-ygoulu ya liri ya liri ya liri	And call me O my dearest
Manḥibush idansi	I don't want him to dance [European-style]
Inhibu jabri mitlansi	I want him to be observant
W-jini hata lifarshi	And come right up to my bed
Wa-ygouli ya liri . . .	And call me O dearest . . .

The boys dream of going to France, finding a lucrative job, and bringing back a "real" *souriya* wife. Although some farm boys do migrate abroad, most do not. Few have ever met a European woman, but they are convinced that obtaining one is desirable. They believe that a *souriya* wife will raise their standing in Tunisian society, bind them to Europe forever, guarantee their wealth, and lighten the skin color of their offspring. They also believe it is advantageous to have a foreign wife because she cannot mobilize her family in her defense in the eventuality of a dispute or a beating. The dreams of a *souriya* wife have some precedence in Medjerda, for there are two or three European wives in the region—none of whom are the wives of poor fellahin. The best of all possible worlds is the European wife who accepts Islam and dons the *hjab*. *ᶜArbiya* wives, however, are considered cleaner; they know how to cook, have fewer expectations, and are less demanding. They can brew a proper pot of tea, will raise *ᶜarbi* children, and will not sneak pork into the cooking. In addition, an *carbiya* is also the most likely wife—since most marriages in the region are variations on endogamous themes, from father's-brother's-daughter's-marriage to local alliances with distantly-related Medjerdi families.

cArbi weddings take place mainly in the countryside or in one's family courtyard; *souri* weddings take place at public buildings in Medjerda-*souri*. At an *carbi* wedding, the festivities are held in the courtyard of the house. The *darbuka*, *mezwed* goatskin bagpipes, and flute are played. One of the musicians dances with an clay *kanoun* on his head. The *kanoun* is filled with burning coals and incense and, as he dances, the incense pervades and purifies the courtyard. Women sit at the edges of the courtyard on sheepskins and lean against the mud walls of the *gourbi*. Guests chat, sip tea, and share sunflower seeds. In the center of the courtyard, the musicians play and the male guests dance, one-by-one. Later on, a few girls, surrounded by girlfriends, dance within the confines of the women's half of the courtyard. The bride sits alone on a chair inside the darkened, gift-filled *gourbi* that from then on she will call home. She is visited throughout the celebration by female guests examining the gifts and straightening out her hair or gown. Except for basics—a basket of dates, a new *safsari*, and perhaps some *khol* eye-makeup from Mecca—the gifts are generally *souri* and include lipsticks and nail polish, imported perfumes and negligées, or china tea sets that will be displayed—but never used.

Souri weddings take place primarily at the *Salle de Fêtes* in Medjerdi-*souri*, adjacent to the town hall. The groom is paraded around town by a marching brass band as his bachelor friends sing and joke in accompaniment. The bride is brought to the *Salle de Fêtes* and sits on the right side of the hall; she is displayed on a throne throughout the celebration. She is dressed in stiff silver brocade, wears a tiara, and holds an Andalusian fan (even if hers is not one of the Andalusian founding families of Medjerda). An orchestra plays onstage. Women are in the front of the auditorium, close to the stage. They dance, talk, sit in clusters, and snack on Coca Cola and baklava. Men sit quietly in a row at the back of the auditorium behind a long table. They sip their Coca Cola and smoke cigarettes handed out by the groom. The men do not dance. The theme of round/long emerges again in the seating patterns of women/men, but at the *souri* wedding women occupy the central space and dance, while men observe. After photographs are taken of friends and relatives posing with the bride on the throne, people disperse, and the bride is driven to her new home.

Funerals are always *carbi*. Although there still exist old colonial cemeteries, complete with what some Medjerdis have called the "*souri* marabout," or saint's tomb—actually the tomb of a former French leading citizen of Medjerda—no Tunisian has ever been buried there. Despite the many *carbi*/*souri* choices made in a lifetime, one's final destination is always *carbi*.

احنا كل كيف كيف ، احنا كل عربي

كسكس زلاس مآتش كسكس كرواني

3

Local Distinctions

ahna kul kif kif, ahna kul ⁿarbi
we are all the same, we are all Arab

kuskus zlass ma'atch kuskus kirwani
a couscous of the Djlass is not a couscous of the Kirouani

The people of Medjerda have felt pulled between assimilation to the larger society and differentiation into smaller, more local affiliations. The first process has promoted homogeneity—that is to say, the expression of the ideal of solidarity, conformity, and equality; the second has reinforced regionalism and tribalism, and has reaffirmed the diverse origins of Medjerda's population. Other forms of differentiation, such as rank, class, relative wealth and skin color are also present. Local distinctions find expression through the idiom of *nisba*, or collective identity. Local perceptions of Medjerda's social history begin with the social relations between identifiable groups. In so doing, one quickly discovers that though Medjerdis and developers alike share the notion of a model of a homogeneous society, such a model is inadequate for understanding the behavior, values, and responses to change of the fellahin of Medjerda.

One must distinguish between the developers notion of a uniform population and the Medjerdi understanding of their own homogeneity. Fellahin proclaim *"ahna kul kif kif"*—"we are all the same"—or *"ahna kul ⁿarbi"*—"we are all Arab." Developers have perceived this avowal of uniformity as traditionalism and thus have interpreted it as an expression of opposition to progress. But the Medjerdi profession of homogeneity celebrates emancipation from colonialism and serves as a reminder that whereas Medjerda's population once included Jews, as well as the French, Italians, and Maltese, today there are only Arabs. The statements express solidarity with Tunisian nationalism and by extension, proclaim identification with Islam and pan-Arabism. For some, it has been a further statement of opposition to external forces in general and for these, the developers' assessment may be correct.

Conformity is highly valued in Medjerda. Acting as a member of the community displays solidarity, while expressing individuality does not. This is not to say that individuality does not exist; it does, but it is not positively reinforced. On the whole, conformity has been valued more in a woman's behavior than in a man's. Women have been expected to be inconspicuous. Individuality and identity have been hidden under an enveloping white veil, the *safsari*, when out-of-doors, or the more contemporary Islamic headcovering, the *hjab*. At home, women have continued to value performing tasks in common to the extent that individual identity is lost in the final product. In matters of cooking, sewing, weaving, cleaning, and childcare, collective participation has left little room for idiosyncratic behavior. It would have been unthinkable, for example, for stylistic changes to show up in embroidered pieces. The women of Medjerda have been adamant about the "right way" and the "wrong way" of doing things; they have ridiculed non-conformists and teach their children the proper path.

Women also have emphasized the uniformity of Medjerdi society in their discussions of kinship matters. Each woman can demonstrate her own connections with any family in the region by tracing marriages between members of one tribal grouping and another. Medjerda's families are considered as a unit: "chained links on a necklace," they say; "metal teeth on a zipper." When the zipper is closed it appears to be a solid mass, flexible but firm—but it can be undone and split apart at any moment.

Medjerdis have tended to use regional and tribal sayings to describe and account for behavior which differs from their own. Medjerdiya women, for example, would first establish that "we eat couscous here" and only much later allow that "a couscous from Djlass is not a couscous from Kairouan." This statement, when made by a Kirouaniya, is a disavowal of any connection between the Djlass and the Kirouani despite their territorial proximity. Every assertion of uniformity is countered by a later demonstration of ʿarsh distinctiveness. Regional stereotypes are used not only to articulate differences but also to admonish others to conform to a national ideal. Regionalism and tribalism have persisted as dominant factors in the social relations of Medjerdis; they continue to provide values as well as models for behavior.

Like the notions of solidarity and conformity, the ideology of equality has served to mask differences—in this case, differences based on rank, class, tribe and wealth. Principles of class distinguish wealthy, politically-connected landowners from other fellahin while mechanisms of the local ranking system serve to unite them and establish long-lasting patron-client relations. Despite the egalitarian ethic, Medjerdis nevertheless have recognized stratification—or at least, clear distinctions—within the region's population. They speak of "levels" of society and disparage the individual who seeks an inappropriately, higher status than others accord him. There appears to be consensus that in the post-colonial era, the highest status is accorded the local representatives of the national administration and members of the new agrarian elite. At the next level are the traditional elite, who remain the most respected families in the town despite their loss of political power. These include members of the founding and saintly families as well as religious functionaries. The fellahin, particularly those of tribal origin, tend to see themselves as belonging to a particular extended family or lineage with distinct characteristics and traditions, regardless of whether they live in towns, villages or isolated farms.

Whether or not the locally recognized social categories are thought to form a hierarchy or simply constitute niches of Medjerdi society varies from person to person. In terms of national or regional power—the ability to make, change, or enforce policy—the first group clearly recognizes its own leadership role. In terms of local prestige, however, the second group dominates in the eyes of many Medjerdis. The focus of the delegation's population has been farming; from this viewpoint, those employed in non-agricultural activities function in a supporting role.

Occupation, like class and physiognomy, is also seen through the idiom of *nisba*. The association of a specific tribe with a given occupation may be associated with a tribal appellation whether or not it applies genealogically. Thus, "*nimshi l-djerbi*" means "I am going to the store;" the shopkeeper need not be from the island of Djerba to be associated with the Djerbi, Tunisia's traditional grocers. This tribal or regional identity needs further explanation, for many professions are considered outside the local classificatory boundaries altogether. Here we may find townsfolk of diverse civil service professions—doctors, teachers, postmen, policemen, tax collectors,etc.—who live not only in the town of Medjerda, but also in the smaller towns and villages of the delegation. However, this population is excluded from the local hierarchy because they lack both permanent residency in Medjerda and a feeling of identification with the region. They have come to serve, for a specified duration of time, and look forward to their eventual return to their own regions. So too, the "outsider" permanent residents (e.g. the Djerbi shopkeepers or the Italian craftsman) may live in Medjerda, but do not at all identify with the town or region. On the other hand, merchants and craftsmen who claim Medjerdi affiliation seem to be considered as local because of their affinity with Medjerdi land. In addition to their urban professions, they are also fellahin, for all own, rent or work local land in addition to their entrepreneurial activities.

Nisba and Identity

There is a term or concept in Arabic which acts as an identity marker; it may designate the family, tribe, region, city, religious group, or brotherhood to which one belongs. *Nisba* (plural *nisab*) manifests itself as the suffix "*i*" to designate the masculine and "*iya*" to mark the feminine. According to the dictionary, *nisba* means "ascription, attribution, imputation, kinship, relationship, affinity, relationship by marriage, connection, link, agreement, conformity, relation, [and] reference" (Cowan 1976:960). The term refers to membership within a group or category but one's identity is only relatively fixed within a series of "nested" categories and given contexts. Thus, one can be Arab (ᶜ*arbi*), Tunisian (*tunsi*), Medjerdian (*medjerdi*), as well as Andalusian (*andulsi*) in ever narrowing circles of affiliation. The three attributes of conformity, solidarity and equality apply to all and require adherence to shared rules, beliefs, values, structural relationships, territorial boundaries, origins, and behavior. Behavioral guidelines, however, become increasingly differentiated—and sometimes contradictory—within each circle of affiliation.

Nisba is either reflected in the patronym or is used instead of one's patronym; it is available either as a latent or an overt designation. If one were to classify the population of Medjerda—or that of any Arab town or region—by *nisba*, one would have a good indication not only of the social categories in the area, but also of the origins of a good part of the population.

The post-colonial population (see Figure 3.1), consists entirely of ᶜ*arbi* families with the exception of the few European wives who have been brought to the region and whose children are raised in accordance with local rather than European custom. However, one colonial family—an elderly Italian brother and sister—chose to remain in the town of Medjerda long after the departure of the French, and to live out their remaining years in the heart of Medjerda-*souri*. Foreign development experts working in the region have been dubbed "the authentic *souri* article." They rarely choose to reside in the region; nevertheless, they are visible representatives of European ways. Local fellahin recall with humor the one Dutch extension worker who only took up local residence so as not to be too far to tend his European cattle.

In the valley, a distinction is made between people of nomadic or urban origins. Here we find that, with the exception of the Oueslati, regional leadership has remained firmly within the jurisdiction of families deriving from urban backgrounds. The enigma of the Oueslati is all the more interesting because of the low status accorded them in Testour, another Andalusian town in the Medjerda Valley (see Hopkins 1977:465).

At another level of distinction, those of nomadic background are differentiated by their degree of sedentarization. This level includes families who have remained nomadic as well as those who have partially or wholly sedentarized. Sedentarized nomads—the bulk of the population—are distinguished as either those with Berber or mixed Arab-Berber ancestry and those of Arabic tribes from outside Tunisia. Those families with urban origins have been distinguished as belonging either to the traditional or the post-independence elites. These classifications, as will be seen, reflect local interpretation of Medjerdi social order.

Although the population is almost entirely interconnected by marriage, members of each patronymic group maintain a distinct identity and a proud sense of lineage history; when precise historical knowledge has long been lost, legend and myth are used to fill the breach. The most prevalent *nisba*-groupings are shared identities which cannot consistently be called "tribes" or even "lineages," since some simply reflect urban or rural appellations, and many have lost their former sense of corporate identity. Figure 3.1 depicts a continuum ranging from those with the most political authority to those with the least.

To understand the dynamic within the system is to gain further clues regarding structural relationships, for *nisba* is relational and affirms traditional alliances between groups. Geertz describes the on-the-ground workings of *nisba* thus: "The selves that bump into each other on the street gain their definition from associative relations they are imputed to have with the selves that surround them" (1974:40). Geertz's definition suggests the manipulative aspect of *nisba* when he uses the phrase "imputed to have," for people associate themselves with other groups and are adept at reassigning *nisba*-identities to malign others or to aggrandize themselves: "He's not really Andulsi," claims the Djlassi. "He's really Maltese and we Djlass are not mountain tribesmen [*"riffi"*] but come from the holy city of Kairouan; we're Kirouani." Assertions and counter-assertions reflect the ranking of tribal groupings within the community as well as competition between groups in the formation of marriage alliances.

State Administrators
and the New Agrarian Elite

At the political and economic center of Medjerdi society one finds administrators of the state bureaucracy and landowners who are linked to national organizations. Men in these two categories form a class apart from the rest of Medjerdi society; they neither have kin ties within the region nor

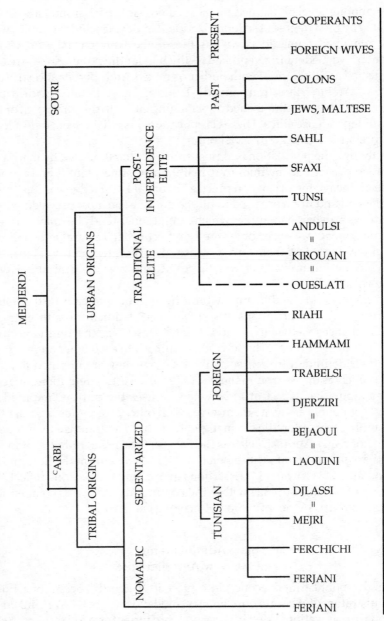

FIGURE 3.1 Predominant Families of Medjerda

── Marriage Alliance   ─ ─ ─ Old Territorial Alliance

do they marry Medjerdiya girls. These men—and their families if they are married—have more ties outside the region than within it.

The Sahli

Two *nisab* are associated with the region's leadership; Sahli in the political sphere and Sfaxi in the economic sphere. A third—the Tunsi, or people with family roots in the capital—have also participated to a lesser degree. The Sahel produced the political elite of Tunisia well before Bourguiba came to power but did not predominate in service in the era of the Ottoman Beys before the arrival of the French. The Sahlis have been posted in towns and villages throughout the country as civil servants, engineers, directors of state farms and cooperatives, agricultural developers, and government representatives (e.g. as judges, tax collectors, police, etc.). As civil servants sent by their respective ministries, they remain for a period of two to five years before being transferred to another post. They arrive with their wives and children if they are married, but their roots remain in the Sahel; they return home every holiday, when they have the opportunity. To them, Medjerda, and places like it, are "stints," merely rungs on the administrative ladder. Most of all, each desires a transfer back to the Sahel; second best would be a post at the central bureau in Tunis. The Sahlis hold key positions in Medjerda because they are outsiders and, presumably, have no local allegiances. Their loyalty is to the administration which they represent and this is said to aid them in carrying out their orders without any contrary pressure from family ties or alliances.

Sahli administrators and their agronomist assistants—who may also be from other parts of the country—oversee the state and cooperative farms of the region. They are the harbingers of national policy and production goals, which are determined each year by the Ministry of Agriculture, and they are on the farms to see that national goals are pursued. The Sahli are both state administrators and outsiders and—according to some fellahin— their role is reminiscent of the *colons* who were the former proprietors and administrators of these same estates.

There is also another kind of Sahli in the region—the permanent settler. These Sahlis were given agrarian reform parcels by President Bourguiba in appreciation for their political activities and support of the Destour Party during the struggle for independence. Like the government workers, they too are present in the delegation by virtue of their political activities; unlike them, however, they are slowly becoming integrated into the region. As may be surmised, Sahli fellahin are perceived by their neighbors as having continued access to political connections (*kteff* or *pistons*) which may afford them greater success in agriculture: in applications for additional land, water, equipment or loans, being well-connected constitutes a formidable advantage.

The Sfaxi

The sale of large French colonial rural and urban landholdings attracted a series of speculators and entrepreneurs from other parts of the country—particularly from the wealthy coastal towns of Sfax, the Sahel and the island of Djerba. The Sfaxis, known as the modern commercial and industrial entrepreneurs of the country, were well prepared for taking over former French farms. Clement Henry Moore points out that

> Modern European farming was only rarely a model that Tunisians imitated. The one exception was in the Sfax area, where the French successfully introduced new dry-farming techniques for the extension of the olive-tree forest, and the Tunisians tended the trees and used half the profits to buy out the French investment. In the fertile northern plains, however, few Tunisians imitated the *colons* to become business-like farmers. (1965:20)

Sfaxis accept French agricultural innovations but also have ideas of their own about agriculture. They experiment with government recommendations—but when they feel that suggestions may interfere with their considered goals, they are neither afraid to reject the recommendations nor to side-step government regulations. It is worthy of note that the Sfaxis have expanded whatever enterprises they engaged in—whether they be of an agricultural or a commercial nature. Although there are only a few Sfaxi families in Medjerda, each of them is engaged in a variety of commercial enterprises. One in particular, a former garage mechanic in his native Sfax, quickly rose to become the key figure in agrarian Medjerda. This Sfaxi began by managing farms for others, drawing on his knowledge of machinery to mechanize the farms, and seeking the advice of government and foreign agrarian advisers. Within ten years, he became one of the largest landowners in the region, president of the Farmers' Union and head of the *Caisse Locale* which loans money to small and mid-scale farmers. His stature in the community has grown over the years, accompanied by an ever-increasing involvement in regional and national politics.

The alliance between large-scale landowners and agrarian bureaucrats is reinforced by the former's active participation in the Farmers' Union. Large-scale landowners comprise the entire leadership within this organization—which acts as a bridge between government and fellahin—and in this role, they both influence and represent their less affluent neighbors.

The Traditional Elite

Medjerdis distinguish clearly between what they consider "traditional" and what they do not. The undisputed traditional elite consists of old established wealthy landowning families, some of whom served in political roles during the pre-colonial and protectorate period. The traditional elite has concerned itself primarily with local leadership rather than national politics; in this capacity its role and influence diminishes each year. However, the old families provide the religious leadership in the town of Medjerda and in this sphere, their authority remains undisputed.

One Djlassi, who earlier had so eagerly classified himself as "Kirouani", explained the difference between Medjerda's traditional and modern elites. "In Medjerda," he said, "we have both kinds. There are the Kirouani, Andulsi, Oueslati and Jendoubi on the one hand, and there are the Sfaxi, Sahli and a few others who are not so important on the other hand. The first are religious; they wear the *jibba* and *chechia* and they go to the mosque. The second drink whiskey, wear European clothes and never say prayers or go to the mosque—unless it's politically motivated. The Kirouani have *baraka* [saintly prestige] and the Sahli have *pistons* [secular/political connections]."

The Djlassi's analysis demonstrates that there is not only a separation of religious and political spheres of authority but also differences of cultural values and personal behavior. His division reflects the separation between *ᶜarbi* and *souri* ways and, indeed, the elites of Medjerda are more polarized than the rest of the region's population in this respect.

The Andulsi

The Andalusian Moors began their retreat from Spain to North Africa in the fifteenth century, yet it was not until the mid-seventeenth century that they became organized into a distinct community in Tunisia. Under the Bey, they were led and represented by their own sheikh (Abun Nasr 1971:158-9). The *sheikh al-andalus* was the political leader of Andalusians throughout the entire lower Medjerda Valley from Galaât-el-Andless on the northern coast to Testour, southwest of Medjerda.

The Andulsi were wealthy, educated, religious town-dwellers who brought both capital and technology with them from Spain. They were able to monopolize certain new industries and introduce lucrative innovations into existing ones. Within a short period, they made their mark in art, architecture, industry and agriculture— especially with regard to the cultivation of olives and in the refining of olive oil (see e.g. Berque 1967:131-132; 157-159). In addition to the foregoing, they flourished in the textile industry and monopolized *chechia* production. Under the Andalusians, Medjerda was a center of textile production. By independence, all that remained was a single factory devoted to one portion of the arduous *chechia* production.

Although the countryside must have been inhabited by tribal grouping before the Andalusian settlement of the region, the Andulsi are considered the only "authentic" Medjerdis. Later immigrants maintained their distinct tribal or urban identification as well as the traditions unique to each. This preservation of distinct traditions was reflected in their perceptions of the land and its potential. The Andulsi compared the land to Spain and found Medjerda suitable for olive production and irrigated gardens. Tribes from south and central Tunisia considered Medjerda to be a rich grazing land for their sheep. Olives, cereals and grazing predominated in the region until the arrival of the French.

The Andulsi elite observed the French transformation of the countryside into vineyards and orchards but were loathe to abandon their own time-honored cultivation practices. Andalusian landowners continued to insist on olive and cereal production well into the post-independence period. Only by the 1980s did some discover it was more profitable to disband their antiquated agricultural enterprises altogether than to invest in moderniz-ing (i.e. mechanizing) their techniques.

The Andulsi mystique in Medjerda is subtle when compared with other North African Andalusian towns like Testour, or Chefchaouen in the Rif Mountains of Morocco. In Medjerda, there are no Andalusian folk festivals, no Andalusian musicians or craftsmen, and no flamboyant Andalusian architecture. The Andalusian families themselves constitute a minority in the town. Medjerda has systematically rejected all efforts to draw attention to itself; nothing should beckon the outsider. There are no hotels, no spectacular weekly markets, no restaurants—not even beaches—and thus no tourism at all. Andalusian identity is not on display; it exists inherently in the home.

The four distinct Andalusian families who remain in Medjerda are the Andulsi, the Bitri (an Arabization of the name Pedro), the Maina and the Ghlaff. Andalusian women who marry outside the four keep their identity alive by giving their daughters Moorish names like Soufya, Sounya and Linya, and by teaching them of their heritage through distinctive cooking and embroidery patterns. The Andulsi primarily intermarry with two other old families of the Medjerdi elite, the Kirouani and the Oueslati. These two families are the core of what continues to be called the traditional elite of Medjerda—and while they continue to provide Andalusian given names for their daughters, they also have maintained distinct traditions of their own.

Medjerdis recognize an "Andalusian physiognomy" which distinguishes descendants of the founding families from tribes who arrived later. Straight hair, light skin, narrow nose, and sometimes blue eyes, characterize the Andalusian physical type and these are desirable features in selecting a bride. Tunisois scoffers in the capital have called these traits Turkish (or Circassian) but locally they are nevertheless identified with Andalusia. Young men, as we have seen, dream of acquiring such a bride—but they have come to identify her more with France or Germany than with Medjerda's own Andalusian heritage.

The Kirouani and Oueslati (Weslati)

Both the Andulsi and the Kirouani originate from the two great centers of early Islamic learning in the Western Mediterranean. Kairouan, founded in the seventh century, was the first Islamic center in the Maghrib and the base from which Islam and the Arabic language spread among North Africa's Berber tribes. In addition, Andalusia and Kairouan were the political centers of independent administrative regions. Their historical link can be traced through the architectural influence of the Great Mosque of Kairouan (*Djam^ca Sidi Uqba*) on Islamic architectural masterpieces such as the *Mezquita* of Cordoba.

The Kirouani families of Medjerda left the holy city of Kairouan before its decline in the sixteenth century and say they have lived in the Medjerda Valley for over five hundred years. "There are no more real Kirouani left in Kairouan," they explain. "We all dispersed centuries ago. The city is now filled with tribesmen like the Djlass." The Kirouani left in part, they say, to take on religious functions in towns throughout the Maghrib. It is they who symbolized the growing sense of convergence among the disparate population, identification with the Islamic community, the *'umma*, which until the arrival of the French had been taken for granted. Prior to the Protectorate period the region of Medjerda had housed too few Jews or Maltese to engender either a strong sense of religious pluralism or fervor.

The Oueslati—a tribe from Djebel Oueslat, just north of Kairouan— followed the Kirouani in dispersing throughout the country, and those who came to settle in Medjerda formed a strong alliance with their traditional neighbors, the Kirouani. The Kirouani and Oueslati both began taking Andulsiya wives, and became prominent landowners in the Medjerda. This is in strong contrast to the position of the Oueslati in Andalusian Testour in the central Medjerda Valley:

A legend is often recounted to explain the dearth of *thiqa* [trust] in Testour today. It seems that when the Andalusians first settled in the town, they were its only inhabitants. In those days, there was a great deal of trust because everybody was conceptually equal. So much so, in fact, that when a man working in his garden wanted to send produce to market he would simply load up the saddlebags of his donkey and send the animal to a regular shop in the Testour market. The shopkeeper would remove the produce and place the correct amount of money in the saddlebags, and the donkey would return to the garden. But then the Wsletia arrived, and pretty soon several incidents occurred in which the donkey returned to the garden with empty saddlebags. The Wsletia were suspected of thievery, and from then on this practice was avoided and there was no longer any trust in Testour. In this tale the

'Andalusians' represent the local people who know and 'trust' one another, while the 'Wsletia' stand for outsiders and newcomers who are outside the system and therefore 'untrustworthy.'   (Hopkins 1977:465)

The difference of status of the Oueslati in Medjerda and Testour is striking. It appears that their ability to form marriage alliances with the Kirouani and the Andulsi was a significant factor in their prominence in Medjerda.

The Kirouani, Qaroui, Grioui, or Sadqaoui family names all indicate origins in the holy city of Kairouan. Differences between these patronyms are matters of accent, which under the French became registered surnames phonetically transcribed. In Arabic, all are written with the letter Q, but pronunciation ranges from the classical Q to the rural G accents. The first three names designate simply origins in the holy city, while the last identifies the holy family whose members have served for generations as *imam* of Medjerda's central mosque. Most of these families maintain homes or connections in Kairouan, a hundred fifty miles to the south, and visit the holy city during religious festivals. Despite their carefully maintained bond with Kairouan, they are Medjerdi and are at the core of the Andulsi-Kirouani-Oueslati alliance which has made up the traditional political leadership of the town for generations.

The Kirouani brought with them a cultural heritage which rivaled that of the Andulsi. They were spiritual and legal experts; they were respected for learning if not for worldliness and technology. The Kirouani came to dominate as religious leaders and have maintained this position securely. Their juridical knowledge further led them into local politics and they came to serve as the sheikhs of Medjerda—alternating in this role with their long-time allies and competitors, the Oueslati. The choice of sheikh was made at least in part according to the age of the next son to succeed; if there were no Kirouani son of age to succeed his father as sheikh, a Oueslati would be elected to the post. In this way, two lines of succession emerged to the position of sheikh, both being passed from father to son.

The last sheikh of Medjerda, a Kirouani, retired in 1975 after eighteen years of service. Shortly thereafter, however, the national government abolished the position and created a new administrative position, that of ^comda, which only in part fulfills the functions formerly carried out by the sheikh.

The ^comda is selected from among candidates who have been elected by the local Neo-Destour and is chosen more for his loyalty to the party and the state than for his family's traditional role in local politics. Nevertheless, the first ^comda to be selected was a Oueslati, immediately following a Kirouani sheikh whose son was as yet too young for political office. In 1981, a new ^comda was chosen who was a clear departure from the past. However, the power and prestige of the ʿ*omda* falls short of that held by the sheikh. For example, it carries with it no authority to resolve local disputes; these are now handled by the court.

The decline of the Griouis and Oueslatis as political forces in Medjerda—which may be temporary—may be linked to their participation, albeit limited, in local administration during the colonial period, when sheikhs were allowed to continue in their role only as long as they cooperated and worked closely with the French. In the formative post-independence period, allegiance to Bourguiba and the newly formed state overrode any local political allegiances. Local allegiances, in fact, were seen as detrimental to nation-building.

Although they claim to have lost their political ascendancy and aspirations in Medjerda, the Kirouani appear to have retained their monopoly on piety and continue to serve as the *imams*, or religious leaders, of Medjerda. There is a belief throughout the countryside that the Kirouani are aided by their *baraka*, or closeness to God, and the Kirouani themselves explain their good fortune in terms of God's will rather than their own labor. In this, they are not alone, for many—if not all—of the successful landowners from the old elite families of Medjerda are religious men who attribute their success to the will of God. They are conservative farmers, primarily dry-farmers, who have persisted in cultivating olives and cereals and maintaining flocks long after this style of farming was deemed economically irrational by developers. They have changed some of their practices, but not before evaluating a good decade or so of positive results.

By working within the system, they were able to withstand colonization of their own land and, at the close of the colonial era, to increase their holdings. After independence and during the cooperative era, they were appointed directors of their own cooperativized land—and when the movement failed, their land was returned to them intact.

Sedentarized Tribes

Although the migration of nomadic tribes into Medjerda pre-dates the establishment of the French Protectorate, the largest influx of nomads occurred during the colonial period. This increase in migration was accelerated by two factors: the coincidence of drought in the central steppe and in the southern desert and the expansion of colonial agriculture in the north. Colonial farmers were motivated to accept these newly available if inexperienced tribesmen in the hope that they could stem the immigration of Italian workers.

It is not possible to catalog all the separate histories and traditions of Medjerda's sedentarized tribes here, but it is important to emphasize the lack of homogeneity among them. Each tribal grouping (ʿ*arsh*) retains its

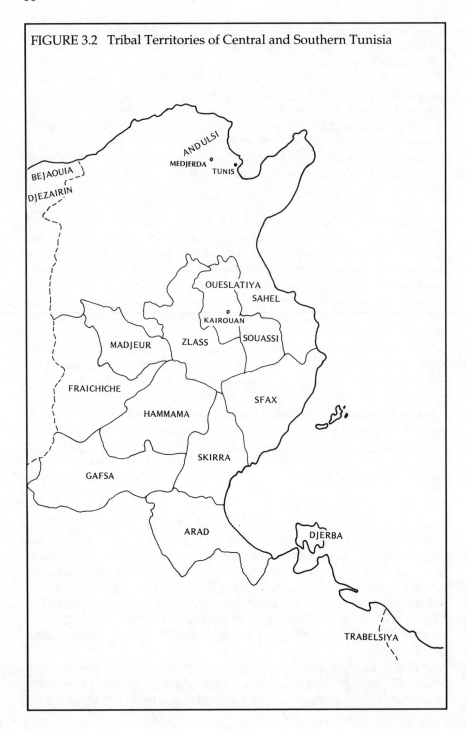

FIGURE 3.2   Tribal Territories of Central and Southern Tunisia

own values, norms, and beliefs, and each tribe differs in the severity of its adherence to their asserted ethical and moral code.

While most of the tribes of Medjerda are connected by marriage, some attempt to maintain strict endogamy while others develop particularly strong diadic alliances. Of the numerous tribal fractions to come to Medjerda (see Appendix C), six tribes are most represented in the region. The Djlass and Mejri are numerous throughout the delegation and base their tradition of marriage alliance on close historical and territorial association.

The Bejaoui and Laouini, who are also quite numerous, intermarry as well, and base their association on their common devotion to a particular saint. The Hammami, who predominate on the slopes of the Djebel El Kebir, maintain a stronger tradition of tribal endogamy, a stricter code of family honor than others in the region, and a life altogether more replete with ritual than that of any of the other tribes. The Riahi, who may be found in the southern districts of the delegation, are conservative in their nomadic attachment to raising and herding sheep. Of the others, it is important to note three *nisba*-groupings, the Djeziri, Trabelsi and Ferjani, who are distinctive in the region. The Djeziri, or Algerians, live in hamlets and villages entirely made up of kinsmen; they rarely intermarry or participate in the mainstream of Medjerdi life, and they have cut themselves off from their roots in Algeria. By contrast, the Trabelsi, or Tripolitanians, are both active in local affairs and connected to their kinsmen in Tripoli.

The Ferjani are Medjerda's contemporary nomads and consist of five separate encampments throughout the region. They are included here because at least two of the Ferjani lineages combine the practice of agriculture with nomadic life. Furthermore, the Ferjani nomads have longstanding relations with local fellahin. They graze their flocks on private land throughout the dry-farming sectors of Medjerda.

The Djlass and Mejri

At the turn of the century, large numbers of central nomadic peoples, including the Djlass and Mejri, migrated north after six years of famine and the loss of most of their flocks. In 1901, the Caid of Zlass (Djlass) described the famine:

> Those who stayed behind gathered roots that they crushed into dough to eat. Without government distribution of seeds they would have starved to death. One consequence of this state of affairs was crime. More and more thefts, especially of sheep, occurred, in order to have something to eat. (Dumas 1912:138, my translation).

In this manner, the Djlass gained a reputation not only for thieving, but also for not being able to grow crops without the assistance of the government. The stereotype was carried even further, as Jacques Berque relates:

... A *colon* has had his donkey stolen. A *béchariste* (a professional go-between) puts him on the track of the thief, who 'like a proper Zlass, stoutly denies everything.' (The eternal Bedouin is here contrasted with the sedentary farmer, in a tension aggravated by the colonial situation). . . The remounting Commission reviews some 350 horses, belonging to the aforementioned Zlass tribe (*good horsemen, but wholly unadapted to the new agricultural order*). (1967:337, my emphasis)

The image of the Djlass as "eternal Bedouins wholly unadapted to the new agricultural order" persists, as does the stereotype of the Djlassi thief. "The Djlass goes in with a dog and comes out with a horse" according to the old proverb, which refers to the Djlassi ability to connive and profit in the animal market.

Despite their image as horsemen and perpetual nomads, the Djlass migrated north two generations ago and quickly acclimated to the life of the fellahin. The ancestral territory of the Djlass shared borders with both the Hammami and the Mejri. In the familiar North African pattern of territorial checkerboard alliances, during the eighteenth and nineteenth centuries the Djlass and Hammami were Husayniya supporters of the Bey and fought against their neighbors, the Mejri and Ferchichi, who were Bashiya rebels (see Brown 1974:38).

It is said that the original Mejri territory was sold to the Berber Mejri tribe by the Arab Hillalians—the Riahis. After this transaction, the Majeur retained the territory, but to this day they often wonder how it was that the invaders managed to sell them their own land, the land they had dwelt in for countless generations (See Dumas 1912). The Ferchichi—another tribal fragment found in Medjerda—also paid tribute to keep their own land. Thus, members of each tribe learned that payment, rather than mere residence, gives one the title to the land one works.

The Djlass of Medjerda claim to come from the holy city of Kairouan, thus denying tribal ancestry and territory. And indeed, Kairouan has been the recipient of a large Djlassi immigration. Perhaps some Djlass did come north by way of Kairouan, but only a few octogenarians remain to recall their ancestral tribal territory south-west of Kairouan. They speak of their origins, which are neither Kirouani as the younger generations claim, nor Bedouin as Jacques Berque states, but rather Berber: the name Djlass stems from a tale told about a nomadic Berber. According to legend, the Berber escaped from the Hillalian invasion, fell off his horse, and ran away to what is now known as Djlassi territory. Two Berber words were combined to describe his descendants: *zqua*, "he cried," and *lass*, "he ran away." Little else is known of the Berber founder of the Djlassi tribe other than that he is buried and enshrined at Khanguet Zegelass. In their disclaimer of tribal, Berber, and nomadic ancestry, the modern Djlass of Medjerda seek to

FIGURE 3.3 Djlassi-Mejri Marriage Alliance

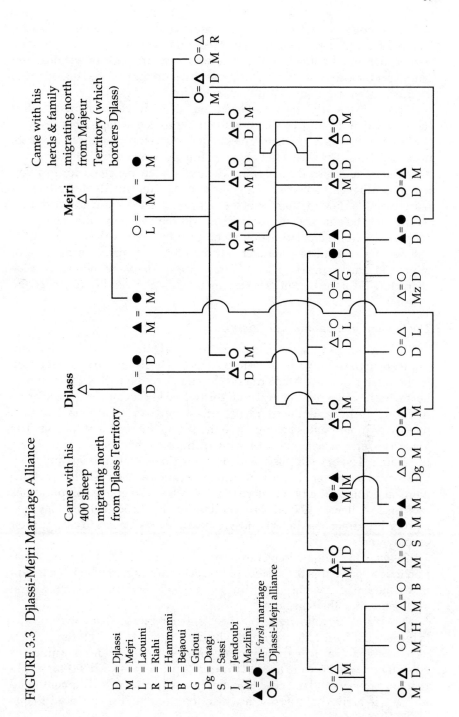

D = Djlassi
M = Mejri
L = Laouini
R = Riahi
H = Hammami
B = Bejaoui
G = Grioui
Dg = Daagi
S = Sassi
J = Jendoubi
M = Mazlini
▲ = ● In-*ʿarsh* marriage
O=△ Djlassi-Mejri alliance

identify themselves with religious, literate and urban origins, as well as the source of traditional leadership in Medjerda. The image of the clumsy Berber, perpetual nomad, or thieving horseman are personifications they would prefer to leave behind. The Djlass cover up the past and take steps to assure a better name for themselves in the future.

Cuisenier states that the Djlass had been "strongly endogamous but after their arrival in the north began making numerous marriage alliances with the Bejaoui in order to rid themselves of their own ethnic identity." (1961:38; my translation). The Djlass, thus, have attempted to merge with the Kirouani, the Bejaoui, and also the Mejri. In Medjerda, their penchant for forming marriage alliances, however, has given rise to an unprecedented preferred pattern of Djlassi-Mejri marriage (see Figure 3.3). The Mejri were accommodating and the alliance enduring. They and the Djlass explain their bond simply: "We were neighbors before coming to Medjerda; we have similarities, and we understand one another." The pattern originated in the face of migration and appears to be a purely Medjerdi phenomenon. It is as characteristic of the region as is Hammami endogamy or Bejaoui marriage customs.

The Bejaoui and Laouini (El Aouini)

The Bejaoui and Laouini are long-time residents of the delegation and originate in the mountains of eastern Algeria. The Bejaoui are concentrated in the western part of Medjerda on the slopes of the Djebel El Kebir and north, to the town of Mateur, about thirty-five kilometers from Medjerda. In the eighteenth and nineteenth centuries, they worked as tenant farmers on fifty or more estates belonging to the Bey in the region of Mateur. The majority were *khammes*, who took one-fifth of the harvest as payment for their labor. The Bey supplied land and sometimes draft animals and seed. The *khammes* were paid in advance and inasmuch as their allotted portions were based upon the previous year's harvest, innumerable complications arose (see Valensi 1977:142-44). The Law of 1847 codified the *khammes*-landlord contract, making it almost impossible for *khammes* to change their employment.

Khammes farming no longer exists in Medjerda. The closest approximation to it at present is the system of *fi-shshtar* farming, in which the tenant takes one-half of the harvest for his labor. *Fi-shshtar* farming is a common arrangement in the delegation.

The Bejaoui are followers of Sidi Bechir, a marabout, or Islamic saint, who is buried just west of Mateur and who distinguished himself through his apparent concern over the high price of securing a bride. Inasmuch as considerable means were needed to marry a proper wife, Sidi Bechir feared that poor men would not be able to marry at all if marriage costs continued to rise. He arrived at a formula which took root and is practiced today.

Bejaoui fathers were forbidden to accept more than sixty-nine millimes in bridewealth for their daughters—about fifteen cents—and the girls could not accept gold, jewelry, or other gifts until after the marriage. Sidi Bechir's followers believe that they will incite the wrath of their saint if they break this canon and further believe that the couscous sauce will turn into gasoline —or something worse—at the wedding if they do not abide by his will. In contrast, bridewealth cash and gifts in non-Sidi Bechir families can run into thousands of dinars, even for a poor family, and may take from five to ten years to pay off before the wedding can take place.

Affiliation with the saint is transmitted bilineally, and thus breaks the local rule of patrilineal descent. Bejaouis may marry whomever they wish as long as the girls observe the Sidi Bechir mandate.

In effect, the marriage pattern of the Bejaoui increases the number of marriages between couples who are still totally financially dependent upon their parents. The common practice of young men establishing themselves financially before starting a family is easily side-stepped in such marriages, and the couple's economic condition is often much more precarious than it would have been otherwise. The overall impact of this marriage pattern is to increase the potential number of children in the course of a marriage. A man who might otherwise delay marriage and endure a lengthy engagement until he was thirty years of age, may marry a Sidi Bechir girl when he is twenty. His bride begins child-bearing during the years that would other-wise have been her engagement— sometimes before she reaches the age of sixteen. Poor families may obtain exemptions from adhering to the minimum age of marriage—which, for a girl, is sixteen—thus, the saint's concern for the marriage prospects of the poor engenders conditions which help to keep them poor.

FIGURE 3.4
Bejaoui-Laouini Marriage:
Parallel Cousin Marriage
and Double-*Nisba* Identity

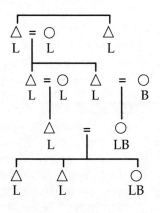

The north-western reaches of the delegation make up Bejaoui territory, and it is here that most of the region's remaining cooperatives are found. Although the labor requirements have long been filled on these farms, families continue to grow rapidly and thus their households continue to expand onto more and more formerly productive land. The population problem on state farms and cooperatives is undoubtedly exacerbated by Sidi Bechir marriages which not only conflict with farm household-space allotments and labor requirements on state farms, but also with national efforts in family planning.

The Laouini predominate in the area around Sidi Mansour on the eastern side of the delegation. They claim to have been fellahin in Medjerda for a long time, despite their continued adherance to values associated with nomads. Like the Hammami, they are preferentially endogamous; the ideal is still to marry the father's brother's daughter. However, the Laouini have also married Bejaouiya girls and their offspring become followers of Sidi Bechir. The combination of Bejaoui-Laouini marriage has led to a double-*nisba* identity for Laouiniya daughters (see Figure 3.4); sons may become followers of the saint, but they are not genealogically bound to the saint unless their father is Bejaoui.

Affiliation with Sidi Bechir is a powerful identity for followers, who see themselves as special in the region. Bejaouiya daughters, rather than feeling sorry at the loss of gifts, self-righteously condemn the elaborate ceremonial gifts of gold, money, and jewelry—to take an extreme example—of the Djerbi. "That's *haram* [forbidden]," they proclaim. "We, the followers of Sidi Bechir, don't do that."

The Laouini, like many other rural tribes of Medjerda, are primarily small-scale fellahin. Because they are numerous in the eastern sector, many live and work on agrarian reform parcels; the cooperatives of Sidi Mansour were short-lived. Those who have no land work for wages as agricultural laborers. Laouini fellahin primarily hire landless members of their own tribe to work their parcels; their reputation for self-help and "clannishness" have led them to be bypassed in development projects which are designed to help those who cannot help themselves.

The Hammami and Riahi

The Hammami—some of whom claim to originate in Syria—and the Riahi—an important clan of the Arabian Bani Hilal—came to Tunisia in the tenth and eleventh centuries to aid the Beys militarily as auxiliary troops. They were rewarded with land: tribal territory in the case of the Hammami, and parcels to work in the case of the Riahi. The Hammami, with their tents and camels, sheep and goats, began migrating north from Hammami territory six generations ago from Sidi Bou Zid in south-central Tunisia (Cuisenier 1961:37-38). Those who remained in the Djebel El Kebir learned to become dry farmers, in addition to grazing their sheep. They later expanded their settlements along the slopes of Es Soujriya, on the Djebel El Kebir, near Sidi Ug⊂ud. They prefer the high grazing ground to the more fertile agricultural lowlands.

The Hammami who settled in Medjerda neither renewed their alliance with the Djlass nor revived their animosity toward the Mejri and Ferchichi.

Instead, they isolated themselves and encouraged new Hammami immigrants from the south to settle on the Djebel El Kebir. Once, the Bejaoui and Riahi served alternately as sheikhs of the Djebel El Kebir, now the Hammami serve as *comda* in the mountain district of Medjerda—characteristically preferring to still be called "Sheikh."

The Hammami say they adhere to the old ways. Their preferred marriage pattern is father's brother's daughter's marriage or tribal endogamy. They live by a stringent code of honor and shame long discarded by other tribes of the region—if indeed, they were ever so strict. Among the Hammami, a son does not speak in his father's presence, he may not dispute his father's decisions, and he may not touch his own son or speak to him in his own father's presence. This deference is extended to the father's brother as well, particularly if he is one's father-in-law. Strict adherence to this code can be dramatic: I once observed a Hammami father freeze in front of his year old son who was playing dangerously with a long, sharp knife: The father could not bring himself to take the knife away in front of his father-in-law/father's brother. His father-in-law could not himself discipline the child without undermining the authority his son-in-law should have over his own son. It appeared as if the toddler would injure himself, or others, if rapid intervention did not occur soon. The dilemma seemed at an impasse until the older man walked deftly out of the room. The child's father thus was allowed to discipline his child without dishonoring the authority of his uncle.

Ideally, girls follow the same code with regard to their mother and mother-in-law. Few, if any, Hammamiya girls go to school in the region. They learn household tasks, prepare for marriage, and await their father's arrangements for their marriage. In some Hammami families, if no acceptable husband presents himself, the girl remains unmarried and serves her father.

In matters of agriculture, too, the Hammami continue to adhere to tribal tradition: they value their sheep above other possessions and prefer raising sheep over other rural occupations. The grazing of privately owned sheep on state land, however, conflicts with the regulations of state farms and cooperatives, where many Hammami live. The Hammami—once upholders of law and order for the Beys—find themselves continually at odds with state farm regulations; for example, they assert their right to graze their own sheep on state land in the hope of establishing a claim to the land. Should such an opportunity arise, they are prepared to take advantage of it.

The Riahi, like the Hammami, had been awarded land for their military aid to the Beys of Tunisia. The land they were given was in the north-eastern part of the country—i.e., in the lower Medjerda Valley—under a contract of fixed tenancy. They were in a better position than the *khammes,* for although they did not own the land they worked, they paid only a small rent and realized far greater autonomy. The reduction of the Riahi to tenancy farming, however—after having been a great military power—left its mark. As Valensi (1977:57) points out, their image of themselves as conquerers of North Africa hardly compensates for the indignity of working someone else's land.

The Riahi are fellahin who are well accustomed to dry-farming and shepherding. Many, however, live on small private farms and agrarian reform parcels scheduled for irrigation by the Ministry of Agriculture. Like the Hammami, their investment in sheep has been an important part of their family-farm economy, but flocks cannot be maintained on irrigated farms without destroying the delicate crops and irrigation system. Thus, the problem for the Hammami on large-scale state farms and for the Riahi on small-scale private and agrarian reform parcels is the same: how to pursue time-honored agricultural and animal husbandry practices in the face of state constraints and admonitions to change.

The Trabelsi and Djeziri (Djezairin)

Before the French Protectorate came into existence, there was no well-defined eastern boundary between Tripolitania—western Libya—and Tunisia. People moved freely between the two countries, and Libyan migrants flocked to Tunisia seeking work. By 1881, when the protectorate was established, the trend was reversed: over one hundred thousand Tunisian tribal people, including all of the Hammama, migrated to Tripolitania to escape the French (see Abun Nasr 1971:282; Cuisenier 1961:38). Over half the emigrés were repatriated by the French in 1882 and the border was defined in 1910. Those who are called Trabelsi are a conglomerate of families with roots or connections in Tripoli and Tripolitania. Some came to Tunisia as long ago as seven generations, others arrived recently; they comprise numerous families with Tripolitanian connections.

The Djeziri, or Algerians (also called El Djezairin) originate from Tunisia's western border. They are actually a fraction of the Bejaouia and followers of Sidi Bechir. The Djeziri migrated across the mountainous Algerian-Tunisian border near Ain Draham at the turn of the century, travelled eastward, and settled their own clustered communities throughout the Medjerda Valley. The Djeziri, unlike the Trabelsi, rarely if ever return to visit their homeland across the border. Many migrated to Tunisia after France had colonized Algeria and had a greater knowledge of the French language and culture than other fellahin in Medjerda. Colonial farmers in Medjerda found them useful and placed Djeziri in managerial positions on their farms. These Djeziri later earned managerial positions on the post-independence cooperatives, and have since become managers of privately-owned farming enterprises.

While the Djeziri have cut themselves off from Algeria, the Trabelsi have maintained links with Tripoli—and Libya, in general. The long history of migration between Tunisia and Libya continues. Oil-rich Libya provides jobs for large numbers of Tunisian migrant workers, paying them wages many times higher than they could receive at home. Farm boys dream of migrating either to France or Libya and many uneducated, illiterate sons of fellahin have made their fortunes across the border. For the Trabelsi, migration is simplified by family ties in Libya and migration is an option they can exercise when life on the farm becomes tedious and impoverished.

The Ferjani

The delegation of Medjerda remains one of the fertile stopping-grounds for Bedouins who migrate north with their flocks. In the late summer and early fall their tents dot the countryside and their flocks (ranging from two to four hundred sheep per extended family) graze on the farms of Medjerda. The nomads are members of the Ferjani tribe, who originate from Gafsa, in south-central Tunisia. They rent land from cooperatives, state farms, and large-scale private landowners and sign written rental contracts, although they, like most of the fellahin, are illiterate. Rent is paid in installments and is based upon both the number of hectares and the condition of the land. Landowners with a stretch of uncultivable, salinated land frequently allow the Ferjani to camp for as long as they wish, in exchange for a few sheep. Agreements are generally made the previous year and the Bedouins return to the same parcels after each year's harvest. In a poor year, the nomads must supplement harvest stubble with fodder purchased from the market. The fellahin take back their land in time for the fall planting, and the Bedouins move on to their next site.

A few Ferjani households remain in Medjerda for six months of the year. They farm small garden-plots on their rented land, and then move with their sheep for the second half of the year. This pattern may be a form of transitional sedentarization; it is a pattern born of personal choice and is not related to any government program to settle the nomads. Not coincidentally, the land rented by these semi-nomadic Ferjani is privately owned by Ferjani fellahin who seasonally harbor a number of fully nomadic Ferjani bands as well.

The spread of irrigation throughout the lower Medjerda Valley disrupts the long-term relationship between nomads and fellahin. As more and more land is irrigated, the Ferjani and other nomadic bands will have to establish new migratory routes and relationships with unknown and unrelated farmers. Only the fellahin's reluctance to accept irrigated farming has left these long-standing relationships between nomads and farmers relatively unchanged.

^c*Arbi* Successors

Since independence, a new political and economic elite in Medjerda has formed. The regional leadership and agrarian elite are composed of nationally-linked Tunisians who remain "outsiders," with neither kinship ties nor marriage alliances binding them to Medjerda. They have undermined the traditional authority and political leadership of the old elite families, and maintain a separate, indeed, nationalist identity and a clearly articulated sense of class consciousness.

During the Bourguiba years, local representatives of the national bureaucracy promoted modernization, initiated change, and rejected the ways of the past—which the traditional elite represented. The latter, which has provided Medjerda with centuries of leadership, continued to be dominant in the religious sphere. Their relationships within the region are characteristic of a ranking system in which vertical links are maintained between patron landowners and their clients.

The majority of the population continues to be composed of sedentarized tribal people who, far from being a homogeneous mass, represent diverse origins and cultural traditions. These traditions include distinctive approaches to agriculture, development, and many other aspects of social and economic life. Diversity of outlook and approach belie the notion of uniformity, and in particular, the possibility of a universal *mentalité des fellahin*.

﷽

```
شـوقلت يالطبيب/آنانِدّاوي والمرَض يزيد
```

4

Debates over Mentality

sh-goult, ya ṭbib, 'ana ndawi, wil-marḍ 'izid
what did you say, Doctor? I've got the medicine, but the disease is worse

The Ministry of Agriculture's prime concern in Medjerda is the maximization of land use, and the only way to effect this—short of expropriation—is to influence and transform the mind of the fellah himself. The objective of "outreach" projects such as agricultural extension services like these is to transform the ideology of the farmers and, as a consequence, the technology of the region. The methods employed provide directives, suggestions, and examples for fellahin to follow; and subsidies or other financial aid (e.g. loans, credit, or in-kind aid) to encourage farmers to strive for the farm output desired by the government. A priority of the Tunisian government, long in the process of constructing an irrigation network throughout the Medjerda Valley, is to use extension programs to convert dry-farmers to irrigated farming. In the Medjerda Valley, the threatened penalty for non-compliance is expropriation. This is not the case in drier, less fertile parts of the country.

There are four types of extension services offered in the region: large-scale state farms, specialized and generalized extension centers, and decentralized extension services. The most influential project in the region, the Tuniso-Belgian Extension Project, is examined at length in the last section, while Chapter 5 is devoted to specific examples of farmer strategies and responses to the agricultural projects described herein.

The extension services available in Medjerda are outlined in Figure 4.1 in the order of their presentation. Regional geography is topographically outlined on the chart in order to display the higher concentration of extension services in the irrigated sectors. The lowest topographical points correspond to land along the banks of the Medjerda River and thus, to where the land is the most fertile.

Large-scale State Farms:
The Centralized Extreme

These farms of the dry, hilly, western reaches of the delegation are reconsidered here because even well past the Cooperative Era, the Ministry of Agriculture has expected them to be "model farms"—examples to be followed by fellahin in private agriculture. There were, of course, not more than ten fellahin in the private sector with extensive enough land-holdings and capital to duplicate the production methods of the public sector; nevertheless, their combined hectarage was significant. Most of these landowners—while maintaining their preferred blend of cereals, olives, and sheep—boasted of higher output and profit than the state farms they were expected to emulate.

Only one large-scale dry-farmer admitted that his farm was less productive and profitable than the state farms. And although he claimed that he was too old to change, in 1979 he bulldozed his olive oil refinery and began construction on an apartment building in its place, and planned other changes on the farm as well. Of the score of wealthy landowners of the region, only two collaborated with foreign and domestic projects. Both farmers were originally from Sfax, and were considered by their Medjerdi neighbors as the *"souri* farmers" of the region. They radically altered their farm practices—yet in no way did they model their farms after the agro-combinat or cooperatives.

There was consensus in the region that of all of the large-scale state farms and cooperatives, only UCP Sidi Ug^{c}ud and the Agro-Combinat of Medjerda were possible candidates for the status of "model" farms. Although production was high at Sidi Ug^{c}ud, *cooperateur* dissatisfaction prevented fellahin in the private sector from emulating the farm practices of the UCP. The agro-combinat, however, was the pride of the region.

The Agro-Combinat of Medjerda

In 1976, the OTD began collaboration with the Dutch government to establish a livestock and dairy industry at the Agro-Combinat of Medjerda. The Tunisian government contributed two and a half million dinars to the nine million dinar project. In 1978, the Dutch supplied the agro-combinat with a team of seven experts in cattle-breeding and dairy production. They

FIGURE 4.1 Agricultural Extension Services: Delegation of Medjerda

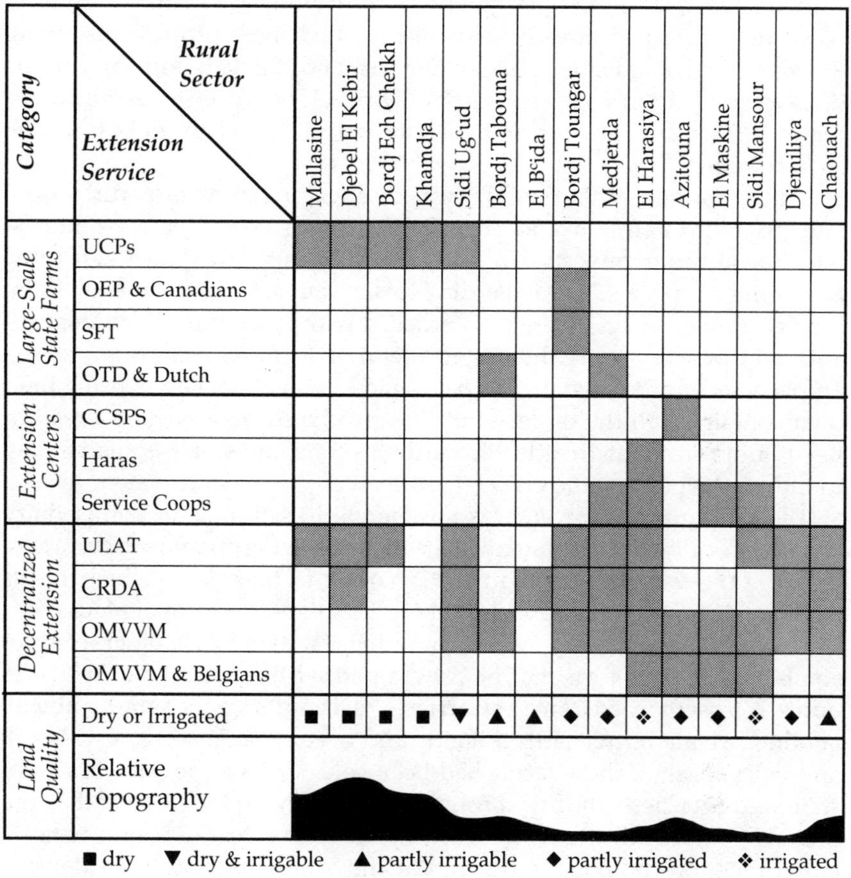

Category	Extension Service	Mallasine	Djebel El Kebir	Bordj Ech Cheikh	Khamdja	Sidi Ugᶜud	Bordj Tabouna	El Bᶜida	Bordj Toungar	Medjerda	El Harasiya	Azitouna	El Maskine	Sidi Mansour	Djemiliya	Chaouach
Large-Scale State Farms	UCPs	▓	▓	▓	▓	▓										
	OEP & Canadians								▓							
	SFT								▓							
	OTD & Dutch						▓									
Extension Centers	CCSPS										▓					
	Haras											▓				
	Service Coops									▓	▓	▓	▓	▓		
Decentralized Extension	ULAT	▓	▓									▓	▓	▓	▓	▓
	CRDA		▓					▓	▓							
	OMVVM						▓	▓	▓	▓						
	OMVVM & Belgians										▓	▓	▓	▓	▓	▓
Land Quality	Dry or Irrigated	■	■	■	■	▼	▲	▲	◆	◆	❖	◆	◆	❖	◆	▲
	Relative Topography															

■ dry ▼ dry & irrigable ▲ partly irrigable ◆ partly irrigated ❖ irrigated

Large-Scale State Farms
Found primarily in the Djebel El Kebir. They are extension facilities in that they are considered by the Ministry of Agriculture to be "examples for the fellahin in the private sector to follow."

Specialized Extension Centers
Located between Medjerda and Sidi Mansour, in the most highly irrigated part of the delegation. These centers provide farmers with a nursery, a breeding stable, and places to rent farm machinery.

Decentralized Extension Services
Exist throughout the Delegation of Medjerda, but are more highly concentrated in the irrigable regions. In addition to central offices, all have "outreach" services with extension workers who visit fellahin directly on their farms.

constructed four barns, one equipped with a milk-processing plant, and air-shipped over six-hundred head of cattle from Holland to Tunisia. By 1979, the Dutch team had already departed for their next project, improving Fulani herds just outside of Kano, Nigeria, and the fledgling dairy of the OTD was on its own. By the spring of 1979, the OTD opened a discount dairy outlet in Medjerda-*souri* to sell OTD products, especially milk from the agro-combinat.

During the late 1970s, the OTD was disengaging from its landholdings, and expanding its role in other areas. Establishing sales outlets was amongst the diversification projects of the OTD, and the outlet in Medjerda became an overnight success. As Medjerdis explained it, prices were the lowest in the delegation, shelves were well- stocked with items previously unavailable, and products were the perfect blend of *carbi* and *souri*. Milk, for example, was unprocessed and unpackaged—consumers had to bring their own containers to the outlet—but was produced by a healthy breed of newly-imported Dutch cattle. Medjerdis, as consumers, at least, had finally found kind words for the OTD.

The OTD goal, however, was not merely to sell milk and other dairy products locally, but to stimulate dairy farming in the private sector. In this, too, the OTD was successful. In 1979, a yogurt factory, Safi—which means healthy, or pure—was established at Les Carrières, the farm of Medjerda's last colonial mayor. Safi quickly became one of the major customers of agro-combinat milk; in return, the yogurt was sold at a discount at the OTD sales outlet. Across the road from Les Carrières, just bordering the agro-combinat, another private farm changed hands and began specializing in livestock and dairy. Both of these farms had been sold through the intercession of state land agencies—the first through the OMVVM and the second through the OTD—and both were purchased by thirty-five year old non-Medjerdi entrepreneurs who lived in the capital and whose families had extensive landholdings and businesses throughout the Medjerda Valley.

Despite efforts to make large-scale state farms function as extension centers and serve as examples for private farmers, large-scale state farming has not produced a model that Medjerdi farmers consider worth following. Instead, the fellahin claim that state farms thrive only as a result of foreign and state subsidies. The fellahin adamantly maintain that livestock and dairy are inherently unprofitable both in the private and the public sector. Perhaps in response to this failure, state agencies have helped wealthy entrepreneurs from outside the region to acquire land in Medjerda—providing they invest in the desired enterprises. Thus, the ideology and technology of private farmers in the region were "transformed" only by diluting the local farm population with outside entrepreneurs who already subscribed to the patterns of farming promoted by the government.

Specialized Extension Centers:
Focused Interventions

These centers, which are concentrated within the irrigated perimeters of the OMVVM, provide services to large and small-scale private fellahin, as well as to the state farms and cooperatives. They consist of a cooperative nursery, a breeding stable, and a number of service cooperatives. The rationale here is that if the fellahin cannot be themselves transformed, then perhaps some will find focused interventions more palatible.

CCSPS

The cooperative nursery of Medjerda, described earlier, works in conjunction with INRAT, experimenting with plant varieties to develop the most suitable strains for the region. Private farmers may be encouraged by extension workers to try the new strains developed at the CCSPS farm. One advantage to farmers is that the CCSPS seedlings, unlike those provided by foreign projects, are available year after year, whereas, imported seed varieties may be available one year but not the next.

Haras

The state-managed stables at El Harasiya play a similar role for farmers as does the CCSPS farm, but in animal-breeding. However, whereas there are numerous CCSPS nurseries throughout the country, there is only one Haras. It is located twenty kilometers from Kassar Said, the national race track, and race-horse breeders as well as farmers bring their mares to be bred at the stables. The Haras manages fifty-five hectares for maintaining the horses, donkeys, and mules which they breed or stable. Veterinary services are also available and the fellahin are encouraged to use them. The Haras also provides short-term stabling services for fellahin when they come from the countryside to take the El Harasiya bus to Tunis.

Service Cooperatives

These facilities rent farm equipment to fellahin, and sell seed, fertilizer, and insecticide on credit, tax-free, and at low prices. These cooperatives are managed by state agencies, semi-autonomous organizations and foreign projects. In choosing a service cooperative, the farmer must weigh a number of factors which include cost and availability of services as well as distance from his farm.

Consider the following two semi-autonomous service cooperatives, for example: The first is the Service Cooperative of Medjerda, located in Medjerda-*souri*. It was founded by the Ministry of Agriculture in 1965, but later became a non-profit, tax-free public organization with the lowest prices for equipment rental in the region. In contrast, the second service cooperative is administered by the OMVVM at El Harasiya. It is more conveniently located and has more numerous services—at only slightly higher prices. For years, however, using OMVVM services had the disadvantage of having one's supply of irrigation water cut off if payments could not be made on schedule. For this reason, many fellahin avoided the OMVVM services, even if it meant going without services altogether. Few fellahin know that this policy has been abandoned, and those that do know assume that it will be reimplemented one day, also without their knowledge until they discover their own irrigation water supply disrupted. Lacking faith in the OMVVM, fellahin would rather do without, borrow from a neighbor or relative, or use the service cooperative of Medjerda.

During harvest time, the canning, processing and winery cooperatives descend on the fellahin to purchase their harvests. These are processed and sold through other state agencies. Distribution cooperatives are used by fellahin who do not have the time or interest to seek out the markets that will yield higher profits. Marketing at regional souks requires a truck—owned, rented, or shared—and knowledge of prices and distances. Furthermore, the fellah must be able to ensure that his harvest arrives undamaged at the souk. As we will see, some fellahin enjoy the marketing aspect of agriculture more than farming. For others, however, they would rather not be bothered; when the service cooperative truck makes its rounds they accept the fixed rates offered by the state.

Agrarian reform and small-scale private farmers use the distribution cooperatives when convenient, and in addition make private distribution arrangements as well. At El Maskine, for example, fellahin themselves have founded a consortium for what they wryly call "private cooperative" distribution. They plan harvests together, merge their harvests to be sold together, rent a truck, plan which souk would yield the highest profit, and take turns at going off to market. This innovation, despite the plethora of extension workers in the region, was entirely unknown to state development workers—who were still trying to promote sales to the state cannery and blaming fellah mentality for their lack of progress.

The *Dar El Fellahin*:
The Union and the Elite

If extension ideas are to be generalized and popularized in Medjerda at all, they will most likely be disseminated on a Friday. Friday is meeting day in Medjerda. The name of the day itself (*nhar ijjumᶜa*) or Friday, is literally a reminder that it is the day when people gather (*jmaᶜ*), go to the mosque (*jamaᶜ*), hold meetings (*ijtimaᶜ*), or visit the delegation social worker (*murshda ijtimaᶜiya*).

On Friday people gather in the cafés, bathe at the hammam, pay their bills at the post office, pick up remedies at the pharmacy, and visit family or friends. Even the region's *comdas*—or sheikhs—gather in Medjerda and meet on this day. Most important, Friday is market day. Fellahin come from throughout the region to sell their produce at the weekly, as distinct from daily, produce market and to buy needed supplies. Sometimes they bring their produce to town late Thursday night, set up their selling-spot, and sleep in their wooden cart, assuring themselves a good spot and an early start in selling their produce in the morning. While Medjerda's Friday souk is considered insignificant nationally, the town nevertheless swells with rural people and acquires a country-fair atmosphere. It is a good day for the Farmers' Union to attract a large crowd to attend meetings, or to encourage fellahin to drop in at union headquarters and exchange news if no meeting is scheduled.

The Friday produce market as well as the union headquarters, which is called the *Dar El Fellahin* (Farmers' Meeting-House), are located only one block apart from each other in Medjerda-*souri*. The produce section of the market, once situated next to the dry goods section in the main square of Medjerda-*carbi*, was relocated in the mid-1970s, ostensibly because it was "too messy" to be in the center of town. For the same reason, the animal market was moved to the outskirts of town. Thus, Medjerda dispersed and decentralized the Friday souk. Some Medjerdis claimed that the change reaffirms Medjerda-*carbi* as the center of town—protected from chaos and filth, but still the center of local social life. The consensus of the fellahin, however, was that the move made Medjerda's Friday souk not worth the bother. But the move may also be said to symbolize the effort on the part of regional authorities to remove agriculture from the *carbi* domain and place it firmly within the province of the *souri*. In effect, the produce market was moved adjacent to the railway station and silos built by the French, where the grain was stored until it was ready to be shipped to Tunis and abroad. Furthermore, the site chosen for the *Dar El Fellahin* had deliberately placed it at the heart (and soul) of Medjerda-*souri*—for the union offices are housed in the imposing French church which once dominated French Medjerda. Thus, the site of European worship was transformed into the center of the region's Tunisification program, and home of the *Union Locale des Agriculteurs de Medjerda* (ULAT).

ULAT is a branch of the national agriculturalists' union (UNAT) whose main office is in Tunis. At the delegation level, ULAT is composed of four elected officials, four division chiefs, and eleven representatives to the rural sectors. The rural sector representatives are the liaison between the union and the 1700 fellahin who are invited to participate in union functions. The union house functions on at least four different levels. First and foremost— and in contrast to European or American unions—it is a forum for communication of Ministry of Agriculture objectives. Second, it is a meeting-place for the small group of Medjerda's wealthy landowners. Third, it is an arena for articulating problems and mobilizing farmers. And fourth, it is a place where poorer farmers come to make contact with the wealthy—particularly when they are in need of a favor. Thus, the functions of the union should not be confused with those of Western union organizations. The first function of the *Dar El Fellahin* includes provision of the following services:

Rural Development

Like other extension facilities, it is the responsibility of the union to facilitate higher agricultural yields. ULAT provides leaflets—with suitable pictures and diagrams for illiterate fellahin—on such topics as recognizing plant diseases, new seeds, soil preparation, and production methods, as well as on financing agricultural investments. Union division chiefs invite engineers, veterinarians, and plant disease specialists to give talks at the Friday meetings of the *Dar El Fellahin*, answer questions, and show films about agricultural advances and development projects in other countries. When the talks have focused on state policy changes, the meetings have been quite well attended and the old church overflows with fellahin from throughout the region.

Agricultural Extension

In addition to audio-visual and leaflet information, union rural sector representatives visit farms and make specific recommendations for combatting plant parasites and diseases, increasing yields, and diversifying production. The advisers distribute new seeds, which have been developed or selected by INRAT, and help the fellahin apply for loans, discounts, or tax-free privileges to purchase agricultural equipment or for additional allotments of land. In this way, the *Dar El Fellahin* duplicates the role played by many other development organizations in the region.

Trouble-Shooting

The rural representatives are responsible for identifying, isolating and solving problems within their jurisdiction. In addition to technical problems, disputes between fellahin are expected to be brought to their attention. If the representatives are incapable of solving these problems, the disputes are brought to the *Dar El Fellahin* for recommendations by the delegation-level union leaders. These men are the most likely to resolve disputes even outside their union capacities, for, as will be seen, they are the wealthiest and most influential fellahin in Medjerda.

Representation

Whereas the above services provide aid for the specific needs of individual farmers, the Union's role also includes expressing the collective needs of farmers and their opinions regarding recent legislation, programs, price increases, and the like. The *Dar el Fellahin* appears to be in the awkward position of telling fellahin what is expected of them as well as responding to fellah opposition to those expectations.

A typical example of this last function and dilemma of the Farmers' Union brings into focus the multi-faceted role of the *Dar El Fellahin*: When 1979 was ushered in, it was accompanied by a price increase for irrigation water sold by the OMVVM, from six to nine millimes per cubic meter. A ULAT meeting was called that January to inform the fellahin of this increase. The fellahin voted to oppose the price hike by sending a telegram to the Prime Minister requesting a return to the old price. This step proved to be of no avail. When asked if the Union would go on strike in order both to strengthen their protest and obtain their goal, the union leaders—some of whom claimed they had never bothered to become official members of the union—laughed heartily and long. They explained that the union does not strike: their goal is to bring government ideas to the fellahin—and not the other way around.

After the large assembly, a number of small-scale fellahin individually approached union leaders to seek their own solutions to the water crisis. For example, one asked that his water allotment be increased along with the price. Another asked to privately borrow a water pump from one of the union leaders. And still a third requested that—since he was a poor man— his water bill not be increased with the others. A number of fellahin confirmed that there were many private arrangements concerning the supply and price of irrigation water, and that these individual solutions were infinitely more effective than collective action.

The union hall was used to solidify pre-existing patron-client relations between wealthy and poor fellahin at the same time that it created a patina of egalitarianism among them—an ideology of shared status as fellahin. This equivocation is reminiscent of Polly Hill's assessment of the relevance of economic inequality to the development process.

> Perhaps the main reason why economic generalizations should never cover both rich and poor cultivators is that the latter are not free to choose between various options, being always under duress; the small minority of rich people are those who make all the important decisions, while the others trail behind forever adjusting themselves to hopeless situations. The point is that the struggling poor are a universal phenomenon, not an anomaly. (1989:28-29).

The *Dar El Fellahin* appears to be another one of many government agencies devoted to transforming the mentality of the fellahin. In addition, it is expected to provide an organizational base through which farmers confide their problems and seek solutions. The union's collective action appears to be ineffectual in coming to the aid of their client fellahin, or perhaps it is even thwarted by the personal aims of the union elite. However, the *Dar El Fellahin* has demonstrated that it is dormant, but not extinct. The union has erupted when its leadership opposes rather than represents government directives—as the 1969 rebellion against the cooperative movement demonstrated. Under normal circumstances, though, the union is valued more as a means for approaching local men in power than for agricultural extension or collective action.

The union leadership consists primarily of members of the local elite—large-scale landowners with varying degrees of engagement in regional politics. Through their offices, public and private sectors merge. These men are the fulcrum of all agricultural activity in the region. They act in conjunction with directors of other extension services and they are bound to most of the small-scale fellahin in the delegation—if not through union ties, then by patronage links. While UNAT is the weakest of all trade unions in Tunisia, as individuals, the power of the union leadership in Medjerda is formidable.

Decentralized Extension Services: Expanding Centralized Control

Whereas it was up to the fellahin to model their farms after those of the state, or to seek out the services of the specialized centers and union representatives, in this case we find that the services cannot be evaded, for they come directly to the fellahin. Extension workers from four separate agencies visit the farms and tell the farmers how things ought to be done. For this reason, the decentralized extension services have a much more profound impact on the actual farm practices of the fellahin than do the extension centers.

Commissariat Régionale au Dévéloppement Agricole

The CRDA, or Regional Office of Agricultural Development, represents the Ministry of Agriculture at the delegation level. Its role is to monitor and facilitate changes in the agricultural sector, and to this end, CRDA staff collect agricultural statistics, act as extension workers, and set up a small number of Demonstration Parcels for the fellahin in the private sector. The CRDA operation is small, ill-equipped and poorly-funded compared with other extension agencies, such as the *Dar El Fellahin*, OMVVM, and Belgian Project. The CRDA office in Medjerda, which is situated on the outskirts of Medjerda-*souri*, consists of one extension worker for each of the six ᶜomda districts of the delegation, one staff member each for forestry and administration, and a general director. Since well-trained extension workers are available through other organizations, the CRDA staff concentrates on preparing agricultural statistics. Despite their narrow focus, however, their cramped two-desk office overflows each Friday with fellahin asking for advice and assistance.

Most of the CRDA extension workers take the bus or hitchhike to their rural sector, and then walk between farms. One or two own motor scooters. The entire staff is expected to share the single *camionette (Deux-Chevaux* mini pick-up truck) assigned to the delegation office. In reality, this vehicle is primarily used by the Sahli director for trips between Medjerda and CRDA headquarters in Tunis. The director can usually be found in the company of the Sfaxi president of the *Dar El Fellahin,* or with other landowners and administrators who have been assigned posts in Medjerda. These men congregate across from the Municipality, or stroll together through the streets of Medjerda-*souri*. They are rarely seen in Medjerda-*carbi*. By contrast, the remaining CRDA staff consists of young men who were both raised and trained locally. They live in Medjerda-*carbi* or in the villages of Medjerda's countryside and they know the fellahin in their districts well. They are well-liked, respected and trusted by the fellahin they work with, despite their youth.

The statistics collected by the CRDA provide the staff with a glimpse into many aspects of rural life in addition to agriculture in Medjerda, and include: (1) a rural census and a census of agricultural workers; (2) a meteorological survey of daily temperatures and precipitation in each of the six *comdas* of the delegation; (3) a land tenure survey of both public and private land; (4) production surveys for both irrigated and dry-farming, which are charted over a five-year period for long-term comparison; (5) farm animal and equipment surveys maintained for a five-year period, demonstrating the growth of both animal husbandry and mechanization, and (6) a survey of agricultural services and associations, including unions, credit facilities, service cooperatives, produce collection sites, and processing plants.

CRDA statistics pinpoint problems, but they themselves are problematic for a number of reasons. First, their figures do not always coincide with those given by farmers and farm administrators. Second, the census of agricultural workers—which is given by number of hectares—does not distinguish private from state and cooperative farms, and does not distinguish agricultural workers from farmers or cooperateurs. Third, although current production is contrasted to that of the past, production statistics do not reflect who, if anyone, has shifted from dry to irrigated farming. Fourth, production statistics from private and state farms are grouped together so that it is impossible to compare productivity in the private and public sectors from CRDA statistics. Because of these deficiencies, CRDA statistics cannot be used to accurately measure the progress of the land improvement schemes of the Ministry of Agriculture, and therefore, although collected for this purpose, they are unlikely to be seriously considered in planning future development projects.

Office de la Mise en Valeur de la Vallée de la Medjerda

The forceful role of the OMVVM in land management has been discussed earlier. Yet, the OMVVM is most noted for its control over water rather than land resources, inasmuch as its focus has always been on irrigation projects. Between 1959 and 1975, the Office collaborated with the Kuwait Project, which was part of the *Mission du Fonds de Dévéloppement Arabe*. With the aid of Kuwaiti funds and Dutch technicians, the OMVVM and *Bureau d'Etudes GRONTMID* worked on a project to irrigate 32,000 hectares in the Lower Medjerda Valley. By 1979, 23,000 hectares were irrigated. The project included the construction of dams and canals, as well as a network of smaller channels to the irrigable farms of the valley. The OMVVM built rural roads, originally for the transportation of project equipment, and, with the hydro-electric dam at El Athmaniya, introduced the possibility of both electricity and water to the farms. The OMVVM constructed new houses and barns on the agrarian reform parcels and imported Dutch cattle and milking machines, subsidizing them for low-cost sale to the fellahin. The rationale behind these projects was that irrigated farming would require a new ecological balance and that cows would provide fertilizer for the soil. The fellahin, however, could not be expected to build their own barns or purchase their own cows. Furthermore, were the OMVVM to construct only barns, the likelihood was that large farm families would simply use them to expand their own living space and allow the cows to stay in the courtyard. By 1979, cost of the irrigation project, including the subsidiary construction of roads, barns, etc., was well over twelve million dinars.

The OMVVM has been unique as a state agricultural agency in that it is financially independent from the Ministry of Agriculture. The Office supported itself in part through the sale of irrigation water. Therefore, for an irrigation project to be worthwhile, it must not only revolutionize agricultural production in the lower Medjerda Valley, but also be profitable. The agency's double incentive to sell irrigation water gave rise to an OMVVM-sponsored extension program aimed at stimulating fellahin to irrigate their fields. Fellahin, who were used to dry-farming cereals and olives and grazing their sheep, found themselves not only working OMVVM agrarian reform parcels, but also dependent upon OMVVM irrigation water, credit at the OMVVM service cooperative, and instruction from OMVVM extension workers. Some felt that they had had greater autonomy under centralized state control of farms than under the OMVVM.

The extension program was little different from those of the *Dar El Fellahin* and CRDA, except that it was better-funded. During the late 1970s, there was one extension worker for every five-hundred hectares, or for every one hundred fellahin. The OMVVM hoped to double its staff so that the extension workers might work more intensively with the fellahin in each district. To this end, the OMVVM collaborated with the Belgian government to create a training program for agricultural extension workers in the lower Medjerda Valley. The Belgian Project encompassed 6,200 hectares in the valley, half of which was in the Delegation of Medjerda.

The Example of the Belgian Project: From Colonizers to Developers

By far the most influential extension program in Medjerda was the *Projet Tuniso-Belge de Vulgarisation dans la Basse Medjerda*, or "*Projet Belge*" as it was known. This foreign aid project was initiated by the OMVVM as a pilot project in two of the five regions affected by the irrigation project. The seven-year-long project was in its last stages in 1980.

The specific tasks set out by the Belgian Project were: 1) to train Tunisian extension workers both in development theory and in practical experience, specifically regarding the problem of conversion from extensive dry-farming to intensive irrigated-farming, and the breeding and raising of cattle; 2) to introduce the techniques of intensive agriculture to fellahin on small-scale parcels within the irrigated territory, and 3) to organize commercial circuits that might be managed by the agriculturalists themselves, and that would be able to deliver the delicate summer crops to market before they rotted or exploded. This project goal was never developed, possibly because the fellahin already had their own informal produce distribution circuits.

The organization of the Belgian Project within the Delegation of Medjerda differed from other programs in the region, for each position was filled by both a Belgian and his Tunisian counterpart. The Belgian staff consisted of the founder/director of the project, five agricultural sub-field specialists, and three general agricultural extension sector chiefs for the regions encompassed by the project. The Tunisian staff paralleled the Belgian both in form and in function; another Tunisian staff existed for the Delegation of Mornaghia, south-east of Medjerda. The Tunisian staff was being trained to take over the project after the Belgians left the country. In this manner, the Tunisian co-director would take charge of the project, while the Tunisian staff would begin training new speciality and extension workers—preferably in another sector of the lower Medjerda Valley. In theory, the project would continue this process until Tunisia had trained a sufficient number of teams so that each extension worker could remain in his own rural sector.

What follows traces the course of the Belgian Project on through to the unwelcome termination of the project and the reluctant departure of its Belgian staff.

The entire Belgian staff had lived and worked in the Belgian Congo at one time or another, either as developers or as *colons* in the private agricultural sector. When the Congo became independent in 1960, the Belgian government founded its Ministry of Foreign Cooperation and established a foreign aid program—thereby displaying its commitment to a large number of suddenly unemployed experts in African agriculture whose skills were of little use in Belgium. Three of the project's staff, including its founder/ director, came directly to Tunisia from the Congo in 1960 and worked with the OMVVM from that time onward. They had long-standing experience in the lower Medjerda Valley, and helped the OMVVM to shape and reshape the land tenure system of the valley. They not only had helped design the pre-cooperatives, but also had helped orchestrate their dismantling. Quite clearly, the Belgian Project was visualized as a continuation of the dismantling process, in that they would be teaching the fellahin what to do with their parcels of OMVVM land.

Despite the fact that the Belgian *cooperants* had averaged ten years of residence in Tunisia, only one had learned enough Arabic to go beyond the customary greetings. The others spoke entirely in French and therefore had better rapport with those fellahin who had learned French—i.e. those who had previously established good relations with French colonial farmers. Otherwise, they communicated by using their Tunisian trainees as interpreters, or by demonstrating procedures for the farmers to imitate. The Belgians believed that knowledge of the French language, and particularly literacy in French, would be indispensable to the fellahin. Among other things, this would enable them to read the labels and instruction manuals on the imported products and equipment they employed. The fellahin, however, were for the most part illiterate in both French and Arabic, and thus the more foreign products they used, the more dependent they became on project explanations and directives.

In the early period, the project showed the fellahin what to grow and how to grow it. The staff made a miniature demonstration parcel on part of the farmer's land and sent the Tunisian trainees to teach and advise the fellah in intensive agriculture techniques, using this parcel. The fellah was told what seeds or soil preparations to purchase; if these were unavailable, the Belgians supplied them, sometimes importing special items for individual farmers. If the farmer claimed that he could not afford to make the suggested changes, the project contributed part of the cost or extended credit to him. The project entered into a contract, written in French, with each participating farmer. The terms of the contract stipulated what the project would supply to the fellah free-of-charge in exchange for his strict observance of project directives. Fellahin were asked to sign (or mark) the contract in order to guarantee their compliance.

By 1979, a total of 94,000 dinars (approximately $235,000 at the time) had been distributed to the fellahin—10,000 dinars of which had been in seed, soil preparations, and agricultural supplies. An additional 25,000 dinars had been given out to those fellahin whose entire farms had been used as demonstration parcels. This sum was approximately twice the amount designated for the full term of the original project, and yet the Belgian director regretted that he could not provide as much aid as he would have liked. He had discovered that few fellahin were willing to collaborate with the project without the inducement of free supplies.

The project's plan to advise the fellahin and then demonstrate to them how to cultivate their land met with resistance. In addition, the Belgians discovered that the miniature demonstration parcels were not cost effective. After the first year's results, the Belgians changed their methods. They held periodic meetings with a group of seven or eight fellahin at a time, and asked them what they wanted to grow. Together, they discussed how to achieve both the goals of the OMVVM and those of the fellahin. The project now focused on developing the entire farm, and not just a segment of the land parcel. Embarking upon this course increased the amount of farmer participation, as well as the amount of aid given directly to each fellah, and accounted for doubling the project's budget. The new approach had the advantage of being less abstract. Fellahin were given specific guidelines— a master plan to follow for their entire parcel, instead of an illustration of miniature intensive farming on a segment of land.

Nine hundred fifty fellahin, most of whom farmed agrarian reform parcels, took part in the project. The Belgians selected "problem cases"— those fellahin with the least knowledge of irrigated farming and the greatest need for financial, technical, and educational assistance. The "worst" farms were also best for training purposes; they provided both the classroom and subject matter for training the Tunisian staff. Fellahin found it difficult to understand Belgian criteria for inclusion in the project. They attributed the selection of farmers receiving aid to their *"pistons"*— for why else would Belgians "reward" poor farming? The fellahin were further surprised by the ability of the Belgians to seriously explore their needs and priorities, and to change tactics in midstream in order to satisfy those needs. On the whole, those who collaborated with the project spoke well of the Belgian team. Their enthusiasm did not extend to the Tunisian trainees, however.

The Tunisian trainees were selected and employed by the OMVVM, and not by the Belgians. The director-in-training, like most directors of state ventures, was from the Sahel. Both the Belgians and the fellahin were dissatisfied with him. They saw this individual as being more oriented toward climbing the administrative ladder in Tunis than in leading a countryside project in the summer dust and winter mud. The director-in-training frankly admitted that it would be shameful, *hishma*, for him to handle the soil. In addition he was emphatic in his belief that the fellahin had an inferior intellectual capacity which precluded the possibility of advance. Despite all efforts at training, project leadership was considered by one and all to have a poor prognosis after the departure of the Belgians.

The lower-level staff was from the region. Many had grown up on the farms of Medjerda. Like the extension workers of the CRDA and the *Dar El Fellahin*, these young men had local ties and family obligations that were impossible to ignore. Thus, although they were assigned to work with certain fellahin, they found themselves equally bound to aid friends and relatives who pressed them for all kinds of favors. They were, after all, *pistons* to both the Belgians and the OMVVM. Staff members were trapped between the fellahin and the *cooperants*, for the Belgians were both unsympathetic and unresponsive to requests made through personal connections.

After seven years of training, the Tunisian staff still saw its work as directed towards meeting specific agricultural goals, rather than as part of the continuous extension process envisioned by the Belgians. Some staff members also felt trapped because of their limited knowledge and training, and expressed concern that if the fellahin actually advanced to their own level of expertise and really did begin intensive irrigated farming, they would no longer be needed as extension workers. The Tunisian trainees were able to see and articulate the irony of their predicament. Quite plainly, they felt that their job security depended upon the failure of the fellahin.

Project Self-Evaluations

The Belgians periodically evaluated the progress of the project in terms of the goals they had set for themselves. Written evaluations concentrated on production results and percentages of fellahin accepting the new technologies. Oral evaluations, however, revolved around issues of motivation, staff problems, work ethic, and similar concepts. The Belgians rated the fellahin in four different areas of farming: fruit tree cultivation, vegetable cultivation, soil preparation, and livestock. They devised a five-level scale to measure the progress of each farmer. The ratings included:

1. Innovators: Fellahin who take risks—those thoughtful, imaginative and willing to both invest and follow through on new farming ideas;

2. Adopters: Fellahin who follow the pattern of the innovator after a relatively short time;

3. Followers: Fellahin who observe the practices of the innovators and adopters over several years' duration and will follow their example when confronted with evidence for the possibility of a profit;

4. Waiters: Fellahin who observe the results of the others over longer periods of time. Perhaps they will change their methods; perhaps they will not. They observe others, but are not ready to change their methods; and

5. Rebels: Obstinate fellahin who, for whatever reason, stubbornly resist departure from their own practices.

The Belgians were careful to document both their successes and their failures, as well as to speculate on the roots of failure. Written evaluations concluded:

Two zones, North Azitouna and Mohammadiya [outside the Delegation of Medjerda], are often cited as model zones; the former in fruit cultivation, the latter in mixed farming (fruit, vegetables, and fodder-crops). These two zones have certain commonalities; all their agrarian reform parcels have been distributed; all their farmers live within the zone; the roads are good; and little land is used solely for grazing purposes. One zone, North Maskine, has progressed, but without the spectacular results of the other two zones. Road conditions and difficult terrain have contributed to project setbacks. Finally, the Zone of South Azitouna has progressed little. The major fault lies in the zone's lack of application of the agrarian reform laws [the parcels were privately owned fragments of land, with absentee owners, and parcels too small or irregularly shaped to cultivate], and the absence of a full-time extension worker in the zone. It was decided to divide the zone between the extension workers of North Azitouna and South Maskine. In retrospect, however, it appears that this decision was a poor one, in that it accentuated the "semi-abandonment" of the zone.

Project aid given in-kind was both equitably divided between farmers, and generally effective. However, a number of mistakes were made. For example: in 1977, a significant amount of aid given to popularize irrigated winter legume-crops did not produce the anticipated results; popularizing the cultivation of potatoes was both costly and unprofitable for a good number of farmers; and finally, the demonstration parcels produced below average yield.

All in all, the results were largely positive—excluding South El Maskine—and the zones aided are clearly in the forefront of development in the Lower Medjerda Valley. (Belgian Project, 1978:70-71—my translation)

Oral evaluations focused on human problems. As the Tunisian trainees discussed each case during one evaluation session, they referred to the farmers by land title numbers. It would appear that one of the implications of this technique was the Belgian hope of creating an objective atmosphere for evaluation of Tunisians by Tunisian extension workers.

The following cites a verbatim extract from one such evaluation session:

Selim: "1230" is never at home. He's always in the cafés in Medjerda. He has no interest in the land at all. He's definitely a "rebel" [*refracteur*] in all areas.

Mongi: "1231" is old. He lives in that broken down *souri* farmhouse and his grapevines are just as old and no longer profitable. Why won't he rip it all out? He's just content to harvest whatever's there and that's all. He's a "rebel," too.

Selim: Ah, but "1232" is a good one! He asked for cows and he uses the insecticide that we brought him. His mind is open but he argues with his older brother—who always disagrees with him. He is an "adopter" in livestock and soil preparation, but a "follower" in growing vegetables.

Moncef: Very well, but "1232" never did get the cattle he claimed he wanted. He never took action, so there you must classify him as a "waiter."

Evaluation of the 950 fellahin went on for days. When it was over, the staff had not been able to name a single innovator. According to the evaluators, even the project's "model worker" took no initiative, but rather waited for staff direction and staff provision of necessary materials. It was said that the "model worker" had resisted numerous directives and suggestions which were considered essential to the development of his tiny parcel, but as we shall see later, the problem is considerably more complex in terms of communication and expectations.

The results of the evaluation are shown in Table 4.1. According to the project staff, the most successful interventions were those involving the introduction of fruit cultivation. The fellahin of Medjerda liked the idea of fruit cultivation and found it was easy to plant a few fruit trees without dismantling an entire olive orchard; it could be done slowly, without total disruption of family income. Unfortunately, fruit trees were not suitable for most of the region due to the high saline content of the soil.

The least successful interventions were those involving the introduction of livestock. Fellahin resisted raising livestock on several grounds, and although the factors involved were never stated explicitly to the staff, they did enter into the considerations of the fellahin. The fellahin viewed the purchase of livestock as being prohibitive because it required the costly

TABLE 4.1   Extension Workers' Evaluations of Fellahin Participating
in the Tuniso-Belgian Development Project

Category	Fruit	Vegetables	Soil	Livestock
Innovator	—	—	—	—
Adopter	21%	10%	3%	—
Follower	31%	33%	25%	29%
Waiter	24%	31%	31%	42%
Rebel	24%	26%	41%	29%
Total	100%	100%	100%	100%

construction of a barn in addition to the actual price of the livestock. Even
were these to be subsidized or provided free-of-charge by the project,
keeping livestock would still entail providing a continuous supply of
fodder and large quantities of potable water—often remote and therefore
time-consuming—and maintaining good health care, as well as hygienic
conditions for the cattle. Furthermore, numerous farmers who would have
kept cattle in order to sell their milk found that their farms were too remote
from milk collection stations to make the effort worthwhile. Taken altogether, these considerations served to deter many fellahin and they did not
invest. From the Belgian perspective, however, cattle were essential insofar
as they provided the fertilizer instrumental to the prevention of soil depletion.

In due course, the Belgians considered the project a failure in terms of its
ability to stimulate increased irrigation in the region. They claimed that
fellahin had a "dry-farming mentality" which included working "just hard
enough to live, but no more." Irrigated farming required greater labor input
in terms of scheduling, work hours, and number of workers. Thus, the
Belgians maintained that it would take more than a generation to override
this mentality.

With this thought in mind—at least, in part—they had proposed the
self-perpetuating extension program. The long-standing ʿarbi values—
raising sheep instead of cattle, growing grains and olives instead of vegetables and fruit, working to live instead of living to work, and the right of
fathers to prevail over their sons in making farm decisions—were unlikely
to change quickly, and the Belgians hoped to extend the project past its
original 1981 termination date. They were not only reflective and critical of
their own methods, but also disappointed and angry at the response of the
fellahin to their efforts. As the top Belgian and Tunisian staff gathered to
evaluate the project's overall performance, the following shortcomings,
resentments, and prejudices emerged:

Albert: Say you plant fruit trees for them. Their sheep eat the trees. The tractors they rent bruise them. They think fruit trees can be treated like olive trees!

Guy: But each fellah seems happy with what they've achieved with the project. As individuals they have become educated and therefore more successful.

The Chief: But for the government this is nothing. The fellahin do not reinvest in the land with this new profit. They buy clothing or things for the house. The family comes first, not the farm.

Albert: They don't want to take risks. When they sell even olives, they sell them on the tree—not at the market.

Guy: We must educate them about the market. The market is the most powerful factor.

The Chief: We've had some success with those who are motivated, but we made a mistake with too much free aid: if you just give a gift, it's bad. You have to get them to participate [in their own farm development].

Sahli: The fellahin don't follow directives because they don't have the intelligence to do so.

Anthropologist: Some fellahin say they don't reinvest because they are afraid the land will eventually be taken away from them. Many get terrible headaches worrying about such problems, and they spend a fortune on headache remedies.

The Chief: They get headaches? I thought they were all pretty happy.

Sahli: You see, that proves the intelligence theory! There's something wrong with their heads!

Debates over mentality, such as the one given verbatim above, serve more to reaffirm existing preconceptions than to generate new understanding of the predicament of the small-scale fellah.

Termination of the Belgian Project: End of an Era

The OMVVM did not renew the project past its 1981 deadline, despite the Belgian offer. The Belgians believed that the Tunisians—particularly the Sahli director-in-training—were not prepared to take over the project at that point. They also believed that the Tunisian government had neither the desire to give the Belgians a priority in its consideration of projects, nor the financial capacity to fund it properly. As one Belgian on staff stated it, "Tunisia would never accept the team without money; they want the money, not the know-how."

Arabization of the Belgian Project took place on schedule, but no one expected it to flourish. The Sahli, who for six years had been trained to assume directorship of the project upon the departure of the Belgians, instead had himself transferred to a new post in his native Sahel soon after the Belgians left. A new director was chosen who was unacquainted with the history, methods and goals of the project. The Medjerdi staff continued to work for the OMVVM as regional extension workers. Fellahin who had become dependant upon the Belgians were despondent. *Waqt essyada, msha l-gelb yitgada*—just when you need them, they disappear (literally, "when it was time to hunt, the dog left to relieve himself")—for their anticipated loss of technical assistance, financial subsidies, and real or imagined *pistons* was felt to be very serious indeed.

All the forms of state and foreign developer intervention had raised the fellahin's hopes to some extent. Now it appeared that in effect, there had been too many remedies, but not enough solutions.

Firing up the oven: Behind the court-yard walls, women begin the long process of baking bread. Stones are placed inside the oven to keep the interior hot after the flames die down.

The finished product: Fifteen loaves of durum wheat bread are baked and consumed daily on this family's agrarian reform parcel. The farm remains planted with colonial vines and the entire harvest is sold to the winery cooperative of Medjerda.

Lessons on the farm: Rural families enjoyed teaching the author all the tasks of farm life, including the tending of sheep, milking cows, plucking chickens, weeding, harvesting, cooking, washing, and other tasks. Women tended sheep if there were only a few on the farm. Men tended the large flocks.

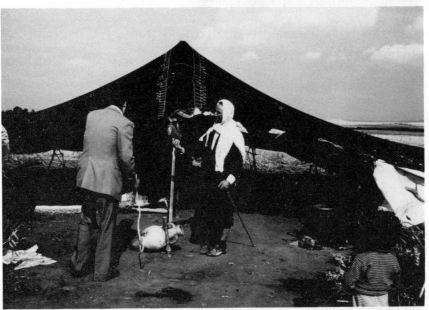

Bedouin encampment: Nomads bring their flocks north for the summer or fall months. They graze their flocks on both private and state land and sell sheep to the local fellahin. Here, a local political leader, dressed *souri*, tries to convince a nomad to send his son to school for the duration of the family's land rental contract in the region.

Spinning with a drop-spindle: Some country women continue to practice crafts such as spinning, weaving, embroidery, and pottery. These are for home use and do not enter the market. Although women do trade craft items with each other, no money changes hands. Homespun wool from ᶜarbi sheep is for domestic use and considered too coarse to be sold commercially.

Sheep-shearing work party: A male member of each household participates in the annual sheep-shearing work party of each family on this state farm. The land worked belongs to the state; the hundreds of sheep are privately owned. The host of this work party was concerned that his neighbors had sent boys who were not yet skilled in shearing.

Outskirts of the town of Medjerda: The path leads from town to the countryside and down to the banks of the Medjerda River. Here fellahin bring produce to market or take their *karitas* down to the river to collect stones. These are sold at market by entrepreneurial fellahin to town people who prefer river stones to cinderblocks when building their houses and courtyard walls. The adobe houses are those of former nomads who have settled in one place.

Smallest viable private parcel in the region: Soil preparation on a half-hectare farm. Farms smaller than this were considered too small to support the average household of ten without an additional source of income. This fellah was desperate to purchase land adjacent to his property.

A fellah of Medjerda: The winter crop consisted mostly of artichokes on this five-hectare agrarian reform parcel. The land was considered too salinated to convert to fruit cultivation. In addition to agriculture, this fellah also ran the only grocery store in a neighboring village.

Aid from the Belgian Agricultural Extension Project: Hybrid *primeur* tomato seedlings at first delighted a "model farm" fellah, who was told to sell them to neighbors with larger land parcels. By the following year, the intervention was deemed a success when affluent neighbors decided to set up nurseries of their own. Large-scale fellahin profited, while the model farmer lost the seedling market promised him. Some fellahin say he was purposefully misled by the foreign developers.

Couscous-making work party: A woman's female kin and friends help her prepare 200 kilograms of couscous for her family's yearly supply. This annual event, parallel to the male sheep-shearing work party, is a week-long process. Both events reinforce lifelong solidarity and obligation to provide mutual aid within the family and community.

Cooking ᶜarbi in a souri kitchen: A Medjerdi woman's unique solution to indoor rainy-day cooking. Although souri housing offers European kitchen amenities such as counter tops, indoor tap water, and sinks, these are ill suited to Medjerdi use patterns and are either removed or awkwardly accommodated. Women are used to cooking at ground level. Many women continue to cook on the ground in the courtyard and only resort to using the kitchen in a downpour.

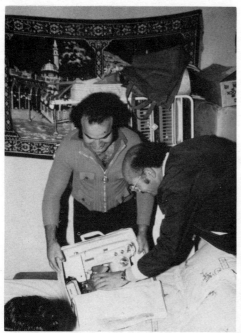

Opting out of agriculture: The son of a farm worker returns home laden with luxuries after five years as a worker abroad. In addition to the sewing machine, he arrived with a gas stove, gas heater, electric fan, synthetic carpets, gifts for all, and a car. Many of the items were not even available in the capital, Tunis.

Women sitting ᶜarbi and men sitting souri: On most occasions, both men and women prefer to sit at ground level when eating or talking. On special holidays, such as the ᶜAid El Kebir banquet depicted here, men sit souri on cushioned chairs at a high rectangular table. They use forks, eat French bread, and have individual settings. The women and children squat around the midah, eat out of a collective bowl, and eat country bread. There was a place for the anthropologist at both tables.

Friday market in the town of Medjerda: The streets swell with fellahin
coming to sell produce, buy dry
goods, pray at the mosque, visit the
medical clinic, and attend meetings
at the *Dar El Fellahin* agricultural
union hall. Schoolchildren are dis-
missed early on Fridays.

Visit of the prime minister: Medjerdis were asked to line the streets one Friday
market day to demonstrate support for Hedi Nouira. Their chants of "Long live
Bourguiba!" were understood as opposition to the prime minister and to his
possible succession as president. Women were encouraged to participate, but the
Medjerdi showing was still less than officials had hoped.

▨▨▨

الأُمـة بالوطن، و الوطن بالأَرضِ، و الأَرضِ بالفلاح

5

Strategies of the Fellahin

li-'umma bil-waṭan, wil-waṭan bil-'arḍ, wil-'arḍ bil-felaḥ
the people depend upon the nation, the nation upon the land,
and the land upon the fellah

The fellahin of Medjerda have been the recipients of policies that had a transformational effect upon their lives. For many, this entailed a unilinear progression from colonial farm worker to UCP cooperateur to agrarian reform farmer receiving direct foreign aid. Those who did not follow this pattern included colonial farm workers who became UCP cooperateurs but who did not evolve into private farmers; those who underwent a full cycle in which they ended once more as workers—this time on farms owned by Tunisian outsiders or the state; those who opted out of farm life altogether, and those wealthy landowners who came full cycle and regained their wealth as landowners. Most fellahin remained where they were while farm categories and boundaries shifted around them.

Their strategies for coping with changes over which they had no control took the form of developing side-line occupations and joint family ventures which had little to do with work on the farm. These ventures offered a degree of control over one's economic destiny through diversification. The occupations chosen and the manner in which they were handled reflected the exercise of individual choice strongly influenced by cultural values instilled through ʿarsh identity. Thus, members of the old Medjerdi elite sought local political offices. Sfaxi and other urban newcomers invested in farming enterprises new to the region, while those of nomadic background engaged in collective activity or some form of migratory labor. Non-agricultural side-lines are a considerable factor in the long-term investment planning of fellahin and yet, these have been ignored by the developers, whose vision is limited to farm output alone. Thus, despite the monolithic view of the developers, the fellahin are not just peasants who can be satisfied with a *promotion paysanne* policy; their solutions to economic problems are as diverse as they are original.

Eight portraits of individual circumstance are presented in the following pages; they consist of four paired cases which contrast the economic styles and strategies employed by the fellahin. These styles and strategies revolve around choices between *ᶜarbi* and *souri* ways and reflect the personal character, cultural values, and historical experiences of each fellah. Here we encounter the ways in which individuals "get through the maze" of economic possibility and impossibility given the myriad of dead ends and wrong turns in the agrarian reforms of the past three or four decades. The first contrast is between two large-scale landowners; the second, small-scale farmers; the third, agro-combinat workers, and the fourth, UCP cooperateurs.

Old Families and Entrepreneurs

The first fellah represents the ways of the old Medjerdi elite who maintain a certain conservatism in personal, religious, and farming styles. For them, landholdings are both a way of life and a link with the past. They are willing to modify non-viable economic practices, but do so with regret and a sense of loss for there are no fellahin in Medjerda who despise what they call progress. Both compliance and resistance to policy directives have been motivated by the same economic rationality. The distinction, therefore between the old and the new Medjerdi elite has much more to do with form rather than content; in Medjerdi terms one could say, perhaps, that while the spices in their couscous may differ, both are equally nourished.

The urbanite newcomers contrast in the manner in which they draw upon European standards to model both their lives and their farms. Their landholdings are big business rather than cherished reminders of their heritage. These two cases contrast fellahin with roots in town or in the city; other fellahin portrayed here derive from nomadic backgrounds— Bedouin, Berber, or a mixture of the two. While almost all of the rural families of Medjerda are bound together, however tenuously, by the bonds of kinship or marriage, here we meet with two exceptions. First is the Sfaxi, who has no local kinship ties, and second are the five sons of Si Sleim, who have rigidly safeguarded their preference for *ᶜarsh* endogamy. All other fellahin encountered here can be linked to each other by at least some traceable bond of kinship or marriage. Thus, they are bound to each other in social, economic and political ways that can only be briefly appreciated here.

The Sheikh and the Hadj

Sheikh Mbarek was considered the most cheerful man in Medjerda; he also was seen as rich, powerful, educated, and religious. The sheikh, who was sixty years of age in 1979, performed his daily prayers at home and went to the mosque each Friday. He dressed in a fine white *jibba* and pantaloons. He wore the distinctive Tunisian red *chechia* on his head at all times. His feet were shod in leather slippers or sandals. Originally, his family had come from the holy city of Kairouan, but had been in Medjerda for nearly five hundred years. His father, grandfather, great-grandfather, and ancestors beyond his memory—for the data survived in archives—had served as sheikh of Medjerda. He, too, held that office for the eighteen years between 1957 and 1975, the longest interval anyone had remained in the post in at least a century. When he relinquished the position of sheikh, ostensibly for health reasons, a new sheikh was elected from amongst the other leading *carsh* of the old Medjerdi elite. These two *caroush* had alternately supplied Medjerda with its sheikh for centuries. The two tribal groupings were in fact intertwined through an equally long history of marriage alliances; Soufya, the sheikh's own wife, was both his mother's brother's daughter and a daughter of this second leading *carsh*. She was proud of her family's historical link both with the sheikhs of Medjerda on her father's side, and with the Andalusian founders of the town on her mother's side.

Sheikh Mbarek was best known for having been on the Hadj pilgrimage not once, but four times, which attested as much to his wealth as to his religiosity. Less renowned were his travels to Europe where, in the company of his wife, he had toured extensively. When traveling, Sheikh Mbarek had never deserted his traditional Tunisian garb; Soufya, on the other hand, traveled in Europe without her veil.

The sheikh's family had extensive landholdings, thought by some to be in the thousands of hectares. Like most of the old Medjerda elite, the family had always lived in the town of Medjerda rather than on the farm. The sheikh owned approximately two hundred hectares of unirrigated land which were planted primarily in assorted cereal crops and four thousand olive trees. Olive trees were planted more densely here in the north than in Sfax, which traditionally had twenty trees per hectare—or in the Sahel, which had twenty-five trees per hectare. Medjerda's olive groves were planted with eighty trees per hectare and therefore the sheikh's olive orchards only accounted for fifty of his two hundred hectares. Interspersed between the olive trees were small vegetable gardens belonging to tenants living on the sheikh's land.

In the transitional period between independence and expropriation of colonial lands, the sheikh had rented some land parcels from colonial farmers. In 1960, he bought a hundred forty-five hectares from an Italian widow whose high price assured the sheikh no competitors. "No one knew that there would be expropriation four years later," explained the sheikh. "The prices did not reflect panic selling; on the contrary, they were exorbitant. But land at that time did not come on the market very often and so I accepted the opportunity when it arose." That same year he married Soufya, built himself a villa, and moved his family from the heart of Medjerda-*garbi* to his prominent new villa at the entrance of Medjerda-*souri*. He was the only Tunisian in the entire delegation who lived in a two-storey house.

In 1968, his Italian farm was incorporated into a pre-cooperative and he was appointed its president. He took the job seriously enough to apply for a bank loan to develop the entire cooperative—and was probably the only UCP president in the region to do so. The cooperatives were disbanded within six months—sooner than it would have taken to process his loan application. When his own farm was returned to him, he abandoned thoughts of development and resumed managing his farms and flocks as he had done throughout his life and indeed, as had been done throughout the centuries.

The sheikh instilled in his children the same values with which he himself had been raised—despite the fact that he recognized them to be ways of the past and not necessarily those of the future. In the political arena, change had meant that sheikhs were no longer elected by the population; they were selected by the governor in Zaghouan from among three candidates presented to him by a committee of the local Destourian Party cell. Furthermore, sheikhs, now called *gomdas*, were no longer local community leaders; they now represented the Party. They had become administrators, rather than intermediaries. In the economic sphere, olives—the traditional symbol of Tunisian agriculture—were now the most unprofitable of agricultural products.

Sheikh Mbarek's father-in-law, Hadj Khemais, was a victim of the demise of olive cultivation and is a case in point. Hadj Khemais was seventy years old and owned about fifty hectares of olive orchards—about four thousand trees—just like his son-in-law. He had purchased the *Pères Blancs Huilerie* during the same time as his son-in-law's land purchase and used the olive oil refinery only for his own crops. Because the refinery was located in the heart of Medjerda-*souri*, the hadj was obliged to transport his olives by truck from his farm at El Maskine, a forty-five minute drive for each trip. Many of his trees were as old as five hundred years and had been planted by the Andalusian settlers of the area. He cultivated the orchards in the mode of the past and he continued the operation of the refinery without modification. He continued to use the original presses and scales brought to Medjerda in 1904 by the White Fathers and did not alter production methods. Symptomatically, the telephone at the refinery was an antique that had to be cranked up in order to be connected with Medjerda's operator.

In a sudden awakening borne of retrospect, the old hadj had one day become aware of the cost of his excessive conservatism: "Not even my son wants the refinery," Hadj Khemais admitted, his mind now a flurry of calculations. He continued:

Not only that but why would *anyone* in these days want a refinery so far from the olives? Look at the cost. Say you had only thirty hectares planted in olives, that's twenty four hundred trees. Each tree yields about five kilos of olives—averaging over five years—which is twelve thousand kilos, or three thousand two-hundred eighty eight kilos of olive oil. Now, say the quality of your oil is a low super (say, point seven acidity) and you sold it to the Office of Olive Oil at three hundred ninety three millimes per kilo. That means that you would get twelve hundred ninety-two point one-eighty four dinars for the whole crop—already turned into oil. Well, that's not including the cost of production, transportation, hiring workers, running the refinery, and all the rest. It's just not worth the bother. Besides, the kids are not interested in an out-of-date refinery. My son here works for the state: what does he need it for? But I have a big family and this property is valuable. Look at this fossil taking up all this space right in the middle of town, and right between the Municipality and the Delegation. I'm an old man now. My kids want something modern so I'm going to do something modern. I'm going to tear down the whole thing and put up some villas for my children.

All this, Hadj Khemais recounted rapidly off the top of his head; he had forty years experience analyzing his crops' profitability. Once the Hadj had made up his mind, he set out to dismantle his entire olive oil production at once. After the olive harvest, Hadj Khemais' very last crop was turned into oil and sold. He tore down the old refinery and began construction on a few villas so that his children could either live in them or rent them out. At the same time that this was taking place, Sheikh Mbarek began reconsidering irrigating his own fields and replacing his ancient and beloved olive groves with fruit trees.

The Accidental Entrepreneur

Si Hedi, who illustrates the *souri* way par excellence, came to Medjerda by virtue of his connections with wealthy entrepreneurs from his native city of Sfax. His personal style, punctuated with whiskey and hard work, led him to build a peerless agricultural empire in Medjerda. His farms were founded on the principles of experimentation and mechanization, themes which pervaded the non-agricultural enterprises he engaged in as well. Si Hedi kept himself out of what he called "local Medjerdi politics"; instead, he held positions at the delegation-level and mingled with the regional authorities posted in Medjerda who originally came from Tunis, Sfax, or the Sahel. Despite his avowal of non-involvement, Si Hedi was the most sought-after man in Medjerda.

Wearing his perpetually furrowed brow and rumpled gray suit, Si Hedi made the rounds at Domaine Azitouna, a task which he performed daily. He drove one of his older Peugeots down the dirt road at a snail's pace, inspected the work in progress from the window of his car, and scolded a young worker for carelessness in allowing too much water to flood the tomato seedlings. An older worker came to the boy's aid, patched the flooding row with dirt, and opened a gap for water to flow into the next row. The Sfaxi, now satisfied, hailed the old worker and drove on. The Domaine employed seventy permanent and eighty seasonal workers on its five hundred seventy hectares. Si Hedi often complained that he could not hire enough workers, despite the fact that he supplied transportation and offered the highest wages.

> They just don't want to work. They'd rather be *chomeurs deluxe*—dress nicely, sit in the cafés unemployed all day long, and keep their hands clean. I started out as a mechanic in a garage in Sfax. Oh, my father had olive orchards down there, but we lived in the city of Sfax itself. In 1959, my brother and a number of others wanted to buy the Domaine Azitouna. It was one of the seven properties owned by the *Société Immobilière Française*, their only farm in debt. They sold Azitouna to be rid of it, but, as it turned out, the other six were expropriated in 1964. We paid four thousand dinars for it, but now it's worth a million.

> My brother's partners said they would only buy the property if they could find a good manager for the farm, someone who would stick to it and do a good job. They didn't want to work the farm themselves, of course, they just wanted it as an investment. So my brother recommended me, but I wasn't sure about it. I said that I would try it for three years and if I didn't like it I would go back to my garage in Sfax. I became a partner and manager of the farm. The others never even visit. I doubt if they could find Azitouna alone.

A storm came up and Si Hedi cursed and worried that it would hail and ruin all of his delicate summer crops. He did not have insurance because he said it was too expensive. He drove down to the Medjerda River—which bordered his land—checked the water pumps, made an adjustment or two on the motors, used a handkerchief to wipe off the excess grease on his fingers, and reflected further. He had not meant to stay in Medjerda, but he could not leave. For fifteen years his family lived in the huge French villa which dominated the farm, but when his children got older, he moved his family to a rented flat in Medjerda-*souri* so they could be near the secondary school. In addition, Si Hedi maintained a house in Sfax and had built a villa in the suburbs of Tunis.

One day, years after Domaine Azitouna had proved to be profitable, the Sfaxi received a telephone call. He recalled the conversation vividly. It was from a Madame Dubois, who told him repeatedly that although she did not like Tunisians, she would have to form a partnership with one or face the consequences—the immediate loss of her farm in El Maskine. She had followed the progress at Azitouna and had decided that Si Hedi was the only Tunisian she would want to secure the future of her farm; title would be transferred to his name and profits would be shared. In this manner, Madame Dubois deferred the inevitable for a period of five years.

In 1964 the remaining colonial farms were "Tunisified" and Si Hedi became one of the major landowners in Medjerda. In 1968, Domaine Azitouna and the Dubosiya Farm were turned into cooperatives. Si Hedi was appointed president of both cooperatives. "You turn the farms into cooperatives and I'll go back to my garage in Sfax," he had threatened the OMVVM, but continued to run the farms and pay his workers as before. Si Hedi explained his position:

> I can't have everyone making decisions like they wanted us to do. I've got to handle things myself. If not, forget it. I can't work by the clock. When there's a job to do, I do it. It doesn't matter how long it takes. I don't stop at 5:00 P.M. I don't take sick days, I don't take vacations. I cannot stop working and I cannot share responsibility—*c'est moi, le responsable.*

The number of Si Hedi's enterprises grew with each year. At Domaine Azitouna, he ran the third largest of Medjerda's seven olive oil refineries. He raised race horses, which he ran at nearby Kassar Said—the only race track in Tunisia. He constructed enormous chicken coops—maintaining the chickens primarily in order to convert wastes into fertilizer—and made a profitable enterprise out of a so-called by-product as he began to market *souri* chicken and eggs. He was a partner, possibly even a founding partner, in *Izdihar*, the oldest cooperative cannery in the country; his trucks transported the produce of the small-scale fellahin to both the cannery and the market. He rented farm equipment to these same farmers and had innumerable transactions with other fellahin—from the poorest to the wealthiest—throughout the delegation.

Si Hedi hired the fellahin and trained their children; he exchanged services and favors with them; he interceded for them in disputes and facilitated their requests; he bought their seedlings and rented their land; he loaned them money and rented equipment to them. Those connected to Si Hedi called him a *rajl b'il-igdeh* —a "complete man," a gentleman—and the poor added that he had a "big heart;" that he came to their aid and was generous. His faults, such as his frequent consumption of hard liquor, were accepted without the comment or condemnation reserved for others. He was in a category by himself; he was not criticized. The livelihood of hundreds of families depended upon him in varying degrees—as did most of the delegation's committees and organizations. As president of the *Dar El Fellahin* and the local *Banque Nationale de Tunisie*, he spent Fridays presiding over meetings and assemblies, and was summoned to appear at other meetings throughout the week. "If I went to every meeting I was summoned to," Si Hedi would say with pride and despair, "my farms would be all in ruins."

Si Hedi attributed his success in farming to his background as a mechanic. He claimed that when he arrived in 1959, most of the farms in Medjerda were not mechanized. He followed French models and incorporated his knowledge of machinery in order to make the farms work. He began taking down the olive orchards—fifty hectares per year—irrigating the land, and planting vegetable crops to replace the uprooted olive trees. "They laughed at me when I started," he sneered, "and now, twenty years later, they copy me—tearing down their olive trees and refineries. They thought I was crazy and now look at them." The "they" he referred to were the landlords of the old Medjerdi elite—conservative fellahin like Hadj Khemais.

In 1979, the summer crops on all of Si Hedi's farms and rented land had strikingly fewer weeds, more water and chemical treatment than those of the agro-combinat. "Those bastards don't work at all so they get nothing," said the Sfaxi. "If you're working for the state for a salary, then why bother? I'm here every day to teach my workers and to make sure that things go right. I learned everything from practical experience. I didn't go to one of those agricultural schools."

In fact, over the years Si Hedi had sought and received a considerable amount of advice from agricultural engineers. His most recent consultation concerned the use of fertilizers and insecticides, and aimed at offsetting the losses he incurred on his 1978 tomato crop. The crop, which cost thirty thousand dinars, only returned twenty thousand dinars at harvest. The agricultural engineers of the OMVVM and the Belgian Project claimed that Si Hedi was going overboard in his enthusiasm for phosphates, nitrates, and the like. Overtreatment of his crops, said one, not only was costing Si Hedi more than was necessary, but also was having the effect of making his tomatoes, especially his first harvests, too toxic to eat. According to one expert, Si Hedi was applying five times the suggested amounts. He was, in effect, using chemical treatment as the insurance policy he would not otherwise buy.

By 1980, the Sfaxi was thinking of diversifying into non- agricultural enterprises and beginning construction of Medjerda's first hotel and a series of shops at the juncture between Medjerda-*carbi* and *souri*. It seemed unlikely, however, that Medjerda—with its provincial aversion to outsiders—

would welcome the implications of a local hotel. The town had voted to disperse the Friday market so as to not attract the dirt of active commerce; the measure had passed and Medjerda's souk was now avoided by all but the most local itinerant merchants. The town was not quite xenophobic; it was more like a mild case of stranger-anxiety—and Medjerdis were proud of it. Villas and shops, however, were a sound investment since the population was unlikely to abate.

Si Hedi discouraged his sons from entering into agriculture and wanted his children to become doctors. He sent his daughters to study in France and was disappointed at their rebellious choice of pharmacy over medicine. His youngest son hoped to become a surgeon—"just like Si Ali, daddy's partner"—but his eldest son, despite forceful discouragement from Si Hedi, was both passionate and adamant about helping his father on the farms to the exclusion of all other interests. The greater the interest this son expressed, the more Si Hedi rebuffed and rejected him. The struggle between father and son increased and Si Hedi swore that he would not relinquish control of his farms to his son—he had worked hard so that his children would never have to farm for a living.

Fellahin with Little Land

Fellahin with any land at all are eyed with envy by their agro-combinat and cooperateur neighbors. Yet, their migraines and obsession with land acquisition are equal in intensity to that of their state employed neighbors. What they lack is the security of agro-combinat wages and benefits as well as the possibility of ever achieving a year end cooperateur's bonus. They have no capital to invest unless they have planned carefully—and no insurance against the pain and magnitude of their losses. The first of these fellahin cannot dismiss the wanderlust instilled in him by his Bedouin ancestry. He finds an ingenious and effective solution to the conflict between nomadism and sedentary farming, one suited to both his temperament and pocketbook. The second fellah presented in this section rejects the ways of his past in favor of dependence upon *souri* methods and patrons.

The Reluctant Farmer

According to his wife, Mabrouka, Si Ismaiel was a weak man. He drank alcohol and could not sleep. He was nervous, had rheumatism, heard a buzzing in his ears, and could not tolerate loud noises. He also was afflicted with frequent, unbearably painful migraines which were accompanied by flashes of light. The family was poor, Mabrouka would say, because her husband was never on the farm and spent their money on drinking or seeing doctors for prescriptions that never worked. Si Ismaiel countered that he got restless on the farm—his *^carsh*, he said, was from Saudi Arabia and travel, not farming, was in his blood. To make his point, he was rarely seen without a colorful embroidered scarf that he either wore as a turban over his *chechia* or, more frequently, draped over his shoulders.

Over the years, Si Ismaiel had developed a routine that satisfied his restlessness, accommodated his drinking, enhanced his income, stilled the noise of his eleven children, and—to a lesser extent— pacified his wife. He left the farm work to his family and went to various distant weekly markets, selling his produce for more money than he could get either locally or in Tunis. He had learned how to drive (and to drink) when he had worked on the farm of Madame Garcia. As a younger man, Si Ismaiel had traveled extensively throughout Tunisia, North Africa, and Europe, and had worked in Belgium for a year. Now, his travels were contingent upon his capacity to rent a truck from any one of his neighbors who might have one available, and he would sell their produce along with his own. He was never gone for more than six days at a time, and while he was on the road he either stayed with relatives or slept in the truck. The circuits he established took him throughout the entire Medjerda Valley and as far south as Kairouan, when he could manage it (*"waqt ^cendi l-courage"*). Most Medjerdi fellahin kept up with the prices of produce at distant rural markets of the interior, where vegetables were scarce and therefore expensive, but they felt that it was either a luxury or a waste of time to market their produce at such places. Si Ismaiel, on the other hand, thrived on it. When harvest time came and other fellahin scarcely left their farms, Si Ismaiel left the cares of the harvest to his wife and children, stayed on the farm only long enough to replenish his supply of produce, and began his cycle again.

Si Ismaiel's circuit generally included the Friday market in Medjerda— especially if he could not arrange for a truck in order to go further away. It was possible to ride his *karita* from El Maskine to Medjerda in less than an hour but, as he put it, "the market at Medjerda is nothing—zero."

Medjerda's convenience, however, made it hard to avoid. Sometimes Si Ismaiel would bypass the pathetic little produce souk altogether; at such times, he would give his *karita*-load—approximately five hundred kilos of produce—to a Djerbi grocer. The Djerbi would then store the entire load in his freezer and sell it out of season when the prices were higher. Instead of being paid immediately for his produce, Si Ismaiel would await the sale and then receive half of the higher profits. Because of the delay in payment, Si Ismaiel worked with the Djerbi only when he was sure not to need ready cash.

Si Ismaiel was far more involved with his marketing schemes than with farming strategies. When the Belgian Project had wanted to teach him improved production methods to develop his five hectare farm, he balked.

They had offered him 600 dinars to encourage him to invest in a tractor. He refused the offer, saying that he could not afford the full 7500 dinars purchase price even with their aid and long term credit. In fact, although he did not tell them so, he had made other investment plans. Si Ismaiel had saved for years and accumulated 600 dinars. His plan was to buy twenty pregnant ewes at the El Fahs animal market, raise the lambs and sell them just before the ᶜAi'd El-Kebir celebration of the following year. Some time later, however, when Si Ismaiel was in the midst of terminating the negotiations for the purchase of the ewes, he discovered that his wallet was gone. He had lost both his dream and his savings in an instant. As a consequence of suffering this severe blow, he was subjected to an onslaught of physical symptoms that kept him ill for weeks. To make matters worse, he had to sell two of his cows in order to prepare his fields for the next agricultural season.

Si Ismaiel cared for his tiny flock of ten sheep more than he cared for his entire five hectare parcel. When he looked at his sheep he knew exactly how wealthy he was; he knew that he could turn his sheep into instant cash—or food—at a moment's notice. Unlike the situation one faced in the sale of a cow, the sum brought in by the sale of a sheep was modest enough to allow a man to adjust sales according to needs. Both farmers and nomads agreed that this was one of the advantages of keeping a flock. Furthermore, sheep could be sacrificed for special family occasions with little worry over food going to waste. Sheep were a perfect size. While fellahin like Si Ismaiel recounted the advantages of keeping sheep, complications set in to disturb their natural proclivities. Thus, when the OMVVM brought irrigation to El Maskine, they were compelled either to rent unirrigable land for their flocks or to give them up entirely in order to devote all their time to irrigated farming. Si Ismaiel chose to rent higher ground from a neighbor who, for a small fee, watched Si Ismaiel's sheep along with his own.

Given Si Ismaiel's attitude and approach to farming, his refusal of Belgian aid to buy a tractor was understandable. For him, purchasing a tractor meant investing in agriculture only. Si Ismaiel thought of his work not only in terms of farming, but also in terms of raising sheep and marketing. If the Belgians had offered him aid to invest in a truck or *camionette*, he would have accepted gratefully. A truck was versatile. It could transport people, animals, and produce. It could go anywhere. It belonged more to the person than the land, and therefore was less likely to be expropriated in the event of future agrarian reform—an event that Si Ismaiel thought was entirely possible.

Once or twice a month, Si Ismaiel took his wife and youngest son with him on short excursions. As a result of these trips, Mabrouka was one of the most travelled country-women in El Maskine. On the Fridays when she accompanied Si Ismaiel to Medjerda, she spent the day bathing at the *hammam* and visiting relatives. Once in a while she would take the bus into town alone, ostensibly to purchase her next three months' supply of birth control pills.

Sometimes Si Ismaiel took her visiting throughout the delegation, to Tunis, and even to the Mediterranean resort town of Ez-Zahra. There, they would visit their former patroness, Madame Garcia, and her second husband, Monsieur Quinet. These visits were journeys into reminiscence at the same time that Ismaiel and Mabrouka helped the elderly couple with their cooking, housework, and gardening. Both had worked for Madame Garcia over a twenty-five year period and they still grew vegetables for her.

In the early 1960s, after the OMVVM had expropriated 50 of her 87 hectares to form the CCSPS nursery, Madame Garcia had divided the remainder of her farm equally between Ismaiel and a second favored worker, giving each of them 18 hectares. Unlike the situation in Si Hedi's case, however, the OMVVM invalidated or expropriated their claims—it is unclear which—and allotted each of them a five hectare agrarian reform parcel which consisted, for the most part, of rocks and weeds. Si Ismaiel accepted the OMVVM's action without protest; the second worker still opposed the OMVVM twenty years later, and adamantly refused to move out of the Garcia villa at the center of the property. The OMVVM sent him threatening letters but took no other action. For his part, Si Ismaiel kept Madame Garcia's few sheep and cows, disregarded paying for his OMVVM parcel, and was satisfied. He did not believe he would be asked to pay for the land; he thought the OMVVM would either cancel the debts of the fellahin or take back the land for some new project. Just in case—Si Ismaiel would wink—he kept his flock on non-OMVVM land. He had learned from the past and was thus prepared for the future: First, if the land were expropriated his sheep would not be, and second, if he were forced to pay for the land, he would sell sheep to meet the payments and hold back at least one or two pregnant ewes in order to start over again.

Four of Si Ismaiel's eleven children were sons. The eldest of these sons followed his father's pattern rather closely. For example, although he was recently married, he left his wife in his parents' care, wandered from place to place, and returned only after a period of days or weeks. He began to drink, suffered migraine headaches which rivalled his father's, and kept himself inside the darkened *gourbi* for days on end. Ismaiel and Mabrouka shook their heads in disappointment. Their two middle sons were perma- nent agricultural workers on other farms in the region—one was at the CCSPS nursery, where his father had worked on the Garcia Farm, and the other was at Si Hedi's Dubosiya Farm. Little choice was left. Si Ismaiel began to groom their youngest son, Sami, to manage the farm. Sami, who was twelve years old, was devoted to the farm, enjoyed the farming lessons he received at the El Maskine primary school and, to Ismaiel's delight, was talented in translating farming principles learned at school into action on the farm. Irrigation was new to Si Ismaiel, but his son had learned such techniques as moving from row to row, opening new water veins without waste or duplication, and lining the dirt canals with plastic to preserve the water for later use.

It may be said that Si Ismaiel was a cheerful man when things went well, and morose when they did not, and that he was at his best in the market-place. He knew the prices he could obtain and carefully weighed those rates against the costs of transportation. He calculated the hardiness of his crops in terms of the distance to market. The relative isolation of the life of a farmer did not suit Si Ismaiel's temperament and he sought and found a satisfactory solution to what would otherwise have been a serious problem.

The Model Farmer

Si Hamadi's most prominent feature was his wide, gullible eyes. He was a believer in the power of individuals, and he religiously pursued men of power. When Si Hamadi reflected on the men who contributed to his success, he spoke chiefly of Monsieur Paul, Si Hedi, and Monsieur Delacourt. The first of these was the *colon* for whom he had worked for twenty years, the second we have already met, and the third was the Director of the Belgian Project. The influence of these men was decidedly European both in terms of values and economic aid, but Si Hamadi was more interested in the power of the advocates themselves than in the utility of what they advocated. He accepted any and all European aid offered—to the point of being considered a mechanical follower by the Belgians—but he had goals of his own, which he pursued relentlessly. An early example of his single-mindedness is told by his neighbors and relatives:

> Hamadi is an only son. He always had big dreams. His father had saved three hundred dinars and knew of a widow selling a tiny parcel of land at Azitouna. This was in 1960, when none of us had land. He said to Hamadi, 'take this money—which is all I have—and buy the widow's land.' Hamadi took the money, went to the widow, and bought the land. But he put the title in his own name only. When his father heard of what he had done, he had a heart attack and soon died. Because of Hamadi's selfishness there was no inheritance to divide with his mother and sisters.

> Now, it happens that Hamadi's wife and mother did not get along well at all. Fatma, his mother, was sick and could not work either on the farm or in the courtyard. Furthermore, her bad stomach could not tolerate Algiya's greasy cooking, and she was forced to cook her own food and eat alone. *Maskina*, poor thing. Hamadi gave her no money for food, so she would go between her four children, staying for a month or so with each one. But they all had lots of children and so she couldn't stay for very long. So Hamadi arranged for his mother to marry again and forced her into it, but Fatma ran away and would not go back to her new husband.

Hamadi had just built that huge house and he had room for her, since his eldest son, Naji, was in the army. He had plenty of money from those Belgians, who helped him build the house. So Fatma came back to live with her son, but she got sicker and sicker, poor thing. Hamadi is an only son, understand me? He makes Algiya have all those children so that he may become the father of a great *ʿarsh*. But when Algiya became pregnant with their eleventh child, she became nastier to her mother-in-law. It was during the tomato harvest and nothing was getting done for all the shouting and problems. Secretly, Hamadi sent for his mother's second husband to come and take her away, *maskina*. These men—you know what they want a woman for—and Fatma was so sick. It's not good for an older woman. Hamadi is a bad man. His father's death is on his head. He forced his mother to go with another man and took away her title. Ḥishma!—Shame! When the *camionette* came to take Fatma away, she kicked and screamed so in the back of the truck that you could hear it all along the road from Azitouna to El Maskine. *Lutf, lutf. . .*

Hamadi's own version of the story follows:

My father gave me three hundred dinars to buy this parcel from the widow. Soon afterward, my father got sick and so I brought him to the hospital in Tunis. It cost me twenty dinars a day—four hundred dinars for twenty days to keep him in the hospital. He wasn't any better so I took him home to die. My mother remarried five years later. Now, you see, we have no more room. Algiya's having another baby and Naji's coming home from the army. Besides, Algiya and my mother fought all the time and my mother couldn't eat Algiya's cooking. So my mother went back to live with her husband. *Hek-heka bratig*—it was the only practical solution.

In a way, Si Hamadi's eagerness to acquire land backfired, for as a small-scale private farmer, he did not work on any of the cooperatives near Azitouna and, as a result, was not allotted a five hectare parcel when the cooperatives were disbanded. His one hectare private farm was soon surrounded by five hectare agrarian reform parcels belonging to his formerly landless neighbors. In comparison with his neighbors, what had appeared as wealth now seemed to him a pittance, and he devised new schemes for acquiring land, preferably land adjacent to his own parcel; his new plan was to acquire the land belonging to his neighbors.

Si Hamadi irrigated his parcel and grew out-of-season vegetables long before any of his neighbors. He had ripped out the farm's long-standing olive and apricot trees during their best harvest year, in order to follow the radical notions espoused by the Belgian Project. Hamadi's "case" was taken up by the Belgians, who felt that if he succeeded on his tiny, overcrowded, overcultivated farm, neighboring farmers would follow the methods introduced on his farm. The project director, Monsieur Delacourt, singled out Hamadi for intensive aid, and Si Hamadi was eager to work for the project.

The Belgians were initially pleased that he was willing to participate in his own development—so much so that he incessantly sought out Monsieur Delacourt—but they soon discovered that Hamadi had reasons of his own for pursuing and ultimately signing a contract with the Belgian Project. His wife was pregnant with his eleventh child, his eldest son had just gotten engaged, and the pressures to obtain a high yield on his tiny parcel were more acute than ever. In addition to these concerns, Si Hamadi was afraid of losing the labor of his eldest son, who had realized that two households could not survive on one hectare. Si Hamadi expressed his dilemma in terms of his expectation:

> Besh yeshuf Msyu Delagor l-khidma imta‛i, wa-yagul l-Msyu Romdan, 'il-felah. l-hadi yikhdim b'il- igdeh.' Wa-yacatini gat‛a kbira. Hek heka, yug‛ud Naji l-kbir bahdani, wa-ma-yimshish il-barra, 'basbor dela lun' [passeport de la lune].

When Monsieur Delacourt sees my work he'll tell Monsieur Romthane, [the director of the OMVVM, who—Hamadi indicated by rubbing his index fingers together—was a close friend of the director of the Belgian Project], 'This fellah does good work.' And he will allot me a parcel. That way, my eldest son Naji will stay by my side and won't go away by using the 'passport of the moon' [i.e. he won't sneak across the Libyan border at night—a practice employed by desperate, unemployed Tunisian young men].

As will be seen, Si Hamadi's dream did not bear fruition and again, his own eagerness was very much to blame. Meanwhile, he followed the directives of the Belgians. Both he and the project staff agreed that given his limited resources it would be better to gear the farm to serve rather than compete with his more affluent neighbors. With this objective in mind, they therefore redesigned a portion of the farm to serve as a nursery for new-strain tomato seedling which he could then sell to his neighbors. In pursuit of this aim, each morning an extension worker would come to visit Si Hamadi's farm. He would check the temperature in the project-supplied hot-house, measure the growth of plants, check for parasites, and tell Si Hamadi what to do next.

Despite the daily control, however, many of the men on the project staff were dissatisfied with Hamadi. "He's breaking the contract," one complained. "He bought the wrong fertilizer, and those seeds should have been planted four days ago." Far more serious was the criticism that he spent his profits on building a new five-room dar ‛arbi for his family to live in instead of remaining in the one-room mud gourbi and using the money to purchase cows for his farm. Dissatisfaction grew to the point that the Belgians debated among themselves as to whether or not Hamadi was truly a model worker or just another worker. After five years of collaboration with the project, some of the Belgians felt that Hamadi had failed to internalize the principles and procedures they had tried to inculcate. It seemed to them that their daily instruction had been considered *only* on the level of daily instructions, without making links between present practice and future plans.

While the Belgian Project contract signed by Hamadi specifically called for both learning and initiative on his part, Si Hamadi nevertheless was criticized by the Belgians both for following directives ("he's just a worker") and for making his own decisions ("he bought the wrong fertilizer"). Indeed, both were true.

The Belgians debated Si Hamadi's progress among themselves but Hamadi was unaware of the controversy; he was not only pleased with himself, but also proud of his status as the project's model worker. His farm had never been this productive and he therefore felt confident that the Belgians would continue to help him prosper. He was an optimistic man, had always built for the future, and did not dwell on the past. Of his many fantasies, the greatest was that when the Belgians eventually left Tunisia, they would take him with them; he visualized himself as their spokesman and saw himself teaching everything he had learned to the fellahin of Africa or America.

Si Hamadi's efforts to obtain more land eventually gave rise to a series of events which deflated most of his dreams. He knew that the OMVVM could expropriate farmers for not irrigating their land and so in his request, he had asked to be allotted one of the parcels owned by neighbors who were breaking the law by not irrigating their fields. He cited his own status as a model worker for the Belgian Project as a further recommendation, and solicited Monsieur Delacourt to act as intermediary on his behalf. In reaction to this threat against their land, a number of Si Hamadi's dry-farming neighbors began clearing their fields for irrigated farming. Naturally, the OMVVM was delighted with the unexpected compliance of these farmers to laws long defied. The OMVVM delayed action on Si Hamadi's request.

Si Hamadi was further disappointed by the director of the Belgian Project who had not facilitated his application before he departed from the country. Contrary to Si Hamadi's expectations, Monsieur Delacourt had indicated that he believed Hamadi had overextended himself and that he should not be allotted a larger parcel. The crux of the matter was that for a number of years, Si Hamadi had been renting a three hectare parcel from an elderly neighbor and had been devoting more and more time to the rented parcel rather than to his own intensive farming. Despite the efforts of the Belgians to convince him otherwise, Si Hamadi was at heart an extensive farmer like his neighbors. Stated simply, it was Hamadi's belief that intensive cultivation would deplete his soil. The Belgians were unable to convince him that "balanced intensive farming" could be implemented indefinitely.

FIGURE 5.1 A Comparison of Marketing Patterns of Two Small-scale Fellahin

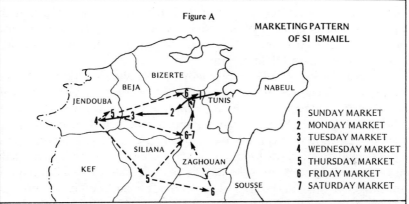

Figure A

MARKETING PATTERN OF SI ISMAIEL

1 SUNDAY MARKET
2 MONDAY MARKET
3 TUESDAY MARKET
4 WEDNESDAY MARKET
5 THURSDAY MARKET
6 FRIDAY MARKET
7 SATURDAY MARKET

Figure A: Si Ismaiel avoided farming by devoting a good portion of the year to marketing produce at distant weekly markets in the countryside. His circuits contrast sharply with the marketing pattern of most of the region's fellahin, as for example that of Si Hamadi, given below.

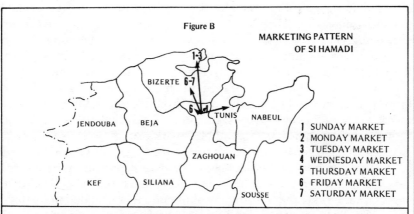

Figure B

MARKETING PATTERN OF SI HAMADI

1 SUNDAY MARKET
2 MONDAY MARKET
3 TUESDAY MARKET
4 WEDNESDAY MARKET
5 THURSDAY MARKET
6 FRIDAY MARKET
7 SATURDAY MARKET

Figure B: Si Hamadi spent most of his time on his own farm and sent his produce off to market on the trucks of his neighbors. He preferred the central farmer's market in Tunis or selling directly to the state. Si Hamadi periodically would market his own produce at the Friday souk in Medjerda. He did this primarily to teach his sons about the market (*besh yeshouf es-soug*) so that they would be familiar with all aspects of farming.

Hamadi faced an additional problem in that the neighbors who were to have purchased his seedlings began nurseries of their own. The Belgians were delighted that using Hamadi as a model for his neighbors had finally succeeded, but felt that it was their responsibility to help him find new markets. As a consequence Hamadi began to rely to an ever-increasing extent upon Belgian aid to market his produce. He invoked the name of the Belgian Project when selling produce on his own by claiming that the superior product of the project's model worker warranted a higher price at the market place. After the departure of the Belgians, however, he would lose both their aid and their prestige.

In response to his cumulative problems and growing isolation, Si Hamadi sought out and renewed his relationship with Si Hedi, the largest landowner in Medjerda, who had once been his employer. Hamadi arranged to sell all of his seedlings to the Sfaxi for that year and to entrench himself as Si Hedi's sole or main supplier over the coming years. He went a step further, and asked Si Hedi to intercede for him in his request for more land, through the power vested in him as president of the *Dar El Fellahin*. In his last request, he arranged for his eldest son Naji to be trained on the Sfaxi's estate. In effect, Si Hamadi renewed his bond with an old patron and reaffirmed his reliance and dependence upon a single individual in order to secure his future.

Workers of the Agro-Combinat

Compared to other rural occupations in the region, the life of the agro-combinat farm worker has remained relatively stable from the colonial to the post-colonial era. They have neither lost nor gained rights to the land they work. They receive steady wages which are dependent upon harvest size, advances or bonuses. Their status is clear; they have no illusions that this status is likely to change and yet they continue to envision that day.

Workers lived either on or off the farm, but were encouraged to live off-farm. The fewer families that live directly on the agro-combinat itself, the fewer requests for land parcels. Laborers were allotted tasks and paid wages, given periodic bonuses and blue work-clothes, and—except for the foremen—would not demand participation in managerial decisions. Workers on the agro-combinat had advantages over those on private land in that they received health and retirement benefits. On the whole, it was clear to any agricultural worker that improvement of one's lot depended upon developing side-line occupations, and this was best accomplished by using the diverse skills of all members of the family.

The first case presented in this section introduces an agro-combinat family nostalgic for the solidary, corporate ᶜarsh of their nomadic forebears. The sons of Si Sleim attempted to revive or reaffirm the extended family as an economic unit. They created what they called their "family cooperative" and superimposed it upon their status as agro-combinat workers. The second case presented here concerns an agro-combinat family also of nomadic ancestry. Quite content with life as an agro-combinat worker, Si Azouz nevertheless finds himself and his family supported primarily by the migrant labor of his eldest son.

The "Family Cooperative"

The seven sons of Si Sleim made earnest efforts to maintain a sense of tribal integrity and cohesiveness, despite their being farm workers. They had lived on the same farm at Bordj Tabouna long before it was incorporated into the Agro-Combinat of Medjerda. Their father, Si Sleim, was originally a Bedouin from the south. He had come to Medjerda with his brother, Si Mabrouk, after drought had wiped out the family flocks. The two brothers began work as agricultural laborers on the Bordj Tabouna farm of the widow, Madame Dumas. After Madame Dumas married the widower Mayor of Medjerda, the Dumasiya Farm was joined to the Mayor's vast estate. The Mayor's workers were often transferred from one to another of the Mayor's five farms and eventually, Si Mabrouk moved his family to the Mayor's Sidi Ug^cud estate. Si Sleim remained at Bordj Tabouna and raised fifteen children there. The three eldest of Si Sleim's seven sons married their father's brother's daughters, who were brought back to live at Bordj Tabouna. His three youngest sons were unmarried and lived in the household of their eldest brother, Si Hamadi after Si Sleim's death in 1960. Upon his father's death, Si Hamadi became the head of the family.

After expropriation in 1964, the Dumasiya Farm became a pre-cooperative of the OMVVM. As in the case of other expropriated farms in El Maskine, Madame Dumas' farm continued to be called by her name. Si Hamadi moved into the unfinished two-storey Dumasiya farmhouse with his wife, children, and younger brothers. As each brother married, the others assisted him in building a *gourbi* that was either attached or adjacent to Si Hamadi's colonial villa. Each household maintained its own courtyard; however, the Dumasiya barnyard behind the villa was shared in common and was used for housing the family's animals, which were owned collectively.

Si Hamadi's house and courtyard served as a gathering place and were continually filled with both his brothers' families and visiting relatives— and this pleased him. He was a jovial and toothless man of sixty; his authority went uncontested and he presided over his domain with ease. A raised eyebrow sufficed to silence upwards of a score of boisterous children who played in the courtyard. In contrast, Si Hamadi's second eldest brother, Moncef, often complained sourly that the children were like a noose choking him to death—but no matter how he threatened, he did not have the slightest effect upon the children.

Si Hamadi and Moncef were made members of the Pre-Cooperative Bordj Tabouna—but when the cooperative era came to a close, the farm was transferred from the jurisdiction of the OMVVM to the OTD without being subdivided. The OTD incorporated Bordj Tabouna into the Agro-Combinat of Medjerda, and the third brother joined the other two working on the state farm. When the younger brothers were ready to seek employment, permanent positions on the farm were no longer available. The fourth brother became a night watchman for the Forest Service in the Djebel El Kebir, a job which he said gave him nightmares; the fifth became a worker on a nearby private farm; the sixth opened a small shop at the agro-combinat; and the seventh became a self-avowed *chomeur-deluxe* with big dreams. On occasion, he worked as a mason's apprentice. In 1979, Si Hamadi retired from the agro-combinat and began collecting a small pension. The position he vacated was not filled; the agro-combinat's new policy was one of mechanization.

The combined households of the brothers grew until over fifty members of the *douar*, or hamlet, lived at the heart of the agro-combinat. They maintained their own farm animals as a collective unit, including ten *carbiya* cows—the agro-combinat specialized in *souri* cattle—and a flock that ranged between thirty and fifty sheep. Four of the brothers rented a private parcel which belonged to the Hadj's farm next door. The rental was *fi-shshtar*; i.e., divided in two. The owner supplied the land, seed, fertilizer, equipment, and transportation—the brothers supplied the labor. At harvest time, the Hadj and the brothers split the profits equally. In this manner, they were enabled to maintain both an individual and a collective income. Cooperation within the family extended beyond farming and the tending of sheep. The wives characteristically worked together and with the children's participation; they were engaged in sewing, baking *khubz tabouna*, and rolling the year's supply of couscous, as well as in working in the Hadj's fields. One of the wives was a fine potter who provided each household and other neighbors with earthenware casseroles, incense burners, and *kanouns*.

The brothers superimposed their kin-based economy on the formal structure of the agro-combinat as if the latter did not exist. Si Hamadi summed up the difference between family collective activity and state farms or cooperatives concisely. "Brothers work well together, strangers do not." Family cooperation entailed trust; state farms did not. Before their eyes, the land they lived on changed hands four times. The brothers attempted to maintain a semblance of *carsh* continuity through endogamous marriage and collective activity. Over the years they ignored attempts by the state farm administration to rid them of their animals, and the issue remained at a stalemate. Thus, while the administration issued periodic orders for the removal of the animals, and while Si Hamadi followed the ritual of selling a few sheep and keeping the remainder out of sight for a short period, both sides knew that the regulations were unen-

FIGURE 5.2   In *ᶜArsh* Marriages of Si Sleim's Five Sons:
The Five Households of the Family Compound

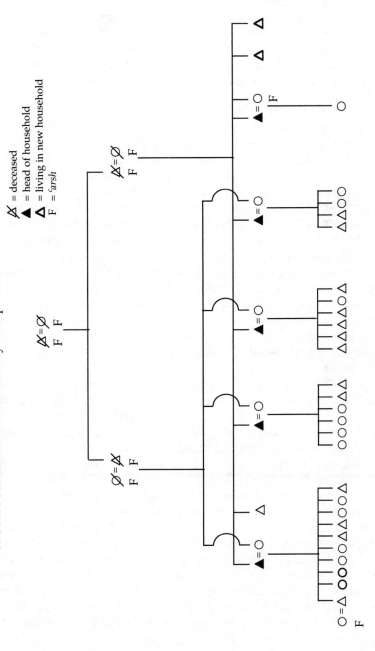

forceable and not likely to be pursued to a definitive conclusion, although they did help to keep the number of animals from increasing. The administration of the agro-combinat never dealt with the larger issue of the growing number of households and the expanding population who lived but did not work on the state farm. The sons of Si Sleim considered the territory they lived on as either their own or—if the state farm were to be dismantled—potentially their own. They maintained a profound respect for the ideal of a land- holding family unit.

The Good Worker and His Son

Si Azouz was both strong and haggard. Like many fellahin of his age, he wore a weary expression that gave him a grim aspect. On special occasions— when he shook hands over the betrothal of a daughter or skillfully sacrificed a sheep for *cAi'd El Kebir*—he was capable of mustering together some gaiety. He dressed in a long faded blue worker's coat and faded blue worker pants. His *chechia* had turned the color of rust from his years of work in the fields. He was fifty-eight years old, had been raised on the colonial farms of Bordj Tabouna, worked as an agricultural laborer all his life, and wished for nothing more than a plot of land to call his own. He was of nomadic stock and the first generation to be born in the Delegation of Medjerda. And, although he was the eldest of fourteen siblings and head of the family since his father's death, he was not master of his own household. His eldest son, desiring to follow any but his own father's footsteps, had left home at eighteen to seek his fortune in Libya. Upon his return, Ahmed outstripped his father in both wealth and authority and lorded his success over all his relatives.

Si Azouz continued to work at the agro-combinat despite his son's success. He commuted to the farm by bicycle and performed whatever was required for the day: he fed concentrate to the cows, acted as watchman and harvested in accord with need. He had little to say about his own work; such tasks had been performed by him when Bordj Tabouna had been the Dumasiya farm, then when it became a pre-cooperative and finally, when it was incorporated into the agro-combinat. Because of the farm's recent emphasis upon developing a mechanized dairy industry, fewer workers were needed. At retirement, Si Azouz would receive 38 dinars monthly benefits; like Si Hamadi, the position he vacated would not be refilled. Si Azouz always expressed satisfaction with his job; he had a secure position which provided health insurance, sick leave, and guaranteed income for the remainder of his life. He no longer dwelled upon his activities; he considered himself an old man eclipsed by the deeds of his eldest son. As an agricultural worker, Si Azouz earned an average of 2.000 dinars per day, including bonuses. As a waiter in Tripoli, his son Ahmed earned ten times that amount.

Ahmed had saved enough from his earnings in Tripoli to buy a small plot of land on the outskirts of Medjerda, where he had a three-room *dar ͨarbi* built on a dirt path leading to wheat fields and olive groves. His parents and five siblings were allowed to occupy the entire house in his absence. On visits home, however, Ahmed and his wife took over the bedroom and his parents were obliged to stay with the children in the sitting room. On each of his three visits, Ahmed had built another room and added various embellishments to his house in preparation for the day when he would return to Medjerda permanently. In carrying out his plans for the house, he hired his father- in-law, a retired mason, and assumed the responsibility of supervising the older man regarding each step to be carried out. In this way, both Ahmed's father and father-in-law profited from the young man's success—the former, by living in spacious new quarters and the latter, by sporadic employment and a small sum for his labors. Although it was customary for sons to support their fathers as they got older, Ahmed's insolence—with his constant references to *his* house, *his* bed, and *his* plans for his siblings—was humiliating for Si Azouz.

Ahmed was his father's opposite in every way. He was tall, confident, fat, and loud. His physical presence appeared to make his father shrink before one's eyes. On his visit home, his relatives sounded as if they were a whispering Greek chorus. They sat in disapproving agreement in the courtyard:

Yitfeshlim!   [He struts like one who has just come back from abroad]

Yitfoukhr!   [He boasts and inflates himself]

Yistili!   [He's putting on the style in front of the women]

Yitgazdir!   [He struts like a peacock]

Yitfafa!   [He wants to show that he's bigger than he is]

Ibonbi!   [He bounces like a woman wearing gold on her breast]

Ahmed had been away for five years this time. He arrived at the wheel of a *camionette* bulging with packages and crates. He unloaded as he greeted his parents and relatives, all of whom had been waiting for him—news of his return had crossed town faster than the vehicle. Ahmed displayed the fruits of his labor: a refrigerator and a stove, an electric heater and an electric fan, a deluxe electric sewing machine from England, a Japanese color television set, a synthetic carpet for the bedroom, a large French pressure cooker, an electric strobe light ashtray, clothes, perfumes, and watches—the total cost of which approximated 1500 dinars. The car rental from Tripoli cost Ahmed 400 dinars—which may or may not have been paid in cash. No one left the courtyard without at least a small gift, and all pronounced Ahmed a very good fellow. Later that evening, when Ahmed returned from the public showers, however, his watch had been stolen. Inasmuch as theft is virtually unheard of in Medjerda, one may easily imagine Ahmed's chagrin and consternation.

More than one young man became convinced that day that emigration was the only way a farm boy could both escape the dreary countryside and make his fortune. The only issue debated was whether to go to Libya or Europe. Ahmed began to make arrangements for his younger brother to accompany him on his return to Tripoli. The younger boy had spent the past two years as a *chomeur deluxe* waiting for someone to take action on his behalf. His heart had been set on migrating to France, but he had not heard from his cousin who lived there. Stories about Tunisians being placed in the Libyan military or being derided and mistreated in some way were disturbing, but Ahmed assured his younger brother that Tunisians would be treated worse in Europe than in a neighboring Arab country. Besides, Ahmed reminded him, he spoke no more than a few words of French. Reluctantly, the boy capitulated, vowing that he would not return home until he had equalled his brother's wealth.

UCP Cooperateurs

The remaining cooperatives are an artifact of government policies no longer sanctioned and of an agrarian system no longer considered viable in the Tunisian context. The few that remained did so partly because they had continued to be highly productive despite the odds against them, and partly because the government was as yet unwilling to relinquish the land. The cooperatives were in an ambiguous position: they were neither fully state owned nor fully autonomous and, as a result, the cooperateurs felt that they were in limbo. The first case introduces a cooperateur (*mut^cadid*) whose loyalty to the UCP did not prevent him from wishing the cooperative would collapse so that he might be allotted an agrarian reform parcel to call his own. Unable to wait for the anticipated day, he "rewarded" himself by incorporating a larger and larger "garden" around his UCP house as his private domain, to be used for his animals and personal farming requirements. The second case introduces an even more cynical and disillusioned cooperateur—one who was unwilling to spend the rest of his life on the farm.

The Loyal Cooperateur

Hadj Mahmoud was in his mid-fifties but already had wrinkled, leathery skin. He dressed in faded worker's clothes and wore a *chechia* upon his head.

His wife and eighteen year old daughter-in-law both wore faded red *meliyas*. He lived with his wife, six children, daughter-in-law, and grandson in a crumbling colonial farmhouse in an isolated corner of the UCP Sidi Ugᶜud at the foot of the Djebel El Kebir. Hadj Mahmoud was outspoken and had an opinion about everything. He could tell his own story and that of the cooperative succinctly:

We have our meetings and elections coming up in just two days and this is what I have to say: We get a director and he stays six months or a year—I don't even know his name. He does nothing, just sits in his office at Sidi Uᶜcud, sits at his desk or rides in a big car to Tunis. He rents a house in Sidi Ugᶜud for fifty five dinars a month. Can you imagine anything in Sidi Ugᶜud renting for fifty five dinars? That's more than double my monthly salary. And where does that 55 dinars come from? From our treasury of course—fifty five dinars of *our* money. And he's never even set foot on UCP soil. He would get lost trying to find the fields. The old director who was here during the sixties took one thousand dinars of our money to give to UCP Mezez or one of the others. He wrote out a check, but for some reason it never got there. To this day the money is unaccounted for—and where did it go?

I was born in a *maᶜamera* made of mud and straw right over there in the Djebel El Kebir. I've worked here my whole life, although my father was a shepherd in the mountains. Everything I have is right here. I don't want to live in one of those houses they built for us on the outskirts of Sidi Ugᶜud (but Manoubiya, my wife, would like it—she's always complaining that she never sees anybody out here). But here I have more space and a bit of garden and nobody keeps his eyes on what I do and what I have. I have my own animals: four sheep, three goats, two cows, and some chickens. Where would I put them in Sidi Ugᶜud? So I don't have electricity. They promise it to the cooperateurs who move to Sidi Ugᶜud, but it'll take them a long time to put it in. Besides, the houses may be subsidized but you still have to pay for them. That's not where I want to put my profit shares. I have enough almond and olive trees for my family—and now that there's irrigation on the cooperative, I'm going to tap into it and use UCP water to grow my own vegetables. Manoubiya lives here like on a private farm—there's no difference for her. But I work for wages and not for myself.

Let me explain how things work here: Say the UCP makes fifty million. Well then, five million goes to the cooperateurs, five million goes to the machinery, ten million goes to the next year's crops, and thirty million goes to the state. The UCP is 'buying' the land from the state and we are the landowners [*patrons*]. Don't I look like a *proprietère*? [He pointed to his worker clothes.]

I work twenty days a month and get minimum wage, one dinar and three hundred thirty two millimes per day, but they call it an 'advance' – not 'wages.' We're going to vote for a higher daily advance. We want one dinar eight hundred and then we can live. They give us twelve sacks of wheat and a hundred liters of olive oil and if you have children in school they give you another ten dinars a year. But none of my children are in school. My son is only twenty-five. He married a Sidi Bechir girl two years ago and they're already having children. He's a temporary worker [*waqti*] waiting to take my place as a cooperateur, but I am still strong—and besides, maybe they won't replace us. Look at Bordj Tabouna.

At the meeting we're going to vote in some competent people. The cooperative used to be profitable, but now it's not. Men don't know how to work anymore—they think that if they just stand there long enough that it's called work... We work for nothing. If they parcelled out the UCP today, I could take my wife to Mecca on the profits from next year's harvests. I went to Mecca four years ago and paid for it out of the year-end profit. I got over three hundred dinars that year. Now, where are the profits? We've already borrowed more than we would get back at the end of the year after the harvest. They mostly reinvest into the cooperative—building those houses at Sidi Ug^cud, fixing the winery, buying machinery, and a lot of things that we didn't vote for. We want to decide where the money goes and we want it to go to *us*. But they limit what we can vote on. We can elect a president and a council, but not much else. If we could, we would vote to split up the cooperative of Sidi Ug^cud and divide it between us like they did with Bordj Er Roumi. They say that we're the *patrons*, the *proprietères*, but we're not—we're nothing.

The general assembly meetings and elections for the UCP Sidi Ug^cud, which Hadj Mahmoud had anticipated with both eagerness and bitterness, did not take place on schedule; instead, they were postponed indefinitely— and were not held at all that year.

The Self-Made Man

In 1949, Si Shedli was an idealistic, energetic, barefoot farmboy on a colonial estate. In 1959, he abandoned regional politics in a dispute with his fellow Destourians. In 1969, he was a disillusioned cooperateur awarded a five hectare parcel of summer dust and winter mud. By 1979, he sought to profit no cause other than his own—he had transformed himself into a train-commuting business representative in the capital. By his forty-second birthday, Si Shedli was an articulate, cynical historian of his time. By 1989 Si Shedli had helped his son to realize his own economic dreams.

Si Shedli's grandfather had come to the delegation as a nomad from the region of Kairouan. His family had lost its flocks in a drought; he and his brother came north and found work on the colonial farms of Sidi Ug^cud. Shedli's father had been the personal attendant of the French "mayor" of Medjerda—the vice-president of the town of Medjerda—and had accompanied him to France in the summers. Shedli, along with his twelve siblings, had been raised in a two-room *gourbi* behind the mayor's villa. He grew up playing soccer with Monsieur Marc's sons and each morning the mayor insisted that Shedli accept a ride into town with his own sons in order to attend school. He learned to read and write Arabic fluently and achieved some competence in French. Shedli loved Monsieur Marc as a father, and was indulged as a favored son. Shedli's own father took pride in the closeness that existed between the two families. The mayor had gone so far as to arrange the marriage of two of Shedli's sisters. When World War II was fought in the fields of Medjerda, the bond between the two families was cemented further when, for a period of months, the mayor's wife and children moved in with Shedli's family to a makeshift *gourbi* which stood in the forest of the Djebel El Kebir. Although Shedli's family had lived in close relation to the *colons*, it was, perhaps, no closer than was the case for many others in the region. However, Shedli was proud, as was his father, to be so intimately associated with the mayor; Monsieur Marc was one of the most prominent French landowners in all of Tunisia. Despite the closeness of this relationship, by the time he was a teenager Shedli opposed the colonial regime. The stance he took proved devastating to his father who considered it not only a rebellion directed against Monsieur Marc, his patron, but also against his own father.

Si Shedli was tall, lean, and balding. He was a man who suffered from extreme myopia and wore corrective lenses. Such lenses were uncommonly worn in Medjerda, inasmuch as eyeglasses were considered undesirable even when needed; to wear them was to acknowledge a weakness that otherwise would have gone unnoticed. He had recalled that the French bore no shame in wearing corrective lenses, and, overcoming his bias, Si Shedli was emboldened to take pride in wearing glasses to the extent that he brought a pair home for one of his daughters who had inherited his vision— thus sacrificing her beauty to enable her to see the blackboard at school. Consciously or unconsciously, Shedli dressed in imitation of Monsieur Marc. During the summer, he sported a white jacket, white slacks, and a shirt which was generally white and worn open at the collar. During the winter, he wore darker clothes—to neutralize splatters of mud—and added an ascot adapted from one of his wife's scarves as a finishing touch to his costume. He frequently bought clothes for himself, making his purchases at Mellasine—the used-clothing souk on the outskirts of Tunis—and continually promised to buy clothes for his wife and nine children. He enjoyed strolling down the streets of Medjerda-*souri* using his umbrella as a walking-stick and being seen in the company of the Sfaxi and other prominent outsiders.

Si Shedli's colonial airs did not go without comment in the town of Medjerda. Some men speculated on what city-held profession might warrant such attire; one man declared that each man had a given position and that Si Shedli kept trying to go beyond his place by associating with people above him. In the countryside, however, Si Shedli had a far better reputation. The fellahin who knew him considered him one of their own despite the façade he went to so much trouble to maintain. They remembered that he had served as president of the UGTT, that he had organized the countryside in the struggle for independence, that he had been a cooperateur in the 1960s, that he was still a fellah of sorts in that he had been awarded a five hectare agrarian reform parcel when his cooperative at El Maskine had been disbanded, and that he still owned that parcel. Somehow through the ensuing years, he had become a man of town and city while they had remained firmly rooted on the farms.

Si Shedli's own five hectare parcel was located in such a remote corner of the delegation that his wife did not believe it existed. It was accessible from the road only with great difficulty. Motor vehicles could reach the parcel only during the driest part of the summer, for the land was so damp, rutted, and eroded that it was nearly a marsh. This obstacle to transporting his produce, particularly in winter, only added to Si Shedli's other difficulties. He could not sell the land until it was paid for, as was true with all agrarian reform parcels, and he had neither begun to make payments nor to inquire about what was owed. His "papers" concerning the land detailed fees for irrigation but made no mention of land payments, because many of the parcel prices had not yet been determined. He had no interest in working the parcel himself and claimed that he would rather lose the land than pay for it since the region had become so desolate. Meanwhile, if he could make a profit from the parcel, it was all to the good. Si Shedli's thoughts concerning his property could be summed up by the maxim "easy come, easy go," for he had observed that agrarian politics were always in transition. One of his friends at the OMVVM even had private parcels marked for land reform on his drawing board. Furthermore, Si Shedli had gotten used to living in one of the new quarters adjacent to Medjerda-*souri* and clearly, he could not commute from town in order to work his parcel of land. So he rented the five hectares to a fellah who lived on a neighboring farm and he himself visited the land only with great reluctance, perhaps once every several years. At such times, it was necessary for him to inquire locally in order to find his own parcel. Si Shedli preferred to confer with his tenant on market day in Medjerda—and this he did approximately twice a year.

Si Shedli initially rented the parcel *fi-shshṭar*—that is, fifty-fifty. Shedli supplied materials and seed, paying for irrigation if needed, and his tenant supplied all labor. At harvest time the two would split the profits. In due time, however, the tenant—who was an old friend of Shedli's from independence and cooperative days— had found the land to be of diminishing quality and productivity. It was situated on what had once been a loop of the Medjerda, but irrigation projects had diverted the river to run a straighter course; the desolate corner of El Maskine was bypassed, and the loop itself had become a marshland. The tenant found it less and less profitable to work the parcel at all, but Si Shedli prevailed upon him to pay a low annual rent and continue to work his land.

Si Shedli retained the nomadic impression that unless one were a big landowner, to be a fellah was to be imprisoned in perpetual poverty. When he scolded his son for getting poor marks in school, he placed a turbaned towel on his head to serve as a symbol of the serious consequences of poor performance. For his own part, with the aid of his ambitiousness, his friends, his literacy, and his fluent spoken French, Si Shedli had sought and found a good job with a construction company in Tunis. Whereas his father had earned two hundred seventy millimes per day and a portion of wheat per month on the mayor's farm, Si Shedli earned a hundred thirty dinars per month, a "thirteenth month" annual salary bonus, sixty dinars every three months of social security for his children, health insurance, and a three week vacation. His wife complained that much of his salary was spent on what she called her husband's egotism (*rajl anani*)—commuting to Tunis by train instead of bus, buying clothes for himself instead of his family, eating in restaurants instead of taking lunch from home; still she was able to boast that he was never among those fathers who refused to buy their children's school books. His selective generosity favored education above the family's food, clothing, and shelter; the house was devoid of ornamental and luxury items. When some household item or other broke, it was generally left unrepaired. Despite Si Shedli's salary which was quite adequate by Medjerdi standards, the family's material life seemed spartan in comparison to that maintained by neighbors, and Si Shedli's wife found that not infrequently she would have to borrow money from a trusted neighbor in order to feed the children.

This state of affairs changed suddenly when Si Shedli's eldest son failed his exams in school and, with the assistance of his father's friends in the capital, quickly migrated to France and got a job in a factory. The evolution of Si Shedli's life from country to town to city thereby reached its apex with his son's emigration to Europe. Within a year, Si Shedli had a television, a refrigerator, a telephone, and a *souriya* daughter-in-law. Given his cynical nature, it certainly must have occurred to Si Shedli that his son was not unlike the cooperatives of Medjerda in the sense that his failure in one area had ultimately resulted in his success in another.

Choice and Constraint

These fellahin give evidence of a few of the diverse responses of Medjerdis to the promotion of rural development in the region. They are caught in a struggle between time-honored concepts and radical change, between conformity and individuality, and between Arab and European ways. They balance short-term goals with long-range considerations. Long-range investment in agriculture demonstrates some degree of confidence in the durability of current reforms; diversification and opting-out of agriculture often reflects the reverse. From among the alternatives, fellahin pick and choose those economic strategies which concur with their individual perceptions of the future. Conservatism and innovation in the Medjerda Valley do not appear to vary according to rank; for as we have seen, there are innovators and risk averse conservatives in all strata of Medjerdi society. Likewise, even the most conservative of fellahin innovate as they see fit.

أناعَلَيَّ بالبِركة، وانتَ عليكَ بالحرِكَة

6

Access to the *Souri* World

'ana 'aliya bil-barka, w-inti alik bil-harka
it is for you to toil and for me to receive the grace of God

The epitome of *ʿarbi* rural life—pastoral nomadism—is present in the region in the late summer and fall. Bedouin or Berber herding families come north with their flocks, rent land from the fellahin or state farms, stay for a month or a season, and then move on to their next destination. The fellahin envy them their mobility, their admitted abundance of leisure, and their liquid capital in the form of ritually sacred sheep. In Medjerda, sheep have become the symbol of opposition to central authority as fellahin refuse to give up their sheep to make way for irrigated farming. The nomads, aware of both the admiration and the derision as "primitives" awarded them, take advantage of their position when in the marketplace. Even their sheep have lineages to be proud of and are priced accordingly.

The herders generally rent the same parcel each year and have established long-standing reciprocal relationships with the fellahin; frequently they are members of the same *ʿarsh* or are related through marriage. The sedentarized nomads, who are now fellahin, enjoy the contractual relations they have with the herders, for it helps connect them to a way of life they remember nostalgically—though one to which they would never return. True nomadism is seen less and less frequently in the lower Medjerda Valley as government policy calls for the expansion of irrigated farming, which is incompatible with maintaining sheep even on a seasonal basis.

ʿArbi farming, as distinct from nomadism, consists of a combination of herding and dry-farming. Before the arrival of the French, the fellahin grew cereals, kept olive orchards, and maintained their own flocks. Women helped harvest in the fields in the summer and in the orchards in the winter. Olives were made into oil, cereals converted into staples. Sheep served as a means of security, investment, and the only way of obtaining instant cash during the growing seasons. To the many fellahin of Medjerda who come from pastoral-nomadic backgrounds, sheep are still valued above all else.

Colon and *Coopérant*

Souri farming began with the influx of the French in the 1880s. The *colons* covered the hillside with vineyards and dotted the countryside with wineries—adding the insult of wine to the injury of expropriation. *ᶜArbi* sheep were replaced by pigs—even more than wine, a symbol of *souri* blasphemy. Throughout the years of the Protectorate, *souri* farming flourished and two separate worlds came to exist in Medjerda. Two political systems were synchronized—one administered by the sheikh, the other by the mayor. Fellahin and nomads became workers on the colonial farms although many *colons* preferred Italian workers. The fellahin fought continually to keep their land, and a few wealthy older families succeeded in doing so. Competition and antipathy between wealthy *ᶜarbi* and *souri* landowners became legendary. A well-known story about the Mayor and the Hadj amply illustrates the antagonism between the two. "Mayor" was what people in the region called the vice-president of the township—the President was always Tunisian:

> The Mayor was the richest of the *colons*. He had more land than any of the others here in Medjerda, and maybe in the whole country. He was president of the town of Medjerda. There was only one rich Tunisian and that was the Hadj. He lived on a farm right next to the Mayor's. They would always dispute and compete with each other. The Mayor wanted the Hadj to sell out his land to him but the Hadj always refused. He said to the Mayor, 'Even though you have two tractors and a car, I am richer than you are.' They went on like this for a while and finally they made a deal. The one of them that was the richer would take the other's farm. So they made a contract in front of the judge saying that the one who could show that he had more money would win the farm. So they both took out their money and the judge counted it for them and there were witnesses. And of course all of them were French and surely would have killed the Hadj if they could. But it was all done legally. When they counted up the money it turned out that they had exactly the same amount. No difference at all. And then the Hadj reached into his *kashabiya*, into the lining of his *kashabiya*, and he pulled out even more money, and that was how he won the bet and the Mayor's farm. The Hadj teased the Mayor for years saying, 'Even though I ride a donkey and you a tractor, I am the richer of the two.' And the Mayor was the greatest colon of Medjerda but the Hadj is greater still.

Another version of this story claims that the Hadj pooled the collective resources of his *ᶜarsh*, or lineage, and thereby won the bet—proving that the

Hadj and his *ᶜarsh* are "greater still." Whereas during the colonial period there was a separation of Arab and French worlds and practices, in the post-independence period, development goals have sought to synthesize them. The fellahin themselves are to be transformed. As the official French-language newspaper typically describes the development process:

> It is the extension workers who do most of the hard work. They're *there*. They actually live in the countryside. They literally inhale the odors of the fields. They unlock the secrets of the mentality of the fellahin. They use psychological techniques in pursuit of their goal: to convert the fellahin to irrigation and modern technology and to force them to adopt these methods once they have been persuaded of the advantages they will reap. (*L'Action* 12/9/78, my translation)

Farmers are urged to use birth control, send their children to school, utilize the labor of their wives and daughters on the farm, and learn the new agricultural methods taught to their sons at school. They are asked to change what they grow and how to grow it, what animals they keep, and, consequently, even what they eat. In short, they are asked to change almost every aspect of daily farm activity and the way of life they consider natural. In this region of former nomads and dry-farmers, *ᶜarbi* values are a source of pride and the fellahin are not enthusiastic about giving up their sheep, working harder at unfamiliar tasks, taking financial risks in areas they do not even want to change, and sometimes being subject to insult or humiliation.

It is in farming that the fellahin have had the greatest experience with *souri* ways; those who came as nomads to Medjerda indeed learned their farming from the *colons*. Exposure to European farming was unavoidable during the colonial period just as it is unavoidable today within the geographical boundaries of state and foreign projects. Many fellahin resent the post-colonial intrusion. Since it appears that they cannot preserve the integrity of their farms effectively, they seek to preserve their families and protect their households from reforms and change.

Parallels and contrasts between the French colonial farmers of the past and the European development workers of the present are not entirely lost upon the fellahin. From their point of view, the *colon* and the *cooperant*, or foreign adviser, are two breeds of foreigners who have come to take over their farms. The *colons* came to stay, owning and expanding their farms and settling in for generations, until they were stopped by independence. They lived in a separate world, but they learned Arabic. They ate pork and couscous, drank wine and tea, and they made farming a way of life and not just a business. They were the original *souri* model, yet in retrospect, they were neither fully European nor were they Arab. The second breed—the post-colonial *cooperants*—neither are farmers nor do they speak Arabic. The *cooperants* eat pork, but only eat couscous under duress; they drink wine but consider Medjerdi tea undrinkable, they live in the suburbs of Tunis and would never consider making a home in the region itself. The farms of Medjerda are academic exercises for them—farms upon which controlled experiments may be conducted.

The fellahin have transferred both their expectations and their ambivalence from *colon* to *cooperant*, and constantly compare their present experiences to the past. Here is one fellah's view:

Sadok: At first I worked as a mechanic and I learned to take care of motor vehicles and repair them. Then I worked for some three years at the vineyard at Sidi Ug‛ud and I learned how to make wine. And then I worked for the Italian *colon* Anternicola and he was like a father to me. He taught me agriculture. He would pick up a handful of the dirt and scowl at it and rub it between his fingers, and say, 'This is the spot for watermelons.' He would say, 'Don't plant that there, plant it . . .' and he would look around the fields, squinting his eyes and finally pointing, he would show me the spot and say 'Plant it there.' He would say, 'Don't plant the oats there; this is the place.' I learned from him—not like the engineers who come here now and they don't know whether they're looking at oats or wheat or barley, but can read in *souri* and write in *souri*, and they've got their diplomas, but if you show them something in a different season from the pictures in the [agronomy] book they don't know what it is. Yes, we wore rags on our backs, we had nothing and we lived in *gourbis*, during the time of *la France*, but I learned everything I know from that *colon*.

And here, another;

Ali: There was a Dutch agricultural engineer who came here to the Chaouach UCP about fifteen years ago to be a foreign adviser and tell us how to run the farm. And he was standing in the fields and he said to me 'Where are your beans?' and I pointed down to his feet where he was crushing the plants and I said '*Ha-ho*' [right there]. He was standing on the beans and didn't even know it. So the fellahin got angry and told Mohammed Ghedira [head of the national agriculturalists' union at the time] and they said to him, 'Look, the man may be an agricultural engineer but he doesn't know any agriculture.' The Dutch engineer claimed that he had studied agriculture, that he knew the theory of how you ought to plant and grow things. And Mohammed Ghedira took him and he took a Tunisian fellah who couldn't even read, let alone read in *souri*, and he asked the fellahin which of the two he thought would make a better director, and the fellahin said the Tunisian who couldn't read or write would, because he had the experience. So Mohammed Ghedira said to the engineer, 'Go back and get on the plane back to Holland. We don't need you.' And the Tunisian who knew the land and the soil and how to plant, but did not know *souri* took charge of the cooperative.

When it emerges, unanticipated nostalgia for the *colons* expresses dissatisfaction with the *cooperants*. After all, it is quite safe to eulogize departed adversaries and inadvisable to publicly criticize current ones. The deep-rooted ambivalence allows the fellahin to commend the *colons* for precisely the same reasons they previously condemned them: their intimate connection with Tunisian soil.

The Semantics of Labor

The *cooperants*, unlike the *colons*, came to transform the fellahin, not just their farms. The proposed metamorphosis focuses on work patterns. The foreign developers enjoy "work for its own sake," and find it challenging—a positive attribute. They are not embarrassed to be seen working. The *cooperants* have chosen their profession and fully believe in the efficacy of their methods. They see work as a means towards a specified end and they are eager to transmit their knowledge, techniques, and funds to help the rural people attain the goals and priorities they have established. They expect that with tools and directives made available, the fellahin will work toward the promised goal of increased farm output. Unfortunately, the *souri* work ethic, as expounded and practiced by the *cooperants*, does not mesh with *ᶜarbi* notions, particularly with regard to the relationship between means and ends. Hard work—promoted by the foreign developers as pleasant and profitable—is, to the fellahin, fruitless at best and shameful at worst. The experience of the fellahin of Medjerda has repeatedly demonstrated that hard work is simply not rewarded by prosperity. On the contrary, it has been frequently rewarded by expropriation or, more recently, by "regrouping" into model state farms.

ᶜArbi and *souri* beliefs about work, what it is, who should do it, and where it leads differ in many ways. The most important of these include basic definitions of work, concepts of shame and modesty, and beliefs about the nature of divine grace, the advantages of personal connection, and the inevitability of fate.

Khidma and Qaḍiya / Work and Chores

The fellahin distinguish between *work* and *chores*. Both men and women have *qaḍiya* (chores), but women should not—and for the most part do not—work. *Khidma* (work) includes all farm tasks such as plowing, sowing, and harvesting, as well as any tasks for which a person is paid. Women's *qaḍiya* includes household tasks such as cooking, washing dishes and clothing, scrubbing floors, sewing, and caring for the children. For men, *qaḍiya* involves going out of the house or going into town to the market or to buy a packet of cigarettes—and generally includes a long stop at one of the town's cafes. Women say this stop is neither *khidma* nor *qaḍiya*—but simply a waste of time and money. Women's *qaḍiya* takes place in the home, and does not include going out or going to the market. Exceptions, of course, are in evidence: there is the rare widow who lives alone and must do her own marketing, or the rare bachelor who lives alone and must cook his own meals. Both *khidma* and *qaḍiya* are alike in that they are rarely performed alone; anyone who comes by is likely to join in the task, which is seen as an opportunity to socialize. Both *khidma* and *qaḍiya* may be compensated for with lunch, dinner, tea or help with other tasks—but only *khidma* is paid.

Women's *qaḍiya* takes place in the courtyard or surrounding rooms of the home; in other words, it takes place in "private" rather in "public" space. *khidma* and men's *qaḍiya* takes place in public—at the souk, in the fields, outside or in public buildings. Women who go to work or go to the souk trespass in men's space.

When women go out into the streets of town, they wrap themselves in their *safsaris* and make every effort to avoid places where men are known to congregate. They take the most inconspicuous route possible. The process of indirection they follow takes them on a circuitous route; they appear to walk in circles, whereas men customarily walk directly, in a straight line to their destination. The fact that the most public places lie at the center of town guarantees the circumlocutions of women. In their passage through town, women generally are accompanied by another member of the family, often a child. In one sense women are afraid to "invade" male space, but in another sense they—as do the men—have an abhorrence of isolation. Women who work—such as nurses, midwives, or teachers—are mostly city girls who commute from Tunis. They are tolerated, even admired, as long as they go directly to and from work, behave modestly, and avoid lingering on the streets. Local Medjerdiya girls who want to work outside the home often go to Tunis instead of getting a job locally.

Countrywomen, however, do not have these options and rarely leave the farm. Those who do work are temporary agricultural laborers; they are transported as a group to and from the fields by cart. Employers supply transportation because they say it is the only way to guarantee a steady work force. For a woman to be an agricultural laborer constitutes an open admission of her husband's poverty; there is no pride in it. Apart from the stigma of poverty that attends this work, women do not relish crossing the line into a male-dominated realm; it is an anxiety-provoking step. When an employer provides transportation, he is easing and legitimizing their right to do so. Foreign developers advocate greater female participation in the rural labor force, and landowners, state farm directors, and cannery managers indeed prefer female workers. Efforts to get them to the work location are worthwhile because the employers find that women work harder, do more careful work, and take fewer breaks. Unlike men, they do not stop to smoke cigarettes; nor do they drink as much tea as the men while they work, and they do not stop work to stare when supervisors visit. In addition, under certain circumstances, women are paid less than men—although this is against the law. The subdued demeanor of women working in men's spaces contrasts greatly to the ease they enjoy while performing household chores together behind the courtyard gates at home.

Samara: There has been only one farm woman—well known in the region—who defies not only the *khidma/qaḍiya* norms, but many others as well. She not only runs her own farm, but also rides a motor scooter, disdains wearing the white *safsari* veil dutifully worn in public by all the women of Medjerda save two (that is, until the 1980s when the *hjab* became an acceptable alternative), and has a loud voice in the regional meeting of the agriculturalists' union. Not surprisingly, she has business contacts rather than friendships, and no extended family in the region; she has been avoided by most of her female neighbors.

Samara has darker skin than is generally found in Medjerda. People of the region, self-conscious of the town's Andalusian heritage (if not their own), tend to associate darkness with roots in the southern villages at the edge of the Sahara. Yet, Samara's identification is with the capital and she is more familiar with the city than the fellahin of Medjerda. She was born on the outskirts of Tunis in a tin shack. Her father had died before she reached the age of ten. With no family in the capital—her parents had indeed migrated from the south—Samara worked outside the home to help her mother support the little family.

During the struggle for independence she became active in the Destour Party and later in the UNFT (Women's Union). In 1961 she was awarded a six hectare plot of land for her political activities and moved to Medjerda to live on her land and become a farmer. She was twenty-one years old, unmarried and with no prospects for marriage. She knew nothing of farming, had only a dry barren field to call her own, and had nothing to lose. Of the four women awarded land by the government—an experiment in itself—Samara was the only one to persist. The others gave their parcels to their husbands or brothers to work, for the land could not be sold.

Like most fellahin of the region Samara could not read or write, but she accepted the help of an American project in the area at the time and the developers helped her to apply for a bank loan that allowed her to get started. They suggested that she build a chicken coop and specialize in raising *souri* chickens. She could have workers in her fields some distance away, and tend the chickens herself close to the house. She followed the suggestion, and twenty years after being awarded the parcel she was turning over approximately three thousand *souri* chickens every three months—in addition to her successful intensive agriculture.

At the age of twenty-four, quite old by Tunisian standards, she married a Sahli who came to Medjerda to work for the region's state farms, testing, inoculating, and treating newly imported cows brought in by a Dutch development project. By 1979, at the age of thirty-nine, Ṣamara managed a prosperous farm. She had three children and planned to have no more. Her oldest daughter was in boarding school in Medjerda-*souri* since the family lived too far away for her to come home each day. Ṣamara had been president of the district UNFT for thirteen years. She remained active in Neo-Destour and regional politics. Her husband said she was a thoroughly modern woman and he proudly displayed clippings about her in the UNFT gazette and photos of her with the American project staff, and said that some people came a few years ago and made a film about her which won a prize somewhere in Europe.

We sit outside the house. There is no courtyard, just farm. As Ṣamara and her husband talk, they never stop working. They are piecing together some old broken chicken crates the Sahli picked up in Tunis this morning. Because they were broken the storekeeper said he could have them for free. The Sahli took ten crates which they would have otherwise have had to buy new at 25 dinars apiece. Repairing them by themselves was a saving of 250 dinars— over $1300.00. As he twists wire Ṣamara's husband says:

> We work with the *Projet Belge* now. We've gotten an automatic drinking trough to give our four cows water. Most of the fellahin don't have this. But cows do not get thirsty at one's convenience: in the winter they must be watered twice a day, but in the summer perhaps five times a day—even at night. With this device you don't have to waste your time bringing them water or taking them out to the canal and you don't waste water either. You are free to go and do something else.

Ṣamara nods in agreement and changes the subject to complain of the high cost of and difficulty finding agricultural laborers. She rehashes an old debate with her husband: "If the children were not in school they would help me more on the farm. Who am I doing this for if they are not interested?" A neighboring fellah comes by on his bicycle to purchase a couple of Ṣamara's chickens. Relatives have suddenly dropped by and he has no time to go to the souk and he does not want to kill any of his *ᶜarbi* chickens just yet. Ṣamara tells him what a good price he's getting and how tender her chickens are. She takes his money and drops it in her pocket. The fellah chats briefly, leaves, and Ṣamara resumes work on her crates.

She complains that the chickens are selling too slowly now; it is getting expensive to keep them and they are getting fat. "Now is the season for fish," adds her husband, "at the souk you can get three kilos of fish for the price of one chicken." Ṣamara says that she cannot afford to lower the price of her chickens or she will make no profit. She presses her hands over her eyes and complains of another throbbing headache. "I have to do the work of a man and take care of the house — *nikhdim, w-naqḍiy fi-dar"* she says. "Would you do it all again?" I ask. "Of course." she answers, looking up in surprise.

"Did you buy any of her *souri* chickens?" a neighboring fellah sourly asks, "They're not as good as our *ᶜarbi* ones—here, have one." "Did she invite you into the house?" asks his wife. "She is not hospitable" says the wife. "She does not want you to see how many chickens she has, or her televisions, or her refrigerators," explains the fellah's wife, "here, take these. Don't go back there" she says, pressing an *ᶜarbi* chicken into my hands and dropping six *ᶜarbi* eggs into my pockets. "Ṣamara is afraid of the evil eye" they agree. The display of her wealth and the ensuing jealousy might bring her misfortune, they explain, as if they had just discovered Foster's theory of the image of limited good.

Ironically, Ṣamara epitomizes the goals of the *souri* developers. She is a woman fellah who is encouraged by her husband; she is hard-working, frugal, values her time, and despite (or perhaps because of) her constant worrying, is economically successful. She is all *khidma* and some *qaḍiya* too. With her war hero status and political activity, she is made an example of by foreign developers and by representatives of the Ministry of Agriculture. Ṣamara is a woman comfortable in man's space without a veil in public and without a courtyard at home. She is praised from a distance, but in her own community she is isolated. Samara began as an outsider in Medjerda; she is still an outsider. For a Medjerdiya woman with local family ties, it would be even more difficult than it was for Ṣamarato begin to manage her own agricultural enterprise. Both Ṣamara and Soufya, however, have had the support of influential men in the community. To illustrate:

Soufya: Soufya is from a founding Andalusian family of Medjerda. Her father owns farms and a trucking business transporting agricultural products for other fellahin, and he is reputed to drink alcohol. The family lives in Medjerda-*ᶜarbi* in a stylish *dar ᶜarbi* elaborately furnished with European padded sofas and antique carved hardwood end tables (probably left over from one of the colonial farmhouses on what is now family property). The furniture is repaired by the sole remaining *colon* of Medjerda, an elderly Italian carpenter. Soufya is eighteen, the third of ten children. Her fifteen year old sister, Sounya, became engaged this year to the only son of another wealthy fellah. "Sounya is too young to marry," said their father, "I am opposed to it. But look at her," and he cupped his hands over his chest to show how developed she was, "If I kept her at home I would have to watch over her every minute." Soufya, on the other hand, is tall and thin "like a man," he says. She has fair hair and blue eyes. Two years ago she dropped out of school and she too would have married but her fiancé broke off the engagement: for Soufya wants to be a farmer like her father, and in this case, she has her father's support.

Because unlike her younger sister she is not noticeably physically developed, her father allows her to wear pants outside her own courtyard. She also rides a bicycle and wears a big straw hat like those worn by male agricultural workers. She has money which she herself has earned: her father gives her a weekly salary and trains her to manage his smallest plot of land—three hectares—as large a parcel as some fellahin have to support a family of ten. It is Soufya who pays the male workers and tells them what to plant and what tasks to perform each day. As in Samara's case, Medjerdis find it unnatural for a woman to handle money, let alone pay men for their labor. Her lack of interest in female tasks has been of some concern to the entire community. But Soufya says she hates being indoors with the women cooking, cleaning, sitting and getting fat. When her mother calls her to help make couscous she jumps in the truck and goes to the beach with her older brother—something else Medjerdiya girls should never do. As she rides her bicycle to "her" land, small boys taunt her, lob stones after her and sing: "*Soufya, Soufya, ṭful w-ela ṭufla?*" [Sofia, Sofia, (are you a) boy or a girl?]Once in the orchard she relaxes, sits on the ground under the shade of an apple tree, hands a coin to one of the workers to fetch some Coca Cola, and reveals her great dream: "Right there I will build a house, right there by the gate of the farm. One part for me and one part for my brother. There we will live together and farm the land."

Soufya's male traits—being tall and thin, wearing men's clothing, liking the outdoors, riding a bicycle, going to the beach, enjoying sports, having money, paying workers—and dreaming of agricultural enterprises—have resulted in teasing, ridicule, and the break-up of her engagement. Unlike Samara, who having dark skin and no family—disadvantages in attracting a husband—and, in her own terms, with 'nothing to lose', Soufya is from an old, respected, reputedly authentic Andalusian family. She has alabaster skin and blue eyes, and had a wealthy fiancé who was from an excellent family. Whereas Samara's choices have upgraded her life, Soufya's would not. Although both Ṣamara and Soufya were considered to be deviants in Medjerda, both of them have had the approval and support of the key men in their lives. And although they cross many male/female boundaries, there is one line beyond which neither will go. Says Soufya: "Here, women and we older girls do not go to the souk." Even for Ṣamara and Soufya, taking this step would be *ḥishma*—or shameful.

Ḥishma / Shame, Modesty

According to the fellahin of the region, being seen working is shameful. Work, particularly in connection with the soil, makes a public display of one's poverty and need to work. Neighbors and strangers alike may witness one's toil in the fields; then, if the land does not produce, one appears foolish or incompetent, or perhaps out of divine favor.

The Belgian Agricultural Extension Project was training a Tunisian counterpart to take over each position held by a foreign developer. The Tunisian counterpart to the Project Director claimed that he would love to work in the orchards of his own land, but that he was afraid his neighbors would see him. Given his "standing" as head of an agricultural development project, it would be shameful for him to be seen touching the trees. And what would his neighbors say if his orchard did not flourish? So instead of doing any work himself, he hired gardeners and others to tend the orchards while he supervised or watched from his window.

Here we meet with an ᶜ*arbi*/*souri* irony: the *colon*/*cooperant* who touches the soil is admired, the Tunisian shamed. In the examples cited, the *colon* is admired for doing something considered ᶜ*arbi*, while the Tunisian project director cannot bring himself to perform the same act. It is bad enough to have to touch the soil oneself, but it is much worse, as has been seen, if one's wife and daughter do so. Thus, the very fact that women are valued and even preferred as farm workers by developers and farm managers is *ḥishma*. Tunisian extension workers have expressed reluctance to convey foreign project directives to increase women's labor on the farms because they themselves do not believe that women belong in the fields. They ask: "How can we tell the fellahin to do something we ourselves believe is shameful?"

When developers advocate teaching sons new farming ideas and techniques so that they can come home and teach them to their fathers, this too is considered shameful. For many of the fellahin this tactic is too much to tolerate; this is especially true in families that are strictest about *ḥishma* in the family sphere: thus, a son should not speak in front of his father; he should never contradict his father if asked an opinion, and he should never display greater knowledge than his father. In fact, under certain conditions, both fathers and sons agree that it is better for a son to lie to his father than to say or admit something that would be shameful.

When developers seek greater female participation in farm labor it is unpleasant, but they can be ignored. When they want sons to teach fathers how to work it is an insult. Furthermore, the respect a son owes his father is, in the ᶜ*arbi* way, generalized or extended to the respect the young should display before their elders. Unfortunately, most of the agricultural extension workers trained by foreign developers are in their twenties and thirties, whereas the fellahin are considerably older. This, too, creates problems. For some of the fellahin it is intolerable to have young extension workers—who have never owned a farm, planted anything, or watched it grow—come uninvited, spouting book-learned directives on how a fellah should run his farm. Conflict involving *ḥishma* has led to more than one extension worker being physically removed from a farm. ·

Baraka / Blessing, Divine Grace

Observant, righteous, and holy men are blessed with God's grace, or *baraka*. They need not toil as other men. God favors their farms and their land produces when others fail. *'Inti 'alik bil-ḥarka w-ena 'aliya bil-barka*—so goes the expression—it is for you to toil and for me to receive the grace of God. However, devout farmers, let alone those endowed with *baraka*, are few. Those who exist are either old, wealthy, saints, or workers on state-managed farms. In other words, they generally have others who perform their farm tasks while they perform their religious duties. Sons, wives, co-workers, or their own workers help on the farm. In addition, saints receive contributions from followers in their order. Most small-scale fellahin say they cannot afford to be observant and, indeed, the fellahin have been notoriously irreligious. They have families to feed and harvests to sell. How, they ask, can we go to the mosque in town, take the time to pray at home, or fast when Ramadan falls during the critical summer harvests? On state farms, however, fasts and daily prayers can be observed without fear of losing one's wages, and without much effect on production.

Toward the beginning of his presidency, Bourguiba tried to encourage people to work harder and to give up fasting during Ramadan in order to make the country more productive:

> ... Bourguiba attacked the strongest of the traditional five pillars of Islam—the hallowed custom of fasting during the month of Ramadan, the one clearly visible manifestation of Islamic social solidarity. Even the Tunisians most deeply influenced by Western education and values adhered to the fast in their country, at least in public. Yet Bourguiba dared to attack it on the grounds that it paralyzed economic activity during a whole month. 'At a time when we are doing everything possible to increase our production, how' he asked, 'can we resign ourselves to give up our efforts and permit the production level to descend to the zero mark? ... I do not believe that religion should be able to impose such a sacrifice... This is an abusive interpretation of the religion. When fasting, man's physical forces are so depleted that he is obliged to cease all activity. No dogma is justification for such a rhythm... All practices of this religion are issues of logical intentions. But when they become incompatible with the necessary struggles of this life, this religion must be amended.'   (Bourguiba Speech 2/5/60, quoted in Moore 1965:56-7).

Moore adds:

> In 1917, when Tunisians were mobilized for agricultural work in war-torn France, the Sheikh El Islam gave them dispensation from fasting because

'these workers have gone to accomplish their mission ... not of their own free will but under compulsion by another and by order of their sovereign.' (Moore 1965:58 note 35).

How can one reconcile the fact that in 1917 the Sheikh El Islam's edict persuaded farm workers to break their fast and work, while in 1960 Bourguiba was unsuccessful? One possible answer lies in the lack of synchronization between the Islamic calendar and the seasonal one: in 1917, Ramadan began June 21—a critical time for the melon, tomato, and pepper harvests (Bacharach 1974). Gathering these crops can hardly be postponed, given the delicacy of the produce; once these crops are ripe, they must be gathered before they burst and brought to market before they rot. In 1960, when Bourguiba called for non-observance, the month of fasting began February 28—in other words, right *after* the olive harvest and therefore a good time to celebrate. In 1979, Ramadan began July 25—one day after the opening of the annual Medjerda agricultural fair, and hardly a time for the fellahin to slacken production. It was also—as in 1917—in the heart of the pepper, tomato, and melon season. Medjerdi farmers in 1978-79 seemed to share Bourguiba's perspective, but by the time Ramadan fell in the off-season, Tunisia was in the midst of an Arabization movement and Islamic revival; fasting became more the rule than the exception. It is possible, then, that the observance of Ramadan by fellahin, especially those who themselves labor in the fields, waxes and wanes according to the seasonal requirements of their crops.

Daily as well as annual religious observances do not fit in well with farm life. Whereas in town some men close their shops, go to the mosque, perform their ablutions, and pray five times a day, it is the rare fellah who prays either on the farm or at the mosque in town. The fellahin say that prayer and work, especially farm work, are incompatible. Their outlook subjects them to criticism; thus, while townsfolk admonish them for not performing their prayers, the developers berate them for not working. Fellahin who till the soil are trapped between *ᶜarbi* and *souri* poles, pleasing no one—not even themselves—while land-owning fellahin who hire laborers, are able to live and pray in town, have workers in their fields, and literally enjoy the best of both worlds.

While the fellahin consider prayer and work to be incompatible, *baraka* and work are seen as complementary. Although prayer and fasting are religious obligations, they do not affect the successful outcome of any task, including farming; one does not pray *for* something, one simply performs one's prayers to express one's devotion and submission to God and as part of one's responsibility as a Muslim. Prayer is an expression of thanks for what one has already received. *Baraka*, on the other hand, is a rare gift that brings results and works to the possessor's material good. Of course, there are still impoverished fellahin who possess *baraka*—but such individuals, say Medjerdis, would be poorer still without their hereditary divine grace. The following illustrates the aid even a small amount of *baraka* can bestow:

Si Maskin: Si Maskin is a marabout, or holy man, in the region. He lives with his wife and eleven children in a mud and straw *gourbi* on a fragment of land between his neighbors' farms on the banks of the Medjerda River. Si Maskin's wife and older children tend their two cows and keep the donkey and *ᶜarbi* chickens off their neighbors' irrigated crops.

Si Maskin dresses immaculately in a white embroidered *jibba*—as is fitting for a saint. He speaks very little—each word is gift. He is rarely at home; his wife says that he goes to Tunis to meet with others of his order and with their followers. At the end of each agricultural season sacks of grain, olives, and peppers appear at the courtyard door. Si Maskin arrives home on his donkey-drawn *karita* carrying a sheep for *ᶜAi'd*, a gift from a neighboring landowner. He goes to the Friday souk in Medjerda with one sack of grain and returns home with holiday clothing for the children, a new *safsari* for his wife, olive oil, vegetables, and a new earthen storage pot. Said a fellah and distant cousin: "Si Maskin is not a major [*kbir*] saint. If he had more *baraka* he would be richer." The impoverished marabout receives gifts in proportion to those he gives, and is considerably less well-off than his neighbors. His *baraka* is innate, and its quantity cannot be changed; indeed, to date, none of his children appear to have inherited any of it at all; he watches each son carefully for the signs of a righteous one [*wld b'iligdeh*]. As the number of his children increases, he and his wife have found another blessing they can bestow on those in need: one or two barren women have been honored to raise an infant born to Si Maskin and his wife.

Despite the fact that Si Maskin is a local marabout, there are non-maraboutic farmers who reap the benefits of *baraka* to a greater extent than he:

Si Nuredine: A farmer in the region who is considered devout is playfully called, "the man who loves his wife." He employs his wife and daughters in the field every day in all seasons. For miles around they are the only people seen picking or planting, pruning or weeding, while those on neighboring farms are indoors or sipping tea. The neighbors laugh at this devout fellah. Some say it is shameful to see his womenfolk in the open all the time. Others explain that he is crafty and is actually protecting their modesty; they are constantly under his surveillance and therefore can do nothing shameful. "He keeps them in the fields to guard them, for why else? He has *baraka* and his fields and sheep take care of themselves." In other words, he does not need their labor.

His name is Si Nuredine. He has thirty-five hectares, half of which are irrigated, half dry-farmed. He lives with his mother, wife, son and four daughters in a *gourbi*. The family has no electricity or running water. To reach the farm one must go three kilometers over an alternately muddy or dusty dirt road strewn with rocks. Si Nuredine was awarded his land because of his active role in both the struggle for independence and in the cooperative movement. He learned agriculture from both his father and from the *colons*. He says that he loves the French but he loves independence too; he was willing to work for the cooperative but he enjoys having his own land better. Nuredine dresses *ᶜarbi* with a red *chechia* on his head and a towel wrapped around it to form a turban. He also wears a long faded blue worker's jacket, pantaloons and plastic sandals. Salha, his wife, dresses in a faded red country woman's *meliya*. The teenage children wear second-hand Western *frippe*. Salha or one of the daughters bakes fifteen loaves of *khubz tabouna* almost every day, although Nuredine sometimes brings back French bread from his weekly trip to town. Salha makes her own clay pots, pitchers and *kanouns* but she has two aluminum cooking pots and a *couscousière* as well. She likes the earthenware better but it does not last as long.

Like his neighbors, Si Nuredine takes some of his produce on his *karita* to the Friday souk at Medjerda, but transports most of his harvests in bulk to the farmers' market in Tunis. He rents a truck at a discount from his brother. Unlike his neighbors he sets aside money each month to pay the installments on his land. Like his neighbors Nuredine has a donkey, a few cows, *ᶜarbi* chickens and a modest flock of about fifty sheep. But unlike them, Si Nuredine's sheep require no shepherd. The neighbors say that Nuredine's sheep, like his fields, benefit from his *baraka*: on their own the sheep stay out of his irrigated fields. They never trespass, do not go into the road, and do not bother anyone. The sheep go out in the morning by themselves and return in the evening of their own accord. Nuredine's explanation for his unique flock is that they are well trained and that he has a good leader-ram. Furthermore, he says, "why waste labor guarding sheep when there is work to be done?"

Si Nuredine smiles a lot but speaks little. He does not invite us into the house to sit and eat and talk but insists that we return frequently to visit while he works. When pressed to explain his success he says simply that it is not *baraka* but rather that he has lazy neighbors. "God," says Si Nuredine, "wants man to work." And so he works.

Si Nuredine's example demonstrates a successful combination of *ᶜarbi* and *souri* strategies, and an interpretation of *ᶜarbi* values rare among the fellahin. His idea of *ḥishma* allows him to employ female labor from his own family without concern. Family labor is further maximized by Si Nuredine's attitude towards his sheep, and his belief that God wants man to be productive. He is also aided by a discount from his brother in renting farm equipment and transportation and from having emerged a hero in the struggle for independence—for which he was awarded a rather large piece of land, initially both rocky and dry. His wife uses birth control, and he only has five children compared with the significantly larger families of his neighbors, many of whom have between twelve and fifteen children. Furthermore, his only son will inherit the entire farm (he will work his sisters' portions and give them their shares of the profits), and keep his land intact. At present, Si Nuredine also benefits from the fact that his children are between the ages of twelve and twenty—old enough to perform farm tasks with little supervision, and not yet old enough to marry or leave home.

The farm itself is half *ᶜarbi*, half *souri*. On his mid-size farm, Si Nuredine has both dry-farmed rocky hills with roaming sheep and irrigated valleys with garden vegetables; both hand and machine labor. His savings are both in sheep and cash; he has both *baraka* and *pistons*. Nuredine is both an admirer of the French and a hero in the struggle for independence. Instead of building a house and moving out of the *gourbi*, he reinvests in the land. Although all the farmers in Medjerda combine *ᶜarbi/souri* features, Nuredine's synthesis is unique in that he combines what is considered by all to be truly the best of both worlds.

Kteff and Pistons / Connections

In Arabic, *kteff* are "shoulders" lifting a person higher than could be reached on his own. *Pistons*—a French word pronounced *"biseton"* in the Tunisian rural dialect of Arabic—are the *souri* equivalents of *kteff*. Both terms refer to intervention by those who can propel another up and forward. The first term, *kteff*, contains imagery which evokes bonds of personal interdependence while the second, *pistons*, implies an impersonal, mechanistic, automatic boost given proper ignition. Just as the fellahin say that men with *baraka* need not tend their farms because God will see that their land is productive, so it is with those who have *kteff* or *pistons*. The aid in this case comes not from God, however, but from well-connected people who can bestow or exchange favors; community or union leaders, farm managers, rich landowners, relatives, friends, extension workers, and foreigners. As one fellah put it: all the hard work in the world will not get you as far as one good *piston*.

> "...How did the Sfaxi get where he is now?" I asked, when I had first been told about him and the effect he had had on the region.
>
> "Because he works?" answered Si Mahmoud's son tentatively.
>
> *"Pistons!"* corrected Si Mahmoud, laughing. "He knows other Sfaxis who know the Sahlis who know the President. That's how. It's like a *silsila*, a chain."
>
> Si Mahmoud linked his two index fingers together. "People are linked together: the rich have their own links and the poor have theirs. But the rich, when they link up into a chain they can pull the others along." And he gave a yank with his hands. "The Sfaxi is one of these."

"What did he do before he came to Medjerda?" I asked.

Si Mahmoud laughed again and so did his son. "He was a mechanic, a car mechanic in Sfax. He knew more about machines than crops so he mechanized the whole farm! And now he is the richest fellah in the region."

The analogy of the chain, or *silsila*, is also the classic way to describe the genealogical transmission of *baraka* through spiritual descent (see e.g. Trimmingham, 1973). But in this case, the *pistons* link people through space, not time, and are activated by human and mechanical implements, not God. Whereas people solicit the intercession of their *pistons* , those who receive *baraka* do so only through the grace of God. *Na*ᶜ*arif il-mas'oul—je connais le responsable* [I know the man in charge], a poor fellah may say to explain a favor done for him. In contrast, a wealthy fellah downplays the role of *pistons*, and either credits hard work or God's will for his success. For a man to acknowledge that he has *pistons*, or can be used as one, is to bring upon himself requests from all quarters. This is exactly the position in which foreign developers find themselves.

Foreign developers have come explicitly to aid the fellahin and are therefore by definition, *pistons*. To many fellahin, however, their criteria for aid appear more mystical than the transmission of *baraka* itself. Those fellahin who are outside the scope of particular development projects view the rejection of aid either as *maktoub*, or destiny, or say at the outset that they did not have enough *pistons* to get themselves included in the project.

The reason for one impoverished fellah's fortuitous inclusion in the *Projet Belge* was beyond his comprehension, despite the fact that he himself had pursued the project director. Si Hamadi's goal in signing a contract with foreign developers was to "*pistoner*" himself to the acquisition of more land: He quite understood his own motivations and he firmly believed that his years of compliance would be rewarded with the additional parcel that would ease the overcrowding of his single hectare.

Si Hamadi's case points to the difference between the goals of the fellahin and those of the *souri* developers. Development goals are to increase production on the farms; fellahin working on the project want "to live better" (see Zussman, 1983). This is why, for example, Hamadi built a larger house for his growing family instead of buying cows for the farm—much to the fury of the project staff. Interestingly enough, Si Hamadi has more faith in the value of his Belgian *pistons* than he has in his own work abilities. He is not alone in this outlook; both his neighbors and the project staff admit that Si Hamadi could never have reached his present position on his own merit. What would happen to Hamadi when the Belgians left the region—as was rumored they would? For despite the benefits of choosing foreign developers as *pistons*, they have the distinct disadvantage of lacking permanence. The Belgian project director left Tunisia; Si Hamadi remained with his mother, wife, ten children, and less than one hectare of land to farm. When Arabization became the policy of the 1980's reliance upon *"souri"* technology and advice came to be disparaged. The Belgian Agricultural Extension Project began its exodus after eighteen years of stewardship, and Hamadi, for one, could only sigh and proclaim that all is *maktoub*. Yet when the time came, it be-came clear that he had also shrewdly preserved his bond with the richest fellah of the region throughout his years of tutelage under the foreign developers.

Maktoub / "It Is Written"

To many of the fellahin, one's material or spiritual wealth reflects a state of innate being like that of being male or female. Saying that something is *maktoub* helps explain great and small injustices. It is common knowledge in Medjerda that neither hard work nor schooling necessarily leads to prosperity. *Baraka* is predetermined by God and heredity. *Pistons* help only those who already possess them. Poor people remain poor. When one farmer is chosen by the *cooperants* as the recipient of financial and technical aid, while his neighbor is not, the best explanation offered for this injustice is simply that it was *maktoub*. *'Allah ghalib*, say the fellahin, in a gesture of despair—God is supreme.

Fellahin claim they continue to be given directives rather than alternatives; as a consequence they feel acted-upon, frustrated and powerless even though independence was intended to be their own. *Ma-ᶜendish foursa* goes the saying—"I don't have any strength." But the fellahin's image of strength—*foursa*— is a French term: *la force*, power, strength, authority, vitality. Thus, this phrase reaches deeply into the erosion of strength that the fellahin feel in what appears to be an increasingly influential *souri* world. The significance of *el foursa* is twofold. Lack of it indicates physical depletion, exhaustion, and inability to work; by extension, it implies loss of virility. State policy makers, attributing these feelings to symptoms of "peasant mentality," had prescribed not only adopting but mastering *souri* models, skills, and technology. For the compliant fellah the result was all too often a sense of futility at having tried and succeeded, but in the end having found himself tilling toxic, depleted parcels of land. The productivity of the land had become dependent on perpetuating the balancing act of chemical treatments, hybridized crops and specialized equipment—all of which were no longer free samples and for which spare parts were suddenly completely unavailable.

Wholesale rejection of all things *souri*, however, was not forthcoming. In Medjerda, each arena—local, national and international—continues to be categorized along ᶜ*arbi/souri* lines. Within the local arena, the dual use pattern is tangible, quantifiable, and visible (see Figure 6.1). Fellahin and their families pick and choose between alternatives, consciously and unconsciously playing out an uneasy syncretism—sometimes on a thespian stage, costumed in ascot and walking stick or *kashabiya* and *chechia*, for there is always an audience in the courtyard or the fields.

Medjerdis tentatively welcomed Arabization as it encouraged trust in inner strength, a return to Islam, and promotion of Arabized education. Thus, French language studies became optional in many secondary schools and were supposed to be deleted from primary school curricula. Foreign development programs, as in the case given above, were either terminated or reduced in duties, jurisdiction and personnel despite the fact that they were quite willing to continue—or expand—their aid. The Belgians, for example had nowhere else to go. Most had come directly from the Congo, had transformed themselves from *colons* to *cooperants* en route and had nothing awaiting them in Belgium. It is possible that the Arabization policies reflected greater aid, influence or financial assistance from Tunisia's Arab neighbors, such as Libya; or an emerging *carbi* self-awareness when Tunisia became the new home of the Arab League. Nevertheless, Arabization did not end the Tunisian proclivity for things *souri*.

cArbi and *Souri* as Metaphor

By their opposition, *carbi* and *souri* have come to define all aspects of the "other." The terms seem to have expanded in the post-colonial world, rather than diminished. They have gained definition, clarity and precision. The *souri* world has become more accessible, more alluring, more desperately wanted in the same era in which Medjerdis have been immersed in Islamic and Arabic revivalism. The colonial metaphor has not gone away, it has grown. And yet, no rural family in Medjerda seeks to live a wholly bifurcated existence. Perhaps they seek the Andalusian merger of the two— the Mediterranean identity—not *carbi* or *souri* alone, but an unselfconscious synthesis.

For now, *carbi/souri* imagery penetrates all aspects of home and farm life in Medjerda. Fellahin debate the merits of various *carbi* or *souri* objects, traits and philosophies, and recognize that each fellah blends the two in a distinctive way. No Medjerdi has chosen an unequivocal path; not the Hadj, not the sheikh, not the manager of the state farm. One father berates his son for poor performance in school by wrapping a towel, turban-style, around his son's head, and calling him "fellah" all evening—implying that lack of success will keep him a country bumpkin like his cousins at Sidi Ug^cud. Soon after, he may belittle his son for too much pointless book-learning and not enough respect. The vacillation played out in the courtyard mirrors the oscillations and reversals of national policy. Fellahin sometimes character- ize each other as either *carbi* or *souri* farmers but their classifications are based more upon personal characteristics—such as dress, religiosity, house

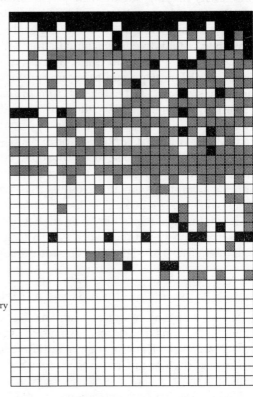

FIGURE 6.1 The *ᶜArbi-Souri* Continuum: A Sample of Farm Families of Medjerda

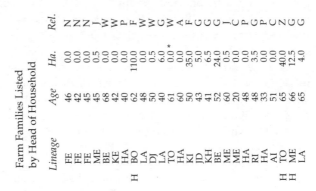

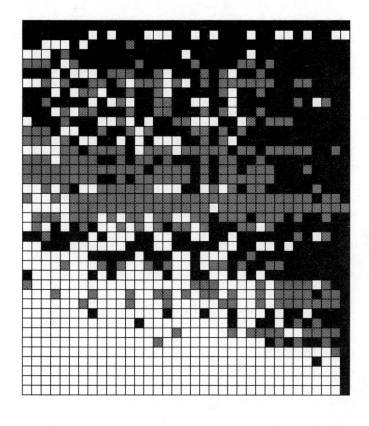

Relation to Land
A Agro-Combinat Workers
C Cooperateurs
F Farmers on Private Parcel

G Farmers on Agrarian Reform Parcel
J Farmers with Farm-Related Businesses
M Managers of Farms
N Nomads, Nomadic Cultivators

P Workers on State and Private Land
W Workers on Private Land
Z Farmers with Non-Farm Businesses
* Fellahin with land outside Delegation

type, social network, tribal affiliation, and strictness in the family—than upon farm practices. Urban, rural, or tribal origins help fellahin to place people along the *ᶜarbi/souri* continuum. Thus, wealthy, religious farmers from respected local families are classed as more *ᶜarbi* than "outsider" urban farm entrepreneurs *even if their techniques are identical*. It is not surprising that the first group dresses *ᶜarbi*, generally lives in Medjerda-*ᶜarbi*, and forms a closely-knit clique which represents the long-standing traditional elite of the local community. This group is bound together by both kinship and friendship, and includes religious leaders like the Imam, as well as members of the two families who in the past alternately held the position of sheikh, or *ᶜomda*. Members of the second group, the outsiders, dress *souri*, drink alcoholic beverages, consider their Medjerdi land-holdings as investments and look upon their Medjerda-*souri* homes as temporary. They, too, form a social clique and an elite in the region, bound by class rather than kinship. However, they represent the leadership only in secular affairs, such as banking, regional politics, and state rural development programs. It is this group of outsiders who, in addition to running their own farms, also hold positions in which they work with foreign developers to transform other fellahin and their farms.

The *ᶜarbi/souri* dichotomy is most apparent in personal and household characteristics because it is in these spheres that the fellah has the greatest freedom of action. Whereas, in the home the fellah initiates family policy, on the farm he is the recipient of state policy. State policies, however, reflect the vagaries of political upheaval and have been far from static. Each fellah's *ᶜarbi/souri* blend reflects both his *ᶜarbi* roots and his *souri* encounters. These encounters give rise to ambivalence and have a profound impact not only upon the fellahin and their farms, but also upon their families and homes. Wives find it difficult to join the work force, sons are sensitive about bringing directives to their fathers and are reluctant to break down traditional areas of respect, daughters—after being enticed by the privilege of attending school—have few options other than those provided by accepted *ᶜarbi* norms, and hybrid homes reflect the display of *souri* influence or affluence amidst still enfolding *ᶜarbi* ways.

The Search for Authenticity

"Souri" may be a colonial intrusion onto the land and into the imagination, yet the fellahin of Medjerda have been alloying *ᶜarbi* and *souri* substances for a great deal longer than the past century. They are well aware of Medjerda's intrinsic Andalusian—and thus, European—bond, as well as its ancient connection with Rome. And unlike neighboring Algeria or Morocco, there are no "pure" Berber peoples in the region, who speak their own

languages and preserve their own customs, thus serving as a model for a truly indigenous identity. Tunisia, maritime power of Carthage and bread-basket of Rome, has always been at the cross-roads.

ᶜArbi imagery invokes a vision of local conditions, practices, subsistence patterns and decision-making as if they at one time existed. Yet northern Tunisia has been accountable to European influence since Carthage ruled the seas, pre-dating the arrival of Arabs in North Africa by almost a thousand years. The dream of autonomy nevertheless remains, poignantly symbolized by the adamant attachment to sheep and shepherding, in-compatible with every national plan for developing the rural sector to create national autonomy through self-sufficient agriculture. Whether the *souri* patina adds or detracts from the search for authenticity may be debated; it is nevertheless difficult to obliterate. The fellahin of Medjerda have been marked by prolonged contact with the colonizer and by his replacement, the foreign development worker. No untainted "traditional man" or pristine peasant mentality exists to be rated on a modernity scale (see Inkeles, 1974:73-83) and transformed, despite the attempt by development workers to portray these fellahin as such and change them. This oversimplification overlooks the fact that in Medjerda the fellahin are well-acquainted with both the theory and practice of European agricultural methods, for so many of the formerly nomadic fellahin—well over half the rural families of the region—were first taught agricultural methods by colonial farmers.

In the interface between developers and fellahin, we find conflicting priorities and values. State officials and foreign extension workers have demanded growth on the part of the agricultural sector in order to feed the increasing urban population and in order to bring about Tunisian self-sufficiency; foreign advisers have demanded that fellahin reinvest in their land in order to meet national goals. The fellahin, however, have viewed development in personal terms as distinct from the collective national good. They have expected to earn higher profits; they have hoped to increase their material wealth, improve their living conditions, and provide greater leisure for themselves, and security for their children. "Peasant oppositionalism" is rational from this perspective. Furthermore, the un-comfortable blur between *colon* and *cooperant*—in which some fellahin firmly believe *cooperants* to be children of the colonizer come back to tend their land until their return—is no ill-founded association. As we have seen, in many cases, the foreign developers were themselves colonizers in another land and have nowhere left to go.

Fernand Braudel would see the persistence of *souri* imagery as the work of the long term historical perspective, the ebb and flow of contact across the Mediterranean; Tunisia as a cross-road intersecting both time and space. The fellah, in this view simply follows the fluctuating current between the two shores:

So when I think of the individual, I am always inclined to see him imprisoned within a destiny in which he himself has little hand, fixed in a landscape in which the infinite perspectives of the long term stretch into the distance both behind and before. In historical analysis as I see it, rightly or wrongly, the long run always wins in the end.   (Braudel 1973:1244)

Pierre Bourdieu, on the other hand, bids the fellah to assume full responsibility for his own hybridized life (1962:157). While fellahin await an era in which the dualism would die out, they continue to endure the intermittent presence of foreign and state rural development advisers. In the region of Medjerda, *ʿarbi* expands in meaning and meaningfulness in opposition to the persistence of *souri* influence). Both images are reinforced by the spread of media and travels abroad. Fellahin reassess and revise their myths, legends and histories of the colonial past and recast them into new authentic visions or versions of their place in the contemporary universe. From their revised vantage point they have discovered that Tunisia continues—and will continue—to be acted-upon by the *souri* world.

دفَعَ اللّـهُ ما كانَ أعظَم

7

Mutual Disenchantments

daf'a 'allah ma-kan 'atham
May God prevent what could well be worse

Developers have described the fellahin of the lower Medjerda Valley as being risk-averse—a condition symptomatic of what they call the *"mentalité des fellahin."* By this they have meant that rural people are "non-maximizers" utilizing the "safety-first" principle when faced with the uncertainty of innovative alternatives (see Scott 1976; Nygaard 1979). Specifically, fellahin have been seen as averse to adopting the methods of the Green Revolution as advocated by agricultural extension workers. To be sure, there have always been good reasons for small-scale farmers to avoid risk. Their tension over the uncertainty of weather, markets, and fluctuating demand has been a perennial source of concern (see e.g. Ortiz 1973, 1979; Barlett 1980; Hill, 1989). But for the fellahin of the Medjerda Valley—and most likely for rural people everywhere—there has been the inescapable additional burden of political uncertainty.

In the Tunisian context, this has manifested itself in the decolonization process and in continuous policy changes during the post-colonial period. As we have seen, for farmers in both the public and private sectors political instability has been a crucial factor in determining both short term economic strategies and long-range goals. Fellahin, however, rarely have been willing to risk overt opposition to the land policies they abhor. Theirs has been a kind of quiet oppositionalism; each individual follows strategies suited to his own personal and family requirements; these have taken precedence over state directives.

The fellahin of the lower Medjerda Valley have witnessed a long history of national policy changes. They have experienced first hand the implementation of national and regional land reform experiments and agricultural development initiatives. Frequent changes in agrarian policy as well as conflict between state and farmer priorities have contributed to a loss of commitment to the development process. The result is removal of long-range investments in agriculture by rural people and massive migration to urban centers which cannot absorb unskilled labor.

The Medjerda Valley presents us with a familiar struggle. Rural people—colonized by European settlers, promised land by post-independence governments, expropriated by cooperative experiments, abandoned by foreign developers, and overtaken by non-local privatization entrepreneurs—have learned to bypass formal mechanisms for reform in favor of unauthorized economic innovations which guarantee personal and family survival. The conclusion that political uncertainty contributes to non-compliance with development programs should be no surprise. This scenario transcends the northern Tunisian pastoral landscape and may be all too easily transferred to a larger canvas—one which depicts the longstanding uneasy global interface of foreign development workers, national policy-makers, and rural people. This larger canvas could perhaps be painted in even more somber hues and longer shadows than official development project reports have yet conveyed. After all, the continuation of programs depends upon evaluations which demonstrate some degree of success or progress.

The dimensions of mutual disenchantment and the ironies which impede the process of development have been shown here to be multi-faceted. First has been the problem resulting from accelerated change—irrespective of the direction of that change. Second have been the problems emanating from the co-existence of residual farm types from failed or superceded national plans. These include a variety of public, private and cooperative farms, both centralized and decentralized. Third, and perhaps the most difficult to eradicate, has been the psychology of disenchantment. This includes the conflicting values, perceptions and priorities of foreign developers, policy-makers, and fellahin. These mutual perceptions reflect concerns over one's own identity and assumptions about the "other." The parallels between colonialism and foreign aid have been painful psychological barriers to full compliance and will come into play in future plans for joint ventures with foreign entrepreneurs. Consideration of these three dimensions will lead to a better understanding of the the relationship between the individual and the state in private, cooperative and state farming. But more than this, locally acceptable rural development begins only when these issues are acknowledged, addressed and resolved.

Accelerated Change

Agricultural policies in Tunisia have mirrored fluctuations of the national political climate as well as shifting trends of international development theory. As a result, the country has oscillated between two competing ideologies—centralization and decentralization—and has produced a succession of incompatible agrarian reforms and land tenure institutions.

The complex sequence of post-independence changes began with the nationalization of colonial estates. These came under the centralized management of a number of state agencies, beginning with the *Office des Terres Domaniales* for dry land and the *Office de la Mise en Valeur de la Vallée de la Medjerda* for irrigable land. As state agencies proliferated for special-use land categories, large-scale farms were transferred back and forth between them. Due to constant administrative changes at the national level, management turnover on state farms sometimes occurred every four to six months rather than the prescribed three-year term. During this initial decolonization phase, some parcels were allotted to heroes of the struggle for independence, others were regrouped into farming collectives made up of former colonial workers, and a minority of parcels were sold outright to private entrepreneurs. Most of the nationalized land, however, was regrouped into semi-autonomous agricultural production cooperatives whose directors were representatives of the state.

When the cooperative movement was expanded beyond the boundaries of nationalized land it was opposed decisively and the movement failed. However, not all of the cooperatives were then dismantled and redistributed to former cooperateurs. The now small-scale parcels were not privately owned but became part of a so-called decentralized agrarian reform program which nevertheless managed to keep the land under the jurisdiction of state agencies. Ironically, at the same time that the cooperatives were "decentralized," a number of large private parcels were nationalized and incorporated into the most centralized of all farming systems in Tunisia—the agro-combinat.

By the 1980s, land reform, like the reforms in other sectors of the Tunisian economy, concentrated on developing the private sector. In this period, agrarian planning came to affect a hitherto untouched category of land-holdings—fragmented, or dispersed, private parcels. Plans were drawn up to regroup private holdings, modifying both their shape and size in order to conform to the state directive to transform the land from dry to irrigated farming.

To date, farm types continue to reflect the era in which development plans were applied to a given parcel of land. Thus, the lower Medjerda Valley retains cooperative, state and private parcels. The valley has mixed farming, ranging from capital-intensive large-scale farms to labor-intensive small-scale ones. The Sixth Plan, long debated in the Tunisian General Assembly in the 1980s, called for some form of compromise between the two outlooks. Throughout the Bourguiba period the result was the continued coexistence of farm types rather than privatization of state land.

The post-Bourguiba era began in November, 1987 with the declaration that the octogenarian president was unfit to lead the nation. Under President Zine al-Abdine Ben Ali, national reforms were once again on the agenda. The anticipated reforms of the 1990s accelerate the trend of mobilizing the potential of private landholdings. The state finally has acknowledged officially what the fellahin have long maintained—that large-scale state-managed farms and cooperatives have failed to raise Tunisian agricultural production to the level of self-sufficiency. The newest land reform proposals call for the gradual privatization and parcellization of the vast OTD and OMVVM holdings themselves. In theory, the proposed dismantling of these two land management "super powers" is exactly what the fellahin have longed for for decades. It remains to be seen to what extent the proposals will be carried out and who will be the real beneficiaries of these reforms. The fellahin of Medjerda are certain to expect "outside" investors, speculators and entrepreneurs to once more gain control over land that local Medjerdis yearn to possess themselves.

Among the major transformations long on the agenda is the as yet incomplete process of Arabization—the move away from dependence on European advisers and technology and toward greater reliance on aid, trade, and loans from within the Arab world. However, the influence and presence of European advisers advocating *"souri"* ways has not only remained, but by 1990, Tunisia has found itself seeking even stronger bonds with the West — particularly with the United States' "Silicon Valley" industries, in order to move in the direction of introducing computer technologies into all sectors of the economy, including agri-business. The lessons of political uncertainty, however, have not been lost upon potential American investors who have remained reluctant to enter into Tuniso-American partnerships.

In sum, oscillations of national policy have continued to leave their mark on rural institutions and to affect the daily lives and long-range plans of rural people. Fellahin have found themselves workers under one national plan, cooperateurs under another, and agrarian reform farmers under still a third. They may soon find themselves workers once again—this time for Sfaxi or Sahli entrepreneurs and foreign investors. Unfortunately, the transitions between each national plan have been accompanied by losses in agricultural production for the state, as well as by reductions of confidence on the part of the fellahin. Farmers respond to changing programs with varying degrees of compliance, innovation, apathy, fatalism, cynicism, and defiance according to their current position and capacity to direct their own lives. Their responses have been less in opposition to specific reforms than in reaction to the turbulence of a lifetime of pendulum-swing policies.

The impermanency of institutions is only one dimension of accelerated change. The proliferation of supposedly enduring reforms is yet another. Agrarian reform laws in the lower Medjerda Valley have required irrigation of all irrigable land; the law has specified what to grow on any given category of land, and has even gone so far as to indicate how far apart to space trees and crops. Non-compliance has been threatened with expropriation. While technological changes have brought about the mechanization of many remaining cooperatives, as well as the transformation of high yield seed varieties, the construction of plastic greenhouses and the extension of an irrigation network throughout the Medjerda Valley, these have led to greater dependence on foreign aid. Foreign projects and agricultural extension services have converged on the region in order to install the new technologies and to teach people how to use them. Parts and seeds must be continually reordered from abroad. Change has been planned not only in agriculture but also in every sphere of life. Family law (based initially upon the reforms of the Personal Status Codes of 1958) has continued to advocate specific women's rights and—like the agrarian laws—to allow for legal recourse in cases of non-compliance. In addition, the growing availability of health care, birth control, education, and high technology opportunities in the country provide further incentives—or pressures—to change. Tunisia's population is more literate and better informed than ever before. Despite the foregoing, customary practice has continued to diverge from or lag behind statutory regulation in all spheres. It should be noted, however, that these reforms have not gone without effect. Policy changes have become identified more with increasing uncertainty rather than with progress. Furthermore, greater literacy in the rural sector has had the side-effect of producing a growing population of *chomeur-deluxe* youths unwilling to participate in agriculture.

Centralized, Intermediate, and Decentralized Farms

Tunisian policy of the 1990s promises to bring private enterprise to the forefront of the development process. The checkered history of post-independence agrarian reform invites a guarded reaction on the part of the fellahin to the current emphasis on revitalizing the private sector of the fertile Medjerda Valley.

The diversity of farm types per se has not been objected to by the fellahin; rather, it has been the lack of resolution of the ambiguities and contradictions in the application of reforms which has led to resentment and oppositionalism. Thus, while the implications of the term 'centralization' have been unmistakable to fellahin and policy-makers alike, 'decentralization' has been an ambiguous term which has generated a good deal of misunderstanding. Nor has 'privatization' ever meant a policy of total farmer autonomy and the fellahin of Medjerda will be greatly suprised to see privatization actually lead to land title in their own names.

The agricultural production cooperatives—which are in theory midway between centralized and decentralized systems—have remained the most problematic of farm types in Tunisia. Ideally speaking, the UCPs were to have been semi-autonomous organizations; their members not only were to have had authority to make decisions through their general assembly, but also to have been considered share-holding owners of the farm. Lilia Ben Hamza reminds us that a major goal of the Tunisian cooperative movement in the 1960s was "an almost utopian *decentralization* of decision-making" of agricultural production (Ben Hamza 1976: 279). Yet, even at the height of the movement, decision-making remained centralized under the supervisory control organisms of the Ministry of Agriculture. This contradiction between cooperative theory and practice has continued to plague the cooperateurs who live and work under ambiguous status. During the Bourguiba era, the struggle between policies aimed at maintaining state control and those advocating greater farmer autonomy persisted well past the demise of the cooperative experiment.

The case in point is the Fifth Plan era, in which decentralization and entrepreneurship in the private sector were first tentatively encouraged. During this period, state agencies like the OTD continued to manage hundreds of large-scale farms under their jurisdiction despite protests that this was in violation of the Fifth Plan promise of decentralization. Instead of parcelling out state farms and cooperatives, these state organisms interpreted the policy as *decentralization of sub-agencies, not parcellization of farms*. This interpretation led to a further proliferation of specialized state organizations under the Ministry of Agriculture, including the formation of a new Bureau of Control (BCUPN) to direct management of the remaining agricultural production cooperatives.

On the local level, if a UCP general assembly is convened at all, cooperateurs have found their authority limited by statute and their decisions circumscribed by representatives of supervisory bodies. The cooperateurs' claim that if they could, they would vote to disband the UCP altogether and distribute the land amongst themselves should not be taken lightly, and may well be sanctioned under the Ben Ali administration. Quite plainly, cooperateurs have felt demoralized and disenfranchised. They have lacked both status and power—being neither farmers nor farm workers; they have possessed neither land nor a union to represent their interests.

In addition, they have derived little comfort from the prosperity of neighbors who have been allotted individual family farms after their cooperatives failed. The dismantling of only selected cooperatives left those who remained behind isolated on residual farms of a once-favored—but later abandoned—large-scale socialist experiment. In full expectation of the continued trend of policy reversals, cooperateurs have attempted to anticipate the politics of the future and to plan for the day when their own cooperatives are dismantled and subdivided. In this regard, they do not wish to be further deceived or disappointed.

The agrarian reform parcels which have been envied by members of the UCP and state farm workers are not without their own distinctive set of contradictions and ironies. They too continue to lie ambiguously between state and private land categories. Fellahin had hoped they were but a single administrative step away from a bonafide private ownership. However, agrarian reform farmers have been reminded daily and emphatically that they are not the proprietors of private family parcels. Fellahin in this situation have been the focus of an elaborate decentralized agricultural extension network which monitors virtually all farm input and output, and has brought development schemes of both an agricultural and a non-agricultural nature directly to the farmer on his own parcel and to his family in its own courtyard. The method of decentralized extension fulfilled President Bourguiba's goal of achieving state control at the family level far more thoroughly than had any of the earlier centralized organs of the state.

To date, the two essential elements in Tunisia's decentralized development schemes have been the attribution of small-scale agrarian reform parcels and the follow-up of extension services. The success of the latter has always hinged upon the attitudes of the fellahin towards the former. Fellahin on agrarian reform parcels have wanted assurances that the land is theirs to keep. Those who have believed that the parcels are as secure as private property—and that they are unlikely to be taken away—have been more apt to make long-term investments in the farm and have been more willing to utilize extension services. Those who have believed that Tunisia will face upheaval through foreign intervention or further national crises of succession—or both—or those who have believed that change is imminent at lower levels have been inhibited from making long-range plans for their farms. Uncertain that their expenditures of energy and money will yield personal gain as a result of their efforts, they have chosen to diversify their strategies.

Conflicting Priorities and Values

If we set aside the problems of accelerated change and the oscillation between political ideologies, we reach at last the interface between developers and local farmers. Here we find that the rural development process has been impeded by the conflicting priorities and values of all concerned. State officials have demanded growth in the agricultural sector in order to feed the increasing urban population and to increase foreign markets; foreign advisors have recommended reinvestment in the land and dependence upon foreign seed, equipment and expertise. The farmers, however, have viewed development in personal terms as distinct from the national good. They expected not only to increase agricultural yield but also to increase their landholdings and material wealth, improve their living conditions, and provide themselves with greater leisure and autonomy.

The fellahin of Medjerda have demonstrated the dangers of type-casting rural people along "modernity" scales. Those fellahin avoided by developers because they appear conservative, risk-averse and traditional— i.e., those who wear the *jibba* and *chechia*, who rely on God's will and whose wives and daughters have been shielded from the developer's eye, those who speak no French, and who emphatically reject development aid—nevertheless have been as innovative in their agricultural practices and economic planning as any of the most *"souri"* farmers.

For the most part, developers and policy-makers have ignored the views of local farmers and have treated them simply as the instruments of national policy. They have acted this way because of their belief that the fellahin are either inarticulate or incapable of advocating anything but traditional agriculture which, in the Medjerdi context of profound colonial penetration, exists primarily in a distant mythical past. Tunisia was, after all, the breadbasket of the Roman Empire, and has for millenia been tied to European tastes and markets.

Persisting in their belief in the applicability of the theory of traditional agriculture, developers have vented their own frustration, proclaiming—in jest—that even were they to transplant a fellah to an apartment in the capital of Tunis, he would still grow wheat and raise sheep on his balcony. While the fantasy is absurd, the frustration is quite real. Developers and state representatives have blamed the nomadic background and traditional values of the fellahin for their lack of compliance with schemes for development. This oversimplification overlooks the fact that such fellahin have been well versed in both the theory and practice of European intensive agriculture—for, as has been demonstrated, these former nomads first learned agricultural techniques from European colonial farmers.

The most conservative farmers have tended to be wealthy landowners from among the old Medjerdi elite, not the sedentarized nomads. However, no farmers in the region can be classified as wholly traditional or wholly modern, along development modernity scales. These categories may be more accurately characterized as European ideal types which do not even correspond to the polar ends of the *'arbi/souri* continuum. Actual experience consists of diverse preferences and practices all of which must be classified as economically rational given the individual goals and technological means available to each fellah. If the *ʿarbi/souri* continuum demonstrates anything at all, it is that personal conservatism, religiousity and adherance to so-called traditional values does not prevent fellahin from rational exploitation of the land. On the contrary, their agrarian strategies may actually prevent long-term soil depletion. At the same time, the economic diversification strategies of fellahin guarantee long term support for large extended families who can thereby remain in the rural sector.

There is an enormously wide range of individual ideologies to be found among the fellahin of Medjerda. There is *not* a uniformity of mind reflecting a shared mentality of obstinate fellah oppositionalism.

One agrarian reform farmer reveals that all he really wants is not a small private parcel of his own, but to keep his sheep grazing on the hillsides without interference. Another claims that the best security is still having plenty of sons so that they can take care of you later. A third states philosophically that a cooperative is a good thing for a poor man but not for a rich man, and "I would rather be a rich man." A cooperateur affirms wistfully that it's always best to have your own land, but adds with a wink, "If you don't have your own, it's best to treat the cooperative as if it were your own private land." In this way, the distinction between private and public land becomes simply *pour la forme*—"for show." Land status is a thing of paper; actual tenure, individual usage, and private profit become the preferable reality (except during those rare official visits by administrators from the capital). The view from one's "private" garden makes official land categories a fictional, or at least only a technical reality.

A dry farmer counts his blessings when describing his own family's idyllic economic strategy and specialization. This, he says, is what a real cooperative is all about; but it is not something that can be created by the state:

> My father, brothers and I each have forty hectares. My father gives the orders. My eldest brother manages the farm. My second brother is a mechanic and runs the tractors and all. My little brother takes care of the cattle and sheep. I work for the state and do the accounting at home. We have trust and land and expertise. Everything is just right now...When the French were here our clothing was torn and full of holes.

Thus, cooperation is to be found only in the family, and state-owned agricultural cooperatives can never simulate the bond.

A small-scale private farmer proclaims that the best thing is to lead a clean life and that God will take care of the rest. A wily fellah lets his older brother till the soil for them both while he manages the accounts. Another claims that it's best to have a truck, transport your neighbors' produce and sleep the rest of the time—like his neighbor the accountant. An agro-combinat worker admits that it's best to get a paycheck and benefits so that you don't have to worry about the harvest. Another is certain that it's best to be a *mas'oul*—the man in charge.

A large-scale dry farmer is convinced that the best strategy is to manage one's own large private estate—but warns that one cannot survive on less than twenty hectares. Another agrarian reform farmer keeps a store. "That way, if the farm doesn't work out I can be a full-time merchant. My son over there shows no interest in the farm. What else can I do?" A fellah on a successful cooperative dreams of nothing but becoming a rich landowner. A small-scale farmer quotes government party line, "Irrigation is better than dry-farming. I follow what the project people tell me." A pragmatic large-scale farmer states that nothing is ever ideal. "I work very hard. If I had to say something was best I would say fruit trees. Fruit trees and hard work. But the soil here isn't good enough for fruit trees, so all that's left is hard work."

An irrigating farmer advises his neighbors to plan everything scientifically, experiment and compare the results. "How else would you know what is best for your own land?" His neighbors think he is crazy to experiment with a crop at stake. A former cooperateur retorts that it's best to work in the city, not the mud. His *chomeur deluxe* friend adds that "Europe, working in Europe is best. But you have to wait for your *pistons* to take action."

There is no consensus and little debate—only individual solutions to the problems of life in the rural sector.

Autonomy has always been highly valued in the Medjerda Valley. In the view of these fellahin, the whole point of having agrarian reform parcels is to be "one's own boss" on a family farm. The fellahin of Medjerda have found dependence on outside aid to be a double-edged weapon against poverty; one can profit for a while, but when the aid, seeds, and supplies cease to arrive, one is left more vulnerable than he was before the intervention. In many cases satisfaction explains complacency, particularly among agrarian reform farmers. They vividly compare their present life with the turbulent past and the uncertain future and find that among the tangible improvements in their lives are higher income, more food, nicer clothing, and—possibly—a new house not made of mud and straw, a television set, electricity or running water—and, most of all, a portion of land (*gat^{c}a*) that they try to believe is their own. Privatization policy is something the fellahin of the lower Medjerda Valley intend to watch very carefully.

Still other fellahin will continue to associate post-independence *coopérants* with the *colons* of the past. Foreign developers and foreign partners will always be seen as a neo-colonial imposition and this is distasteful enough in itself to prevent them from participating in the development process. When Tunisian development workers assume similar roles, they share the fate of being as unwanted and as uninvited as any outsider who manipulates both the rural people and the land.

In the revamping of the Lower Medjerda Valley Extension Project, Belgian developers had sought to provide a remedy for a number of the more glaring difficulties by prioritizing farmer needs. This innovation required listening to the fellahin and working towards a compromise between state and farmer objectives. The experiment entailed the outlay of higher subventions and an increase in the supervisory hours spent per farmer; it thus included fewer farms and did not "maximize" project funds, according to the directorship. A byproduct of the new technique included the creation of a select group of model farmers who quickly gained both affluence and a degree of notoriety. While Belgian evaluation determined that the new methodology did not succeed in bringing farmers closer to state goals, the fellahin who took part in the project were delighted with the results. In addition to providing foreign developers with *"pistons,"* the Belgians supplied these farmers with both materials and profits exceeding their expectations, enabling them to further divert funds to luxury and other non-agricultural ends.

Within the irrigated perimeters, most fellahin have not imitated the practice of balanced intensive irrigated agriculture, the practice advocated for the region, simply because it requires the farmer to work harder for longer hours at unfamiliar tasks towards unforseen results.

Conclusion

The advantages of labor-absorption in decentralized agriculture is lost upon the farmer who perceives and experiences it merely as labor-intensive. *Furthermore, the system advocated by souri developers binds fellahin and their families even more closely to farms they fear they may lose.* It does not—nor does it intend to—free them to pursue other, often more lucrative enterprises.

It has been argued here that the response of fellahin is not one of wholesale conservatism, as has been claimed, and that there is no monolithic "mentality" of fellahin. On the contrary, farmers demonstrate diversity of response, flexibility, and the strength to tolerate an immoderate amount of uncertainty.

Properly defined, innovation has been an essential ingredient in the strategies of fellahin. Developers, however, consider innovative only those farmers who, on their own accord, discover or begin to use new technologies which raise both the quality and quantity of their agricultural production. Given this limited definition, few fellahin have been classified as innovators, and these only reluctantly, after great debate. Their narrow definition ignores a wide spectrum of farmer strategies which, although they do not conform to development models and goals, are nevertheless innovative in a broader sense. I refer here to the vast array of production, distribution and alliance strategies employed by fellahin which include both the specialization and diversification of production, highly individualized marketing practices, and unique methods of opting out of agriculture altogether. While claiming that they have no options, fellahin exercise choices which provide them with viable mechanisms for coping with rapid and continuous change. They are neither unprepared nor reluctant to meet the challenge as they see it.

Appendix A

Glossary of Arabic Terms

ᶜaid el kebir	عـيـد الـكـبـير	The Great Feast
ᶜarbi	عـر بـي	Arab, Arabic; colloq., local traditional
'arḍ	أرض	land, earth
ᶜarsh	عرش	tribe; sometimes also family
ᶜaṣri	عـصـر يـب	modern, contemporary
baraka	بـركـة	holiness, blessing
belediya	بـلـد يـة	municipality
bled el makhzen	بلد المخزن	land of government
bled es siba	بـلـد الـصـبـا	land of dissidence
chechia	شـيـخـيـه	red felt hat or "fez" worn by men
cheikh/sheikh	شـيـخ	sheikh, tribal or community leader, elder
cheikhat/sheikhat	شـيـخـات	territory under jurisdiction of the sheikh (now ᶜomda)
douar	دُوار	hamlet
fellah, fellahin (pl.)	فلاح ،فلاحين	agriculturalist(s)

fi-shshtar	فشـــتار	tenancy with equal shares between landlord and tenant
gatᶜa	قطعـــة	parcel of land
ghelema	غلیمه	herders, nomads, Berbers; lit., youth
gourbi	جـــربي	mud hut
ḥammam	حمّام	Moorish public bath-house
ḥaram	حـرام	forbidden
ḥishma	حشـــمة	shame, modesty
jibba	جـبّـة	white robe worn by men
kanoun	كــانون	clay charcoal burner
kashabiya	قشـــابية	woolen cloak
khedema	خدیمه	workers (agricultural)
khemmas	خمـاس	tenant who receives one-fifth of the harvest
khidma	خـدمـة	work (salaried)
khubz tabouna	خبز الطابون	homemade country-style bread; lit., adobe oven- baked bread
koubba	قـبّـة	saint's tomb
kteff	كتاف	connections, influences "pull"; lit., shoulders
maᶜamera	معمـرة	mud hut
maᶜatmed	معتمـد	governor of the delegation
maktoub	مكـتوب	destiny; lit., it is written

mas'oul	مسؤل	person responsible or in charge
medina	مدينة	city, Arab quarter of town
meliya	ملاية	country-woman's dress
mu^calim	معلم	teacher, boss
mut^cadid	متعاضد	member of a cooperative
nisba	نسبة	collective identity
^comda	عمدة	regional administrator (formerly the *cheikh*); also a territorial subdivision of the delegation (formerly *cheikhat*)
qadiya	قضايا	chores (distinguished from work)
romdan	رمضان	Ramadan; month of fasting
riffi	رفي	bumpkin; lit., of the mountain
safsari	سفاري	white veil worn primarily by townswomen
si	سي	Sir, Mister (used with first name)
Sidi	سيدي	honorific referring to an Islamic saint
silsila	سلسلة	chain, link; relationship
souri	سوري	French; European; lit., Syrian
taqlidi	تقليدي	traditional
waqti	وقتي	temporary worker

Appendix B

Glossary of French Terms

agro-combinat	state-owned and managed agro-industrial farm complex
camionette	small truck
cave viticole	winery
chomeur deluxe	an unemployed educated man or skilled worker; a slacker
colon	colonizer
coopérant	foreign development expert
domaine	estate, large parcel of land once owned by *colons*
cooperateur	member/share-holder of cooperative farm
frippe	second-hand European clothes
gaz	bottled gas, used for hot-plates
huilerie	olive oil processing plant
indigènes	native, Arab population
lotissement	parcellization of land
mentalité	mentality, mind-set, world view
pistons	connections, people who can "push" one higher than he could rise on his own lit., automobile pistons
terres domaniales	state land

Appendix C

Tribal Fractions of the
Delegation of Medjerda (1900)
(Adapted from Protectorat Française)

Type in **boldface** indicates Predominant Tribal Fraction

Cheichat	Fractions
Medjerda (includes Sidi Ugᶜud)	**Oueslati** Zouaoui Djzairin Souahli **Andoulsi** **Trabelsi** Mar'arbi Refarfi Sfaxi **Bedjaoui** Digim **Mejri** Dagi **Oulad Aiar** **Hammami** Aouini **Dridi** **Ferchichi** **Djlass**
Bordj Toungar	**Trabelsi** **Hammami** **Oulad Aiar** Ouled Khezam Htarbia **Medjri** Hdjari

Cheichat	Fractions
Djebel El Kebir	**Bejaoui** Djezairin **Djlass** Oulad Arfa **Trabelsi** **Hammami** Dadja **Riahi** Khazrmi Tlili **Nemamchi** ᶜArbi
El Bathan El Mehrine	**Djlass** Aouini **Trabelsii** **Frachichi** **Hammami** **Ourr'ammi** **Q'ouassemi** **Oulad Aiar** Ouled Khezam Hdjari
Djemiliya	**Trabelsi** Djezairin Q'mata Q'ouazini Djma'i **Hammami** **Jendoubi** **Oulad Aoun** **Oulad Aiar** Oulad Jahia R'raba R'rian Kaoub Safa **Dridi**

Bibliography

I. Archives

Tunisian National Archives, Tunis.

Administration Générale Indigène.	A-6-44
Caidat de Medjerda 1904-1956.	A-6-44
Cheikhat de Medjerda 1891-1892.	A-10-8
Zaouias de Medjerda.	D-73-1 to D-73-8
Ministère d'Agriculture.	E-208-2 to E-220-13
Chambre d'Agriculture et de Commerce.	E-222-1 to E-223-34
Statistiques Agricoles.	E-226
Syndicate Générale des Viticulteurs.	E-227-1 to E-227-9
Police Rurale.	E-240 to E-241
Ghabra et Habous.	E-242 to E-243-7
Coopérative de Foulage.	E-245-12
Ôuvriers Agricoles.	E-250-13, E-250-26
Terres Coloniales.	E-252-1 to 25
Alimentation Hydraulique.	E-344-12 to E-344-56

Archives of the French Ministry of Foreign Affairs, Paris

Agriculture et Colonisation en Tunisie 1885-1897.	NS-223-228
Mérite Agricole en Tunisie 1917-1929.	P-8-3 Nos. 22-24
Agriculture-Ravitaillement en Tunisie 1917-1929.	P-40-1 Nos. 185-193

II. Documents

B.C.U.P.N. *(Bureau de Contrôle des Unités de Production du Nord)*
    1978a   *Liste des U.C.P. par Arrondissement du Bureau de Contrôle.*
            Tunis: Ministère de l'Agriculture.
    1978b   *Resultats de Production Campagnes Agricole 1978-79.* Tunis:
            Ministère de l'Agriculture.

1978c   *Structure Générale des Unités Coopérative de   Production
             Agricole.* Tunis: Ministère de l'Agriculture.
1979   *Perspectives du Ve Plan: Projection de la Production.* Tunis:
             Ministère de l'Agriculture.

C.R.D.A. (*Comissariat Régionale de Développement Agricole*)
1979   *Recensement et statistiques de Medjerda.*

O.M.V.V.M. (*Office de la Mise en Valeur de la Vallée de la Medjerda*)
1959-1975   Kuwait Project Papers. Tunis: Ministère Agriculture.
1961   *Développment de la BVM: Projet et Perspectives Socio-
             Economiques.* Tunis: Ministère de l'Agriculture.
1968   *Secteur Medjerda: Dossier Complementaire sur le Projet
             d'Aménagement du Secteur.* Tunis: Ministère de l'Agriculture.
n.d.a.   *Encadrement des Précoopératives.* Tunis: Ministère de
             l'Agriculture.
n.d.a.   *Fiches Signalitiques des Précoopératives.* Tunis: Ministère de
             l'Agriculture.

O.M.V.V.M. *et* P.P.I. (*Périmetres Publiques Irriguées*)
1968   *Carte des Structures Agraires Actuelles.* Tunis: Bureau
             d'Etudes.
1969   *Carte des Structures Agraires Futures.* Tunis: Bureau
             d'Etudes.
1972   *Recommandations pour l'Élévage.* Tunis: Ministère de
             l'Agriculture.
1976   *Plans Parcellaires.* Tunis: Bureau d'Etudes.
1977a   *Carte Générale des Régions Concernées le Projet Belge.* Tunis:
             Bureau d'Etudes.
1978   *Rapport d'Activité: Projet Tuniso-Belge de Vulgarisation dans
             la Basse Medjerda.* Tunis: Ministère de l'Agriculture.

O.T.D. (*Office des Terres Domaniales)*
1973   *Guide Practique d'une Coopérative Agricole.* Tunis: Ministère
             de l'Agriculture.
1977   *Evolution des U.C.P.A.* Tunis: Ministère de l'Agriculture.
n.d.a.   *Projet des Status-types d'une Coopérative Centrale dans le
             Secteur Agricole.* Tunis: Ministère de l'Agriculture.
n.d.a.   *Statut Générale de la Coopération.* Tunis: Ministère de
             l'Agriculture.

Protectorat Tunisiènne.
1945   *Expropriations.* Tunis: Journal Officiel No. 91.
1951   *Classification des Anciens Combattants.* Tunis: Journal Officiel
             No. 69.
1952   *Vente de Terre Coloniale.* Tunis: Journal Officiel No. 78.

République Tunisiènne.
| | |
1955   *Carte de Medjerda (Ville).* Tunis: Service Topographique.
1961   *Lois Concernant l'OMVVM et l'OTD.* Tunis: Journal Officiel
            No. 61.
1962   *Loi Concernant l'OTD.* Tunis: Journal Officiel No. 62.
1963   *Loi Concernant l'OMVVM.* Tunis: Journal Officiel No. 63.
1963   *L'Unité de Dévéloppment de Medjerda.* Tunis: Gouvernorat
            de Tunis.
1976a   *Code du Statut Personnel.* Tunis: Imprimerie Officielle.
1976b   *Enquête Agricole de Base 1976.* Tunis: Ministère du Plan.
n.d.a.   *Région de Ariana.* Tunis: Service Topographique.
n.d.a.   *Région de Mateur.* Tunis: Service Topographique.
n.d.a.   *Région de Medjerda.* Tunis: Service Topographique.
n.d.a.   *Région de Tunis.* Tunis: Service Topographique.

III. Books and Journals

Abun Nasr, J. (1971) *A History of the Maghreb.* London: Cambridge University Press.

AGEP, eds. (1975) *Annuaire Agricole de la Tunisie.* Tunis: Agence Générale d'Edition et de Publicité.

Anderson, L. (1987) *The State and Social Transformation in Tunisia and Libya, 1830-1980.* Princeton, Princeton University Press.

Anschell, K., et.al., eds. (1969) *Agricultural Cooperatives and Markets in Developing Countries.* New York: Praeger Publishers.

Antoun, R. (1972) *Arab Village.* Bloomington: Indiana University Press.

Antoun, R. and Harik, I. eds. (1972) *Rural Politics and Social Change in the Middle East.* Bloomington: Indiana University Press.

Ayrout, H. (1938) *The Egyptian Peasant.* Boston: Beacon Press.

Bahroun, S. (1968) *La Planification Tunisienne.* Tunis: Maison Tunisiènne de l'Edition.

Bardin, P. (1965) *La Vie d'un Douar.* Paris: Mouton.

Barlett, P. (1977) *"The structure of decision-making in Paso,"* American Ethnologist Vol. 4, No. 2, pp. 285-308.

Barlett, P., ed. (1980) *Agricultural Decision Making: Anthropological Contributions to Rural Development.* New York: Academic Press.

Ben Brahim, A. (1975) *The Tunisian Cooperative Experience: 1960-69.* Master's Degree Thesis. University of Minnesota.

Benedict, B. (1968) "Family firms and economic development," *South West Journal of Anthropology* Vol. 24, No. 1, pp. 1-19.

Ben Messaoud, A. (1974) "Tunisian agriculture," *Phosphorus in Agriculture* No. 63, pp. 41-50.

Ben Salem, L. (1976) "Decision-making in an experiment in agricultural cooperation," in J. Nash, et.al., eds. *Popular Participation in Social Change.* Chicago: Aldine. pp. 277-87.

Berleant-Schiller, R. (1977) "Production and division of labor in a West Indian peasant community," *American Ethnologist* Vol. 4, No. 2, pp. 253-72.

Bernard, A. (1924) *Enquête sur l'Habitation Rurale des Indigènes de la Tunisie.* Tunis: Imprimerie J. Barlier.

Berque, J. (1967) *French North Africa.* New York: Praeger and Sons.

Boserup, E. (1970) *Women's Roles in Economic Development.* London: Allen and Unwin.

Bourdieu, P. (1962) *The Algerians.* Boston: Beacon Press.

———. (1977) *Outline of a Theory of Practice.* London: Cambridge University Press.

Bourrinet, J. (1975) *Salaires et Revenus des Travailleurs Agricoles en Tunisie et en Algerie.* Genève: Bureau International du Travail.

Braibanti, R. and J. Spengler, eds. (1961) *Tradition, Values, and Socio-Economic Development.* Durham: Duke University Press.

Brown, K. (1981) "The campaign to encourage family planning in Tunisia and some responses at the village level," *Middle Eastern Studies.* Vol. 1, pp. 64-84.

Brown, L. (1974) *The Tunisia of Ahmed Bey: 1837-1855.* Princeton: Princeton University Press.

Brown, M., et.al. (1977) "A model of the sexual division of labor," *American Ethnologist* Vol. 4, No. 2, pp. 227-252.

Canal, J. (1914) "Thuburbo Minus et Thuburbo Majus," *Revue Tunisienne* Vol. XXI No. 103 pp. 410-413.

Cancian, F. (1979) *The Innovator's Situation: Upper-Middle-Class Conservatism in Agricultural Communities.* Stanford: Stanford University Press.

———. (1980) "Risk and uncertainty in agricultural decision-making," in P. Barlett, ed., *Agricultural Decision Making.* New York: Academic Press. pp. 161-176.

Chambers, R. (1989) *Rural Development: Putting the Last First.* New York: John Wiley and Sons.

Chayanov, A. (1925) *The Theory of Peasant Economy.* Homewood, Ill.: American Economic Association.

Chelhod, J. (1973) "A Contribution to the problem of the pre-eminence of the right, based on the Arabic evidence," in R. Needham, ed., *Right and Left.* Chicago: University of Chicago Press. pp. 239-262.

Chennoufi, S. (1977) *Mise en Valeur et Réforme Agraire dans la Basse Vallée de la Medjerda*. Toulouse: Le Mirail.

Cohen, A. (1965) *Arab Border Villages in Israel*. Manchester: Manchester University Press.

Colloque International sur les Niveau de Vie en Tunisie. (1957) *Niveaux de Vie liès a l'Agriculture*. Paris: Presses Universitaires de France.

Colson, E. (1971) "The impact of the colonial period on the definition of land rights," in V. Turner, ed., *Colonialism in Africa* Vol. 3. Cambridge: Cambridge University Press. pp. 193-215.

Coulson, N. (1969) *Conflicts and Tensions in Islamic Jurisprudence*. Chicago: University of Chicago Press.

Cowan, J., ed. (1976) *The Hans Wehr Dictionary of Modern Written Arabic*. Ithaca: Spoken Language Services, Inc.

Cuisenier, J. (1961) *L'Ansarine: Contribution á la Sociologie du Développement*. Tunis: Presses Universitaires de France.

———. (1975) *Economie et Parenté*. Paris: Mouton.

Dahmani, H. (1974) *La Politique Economique de la Tunisie*. Tunis: Centre de Recherches et d'Etudes Administratives.

Daves, T. and H. van Wersch. (1976) "Results of agricultural planning in Tunisia 1962-1971," in R. Stone and J. Simmons, eds., *Change in Tunisia*. Albany: State University of New York Press. pp. 39-51.

Debbasch, Ch., et.al. (1971) *Les Economies Maghrébines: L'Indépendence a l'épreuve du développement économique*. Paris: Editions du Centres National de la Recherche Scientifique.

Democratie. (1978-9) *Tunisian Press*. Tunis.

Despois, J. (1959) "Le djebel Ousselet, les Ousseltiya, et les Kooub," *Cahiers de Tunisie* Vol. 7, pp. 407-428.

Dorner, P. (1972) *Land Reform and Economic Development*. Middlesex: Penguin Books.

———. ed. (1975) *Cooperative and Commune: Group Farming in the Economic Development of Farming*. Madison: University of Wisconsin Press.

Dumas, P. (1912) *Les Populations Indigènes et la Terre Collective de Tribu en Tunisie*. Tunis: Rapport du Tribunal Civil de Tunis.

Dutton, R. (1976) "Farming in the Lower Medjerda Valley," in R. Stone and J. Simmons, eds. *Change in Tunisia*. Albany: State University of New York. pp. 3-23.

Duwaji, G. (1967) *Economic Development in Tunisia*. New York: Praeger and Sons.

El ᶜAmal. (1976-81) Tunisian Press. Tunis.

El Ammah. (1976-81) Tunisian Press. Tunis.

El Aouini, M. (1968) "Les lotissements de réforme agraire de la Basse Vallée de la Medjerda," *Revue Tunisienne* No. 15, pp. 75-92.

Erasmus, C. (1955) *Reciprocal Labor.* Unpublished Ph.D. Dissertation. Berkeley: University of California.

Etiènne, B., et.al. (1977) *Les Problèmes Agraires au Maghreb.* Paris: Centre National de la Recherche Scientifique.

Fanon, F. (1965) *A Dying Colonialism.* New York: Grove Press.

Favret, J. (1973) "Traditionalism through ultra-modernism," in E. Gellner and C. Micaud, eds., *From Tribe to Nation in North Africa.* London: Duckworth. pp. 307-324.

Fernea, R. (1970) *Shaykh and Effendi.* Cambridge: Harvard University Press.

Fraenkel, R. and M. Shane. (1974) "Land transfer and technical change in a dualistic agriculture: a case study from Northern Tunisia," *Staff Papers Series* Department of Agricultural and Applied Economics. St. Paul: University of Minnesota.

Gadalla, S. (1962) *Land Reform in Relation to Social Development: Egypt.* Columbia: University of Missouri Press.

Gafsi, S. and T. Roe. (1977) "Adoption of unlike high yielding wheat varieties in Tunisia," *Staff Papers Series,* Department of Agricultural and Applied Economics. St. Paul: University of Minnesota.

Gagnon, G. (1976) *Coopératives ou Autogestion: Sénégal, Cuba, Tunisie.* Montreal: Les Presses de l'Université de Montréal.

Gallagher, N. (1983) *Medicine and Power in Tunisia 1780-1900.* Cambridge: Cambridge University Press.

Gara, M. (1976) *Contribution à l'étude des modes de gestion chez les agriculteurs privés (Cas du Gouvernorat de Tunis-Sud).* Troisième Cycle Thèse. Tunis: Institut National Agronomique de Tunis.

Geertz, C. (1974) "'From the Native's Point of View': On the nature of anthropological understanding," *Bulletin of the American Academy of Arts and Sciences* Vol. 28 No. 1, pp. 26-45.

Goode, W. (1970) *World Revolution and Family Patterns.* New York: The Free Press.

Grissa, A. (1976) *Agricultural Policies and Employment: Tunisia.* Paris: Organization for Economic Co-operation and Development.

Guthrie, S. (1976) "*Essai pour augmenter la production agricole. Le systeme des Unités Coopératives de Production en Tunisie (avec une étude de cas sur l'U.C.P. Methline).*" Unpublished manuscript. Faculté de Sciences Economiques, Université l'Aix-Marseille II (Octobre).

Harik, I. (1974) *The Political Mobilization of Peasants.* Bloomington: Indiana University Press.

Harrison, M. (1977) "The peasant mode of production in the work of A.V. Chayanov," *Journal of Peasant Studies* Vol. 4, No. 4, pp. 323-336.

Hermanson, C. (1976) *Changing Health Beliefs and Practices in an Urban Setting: A Tunisian Example.* Ph.D. Dissertation. Ann Arbor: University Microfilms International.

Hermassi, E. (1972) *Leadership and National Development in North Africa.* Berkeley: University of California Press.

Hill, P. (1966) "A plea for indigenous economics: the West African example," *Economic Development and Cultural Change* Vol. 15, No. 1, pp. 10-20.

————. (1989) *Development Economics on Trial: The Anthropological Case for a Prosecution.* Cambridge: Cambridge University Press.

Hopkins, N. (1977) "The emergence of class in a Tunisian town," *International Journal of Middle Eastern Studies* Vol. 8, pp. 453-491.

————. (1978a) "Modern agriculture and political centralization: A case from Tunisia," *Human Organization* Vol. 37, No. 1, pp. 83-87.

————. (1978b) *Social Soundness Analysis of the Drylands and Irrigation Components of the Proposed Central Tunisia Rural Development Program (CTRD).* Tunis: United States Agency for International Development.

Hoben, A. (1980) "Agricultural decision-making in foreign assistance: an anthropological analysis," in P. Barlett, ed., *Agricultural Decision Making.* New York: Academic Press. pp. 337-369.

Hunter, G. (1969) *Modernizing Peasant Societies: A Comparative Study in Asia and Africa.* London: Oxford University Press.

Hyslop, J. (1970) "The Tunisian cereals sector: an examination of production, prices, and some alternatives for the future," *International Agriculture Series.* St. Paul: University of Minnesota.

Hyslop, J. and R. Dahl. (1970) "Wheat prices and price policy in Tunisia," *Staff Papers Series*, Department of Agricultural and Applied Economics. St. Paul: University of Minnesota.

Ibn Khaldûn. (1970) *The Muqaddimah: Introduction to History.* [1377] Princeton: Princeton University Press.

Inkeles, A. and D. Smith. (1974) *Becoming Modern: Individual Change in Six Developing Countries.* Cambridge: Harvard University Press.

Kassab, A. (1979) *L'Evolution de la Vie Rurale dans les Régions de la Moyenne Medjerda et de Béja-Mateur.* Tunis: Université de Tunis.

Khusro, A. and A. Agarwal. (1961) *The Problem of Cooperative Farming in India.* London: Asia Publishing House.

Kline, B and S. Payne, eds. (1990) *Imperialism and its Legacy.* New York: University Press of America.

Korten, D. (1972) *Planned Change in a Traditional Society: Psychological Problems of Modernizing Ethiopia*. New York: Praeger and Sons.

Kusum, N. (1979) *In Defense of the Irrational Peasant*. Chicago: University of Chicago Press.

L'Action. (1976-83) Tunisian Press. Tunis.

Lancaster, C. (1976) "Women, horticulture, and society in Sub-Saharan Africa," *American Anthropologist*, Vol. 78, No. 3, pp. 539-64.

La Presse. (1976-83) Tunisian Press. Tunis.

Le Houerou, H.N. (1970) "North Africa: past, present, future," in H. Dregne, ed., *Arid Lands in Transition*. Washington D.C.: American Association for the Advancement of Science. pp. 227-278.

Lejri, M. (1974) *Evolution du Mouvement National Tunisien*. Tunis: Maison Tunisiènne de l'Edition.

Lerner, D. (1958) *The Passing of Traditional Society: Modernization in the Middle East*. Glencoe, Illinois: The Free Press.

Lery, F. (1982) *L'Agriculture du Maghreb*. Paris: Maisonneuve et Larose.

Le Temps. (1978-82) Tunisian Press. Tunis.

Louwes, H. (1963) "Organization of markets and marketing procedures in land reform and development programs," in C. Van Nieuwenhuijze, ed., *Markets and Marketing as Factors of Development in the Mediterranean Basin*. Den Hague: Mouton. pp. 93-105.

Maher, V. (1974) *Women and Property in Morocco*. New York: Cambridge University Press.

Maine, H. (1971) "The primitive family and the corporation," from *Ancient Law*. [1861] Reprinted in N. Graburn, ed., *Readings in Kinship and Social Organization*. New York: Harper and Row. pp. 11-12.

Makhlouf, E. (1971) "Les coopératives agricoles en Tunisie: structures et difficultés," *Revues Tunisienne de Sciences Sociales* No. 26. pp. 79-114.

Mann, H. (1958) "Cooperative farming and individual farming in the Punjab: A comparative study," *Indian Journal of Economics* Vol. 38, Pt. 3, pp. 287-295.

Mardin, S. and I. Zartman. (1976) "Ottoman Turkey and the Maghrib in the 19th and 20th centuries," *Social Science Research Council Bulletin*, Vol. 30, No. 4, pp. 61-66.

Mellor, J. (1969) *The Economics of Agricultural Development*. Ithaca: Cornell University Press.

Micaud, C. (1964) *Tunisia: The Politics of Modernization*. New York: Praeger and Sons.

Michalak, L. and J. Selacuse, eds. (1986) *Social Legislation in the Contemporary Middle East*. Berkeley: Institute of International Studies Press.

Michel, H., et.al. (1978) *Technologies et Développement au Maghreb*. Paris: Editions du Centre National de la Recherche Scientifique.

Minge-Kalman, W. (1977) "On the theory and measurement of domestic labor intensity," *American Ethnologist*, Vol. 14, No. 2, pp. 273-284.

Moati, P. and P. Rainaut. (1970) *La Réforme Agricole: Clé pour le Développement du Maghreb*. Paris: Dunod.

Moerman, M. (1968) *Agricultural Change and Peasant Choice in a Thai Village*. Berkeley: University of California Press.

Moore, H. (1965) *Tunisia Since Independence: The Dynamics of One-Party Government*. Berkeley: University of California Press.

Murdock, G. (1973) "Factors in the division of labor by sex: A cross-cultural analysis." *Ethnology* Vol. 12, pp. 203-225.

Nash, J., et.al., eds. (1976) *Popular Participation in Social Change*. Chicago: Aldine.

Nassif, H. (1976) "Women's professional roles in Tunisia" Paper presented at the meetings of the Middle East Studies Association, Los Angeles.

Nygaard, D. (1979) *Risk and Allocative Errors Due to Imperfect Information: The Impact on Wheat Technology in Tunisia*. Unpublished Ph.D. Dissertation. Ann Arbor: University Microfilms International.

Ortiz, S. (1967) "The structure of decision-making among Indians of Colombia," in R. Firth, ed., *Themes in Economic Anthropology*. London: Tavistock Publications.

―――. (1973) *Uncertainties of Peasant Farming*. New York: Humanities Press.

―――. (1980) "Forecasts, decisions, and the farmer's response to uncertain environments," in P. Barlett, ed., *Agricultural Decision Making*. New York: Academic Press. pp. 177-202.

Poncet, J. (1962a) *La Colonisation et L'Agriculture Européennes en Tunisie Depuis 1881*. Paris: Mouton.

―――. (1962b) *Paysages et Problèmes Ruraux en Tunisie*. Paris: Presses Universitaires de France.

―――. (1977) "Les structures actuelles de l'agriculture tunisiènne" in B. Etiènne, et. al., *Problèmes Agraires au Maghreb*. Paris: Centre National de Recherches Scientifique. pp. 45-56.

Popkin, S. (1979) *The Rational Peasant: The Political Economy of Rural Society in Vietnam*. Berkeley: University of California Press.

Protectorat Française. (1900) *Nomenclature et Répartition de Tribus de Tunisie*. Chalon-sur-Saone: Secretaire Général du Gouvernement Tunisiènne.

Prothro, E. and L. Diab. (1974) *Changing Family Patterns in the Arab East*. Beirut: American University of Beirut.

Purvis, M. (1976) "The adoption of high yielding wheats" in R. Stone and J. Simmons, eds. *Change in Tunisia*. Albany: State University of Press. pp. 25-37.

Ralston, L., et.al. (1981) *Voluntary Efforts in Decentralized Management*. Berkeley: Institute of International Studies Press.

Reese, H., et.al. (1970) *Area Handbook for the Republic of Tunisia*. Washington D.C.: US Government Printing Office.

Richards, A. and J. Waterbury. (1990) *A Political Economy of the Middle East: State, Class and Economic Development*. Boulder: Westview Press.

Rosenberg, C. (1976) "Kautsky's The Agrarian Question," *Economy and Society* Vol. 5, No. 1.

Sahlins, M. (1976) *Culture and Practical Reason*. Chicago: University of Chicago Press.

————— . (1981) *Historical Metaphors and Mythical Realities*. Ann Arbor: University of Michigan Press.

Schneider, H. (1975) "Economic development and anthropology," *Annual Review of Anthropology* Vol. 4, pp. 271-292.

Schultz, T. (1964) *Transforming Traditional Agriculture*. New Haven: Yale University Press.

Seddon, D. (1974) "Aspects of underdevelopment and development in northeast Morocco," in J. Davis, ed., *Choice and Change*. New York: Humanities Press. pp. 134-160.

————— . (1976) "Aspects of kinship and family structure among the Ulat Stut of Zaio rural commune, Nador Province, Morocco," in J. Peristiany, ed., *Mediterranean Family Structures*. Cambridge: Cambridge University Press. pp. 173-194.

————— . (1981) *Moroccan Peasants: A Century of Change in the Eastern Rif 1870-1970*. Folkstone, Kent: Dawson and Sons.

Simmons, J. (1972) "The political economy of land use: Tunisian private farms," in R. Antoun and I. Harik, eds., *Rural Politics and Social Change in the Middle East*. Bloomington: Indiana University Press. pp. 432-452.

————— .Ed. (1974) *Village and Family: Essays on Rural Tunisia*. New Haven: Human Relations Area Files.

Soren, D., et.al. (1990) *Carthage: Uncovering the Mysteries and Splendors of Ancient Tunisia*. New York: Simon and Schuster.

Spicer, E. (1952) *Human Problems in Technological Change: A Casebook*. New York: Russell Sage Foundation.

Stevens, R. (1977) *Tradition and Dynamics in Small-Farm Agriculture*. Ames: Iowa State University Press.

Stone, R. and J. Simmons, eds. (1976) *Change in Tunisia*. New York: State University of New York Press.

Talmon, Y. (1972) *Family and Community in the Kibbutz*. Cambridge: Harvard University Press.

Tekara, B. (1981) *Du Cheikh à l'Omda: Institution Locale Traditionelle et Intégration Partisane*. Tunis: Centre d'Etudes de Recherches et de Publications.

Tessler, M., et. al. (1973) *Tradition and Identity in Changing Africa*. New York: Harper and Row.

Tessler, M. (1978) "A longitudinal analysis of Tunisian attitudes toward women and childrearing" in J. Allman, ed., *Family, Fertility and Social Change in the Middle East and North Africa*. New York: Praeger and Sons.

Thorner, D. (1964) *Agricultural Cooperatives in India*. Bombay: Asia Publishing House.

Touscoz, J. et.al. (1982) *La Communauté Economique Européenne Elargie et la Méditerranée: Quelle Coopération?* Paris: Presses Universitaires de France.

Tute, R. (1927) *The Ottoman Land Laws with Commentary on the Ottoman Land Codes of 7th Ramadan 1274*. Jerusalem.

United Nations. (1971) *Studies on Social Development in the Middle East*. New York: United Nations.

————. (1973) *Urban Land Policies and Land-Use Control Measures. Vol. V: The Middle East*. New York: United Nations.

U.S.A.I.D. (1976) "Building an economic analysis organization in Tunisia" in *Ministry of Agriculture Project*. St. Paul: University of Minnesota.

Valensi, L. (1969) *Le Maghreb: Avant la prise d'alger (1790-1830)*. Paris: Flammarion.

————. (1977) *Fellahs Tunisiens: L'Economie Rurale et la Vie des Campagnes aux 18ᵉ et 19ᵉ Siècles*. Paris: Mouton.

Vincent, J. (1970) "Local cooperatives and parochial politics in Uganda," *Journal of Comparative Peasant Studies* Vol. 8 pp. 3-17.

————. (1973) "Rural competition and the cooperative monopoly: A Ugandan case study," ICAES Symposium, Chicago: unpublished manuscript.

————. (1976) "Agrarian society as organized flow: processes of development past and present," unpublished manuscript. Sussex: Institute of Development Studies.

Violard, E. (1906) *La Tunisie du Nord: Les Contrôles Civils de Souk el Arba, Béja, Tunis: Bizerte, Grombalia*. Tunis.

Warriner, D. (1948) *Land and Poverty in the Middle East*. London: RIIA.

————. (1966) "Land tenure problems in the Fertile Crescent in the 19th and 20th centuries" in C. Issawi, ed., *The Economic History of the Middle East*. Chicago: University of Chicago Press. pp. 71-78.

Worsley, P., Ed. (1971) *Two Blades of Grass: Rural Cooperatives in Agricultural Modernisation.* Manchester: University of Manchester Presss.

Yang, C. (1965) *Chinese Communist Society: The Family and the Village.* Cambridge: Massachusetts Institute of Technology Press.

Zamiti, K. (1970) "Les obstacles materièls et idéologiques à l'évolution sociale des campagnes tunisiènnes," *Revue Tunisienne de Sciences Sociales.* No. 21, pp. 9-55.

Zartman, I.W., ed. (1991) *Tunisia: The Political Economy of Reform.* Boulder: Lynne Rienner Publishers.

Zghall, A. (1974) "The reactivation of tradition in a post-traditional society," in S. Eisenstadt, ed., *Post-Traditional Societies.* New York: Norton. pp. 225-237.

——— . (1977) "Pourquoi la réforme agraire ne mobilise-t-elle pas les paysans maghréhbiens?" in B. Etiènne, et.al., *Problèmes Agraires au Maghreb.* Paris: Centre National de la Recherche Scientifique. pp. 295-312.

Zussman, M. (1986) "Pendulum swings in land laws and rural development policies in Tunisia: History and consequences" in L. Michalak and J. Selacuse, eds., *Social Legislation in the Contemporary Middle East.* Berkeley: Institute of International Studies Press. pp. 161-190.

——— . (1990) "From *colon* to *coopérant*: A case study of cultural conflict from North Africa" in B. Kline and S. Payne, eds., *Imperialism and its Legacy.* New York: University Press of America. pp. 39-79.

Index